Culture and Inflation in Weimar Germany

Weimar and Now: German Cultural Criticism
Edward Dimendberg, Martin Jay, and Anton Kaes, General Editors

Culture and Inflation in Weimar Germany

Bernd Widdig

UNIVERSITY OF CALIFORNIA PRESS
Berkeley · *Los Angeles* · *London*

Cover: Max Beckmann, *Vor dem Maskenball,* 1922.
Oil on canvas. © VG Bild-Kunst, Bonn, 1999.

All photos are from Hans Ostwald, *Sittengeschichte
der Inflation* (Berlin: Neufeld und Henius, 1931).
Figures 1, 4, 6, 11, 12, 13, 17, 19, 24, 25, 27, 28
are courtesy of Harvard University Libraries. Figures 14, 15, 16 are courtesy of the Friedrich-
Wilhelm-Murnau Stiftung, Frankfurt. Figures 5,
18, and 20 are reproduced by permission of Artists
Rights Society, New York.

University of California Press
Berkeley and Los Angeles, California

University of California Press, Ltd.
London, England

Library of Congress Cataloging-in-Publication Data

Widdig, Bernd.
   Culture and inflation in Weimar Germany /
Bernd Widdig.
      p.   cm. — (Weimar and now ; 26)
      Includes bibliographical references and index.
      ISBN 0-520-22290-3 (alk. paper)
      1. Inflation (Finance)—Germany—History.
   2. Germany—Economic conditions—1918–1945.
   3. Germany—Economic policy—1918–1933.
   4. Germany—Social conditions—1918–1933.
   5. Germany—History—1918–1933.   I. Title.
   II. Series.

   HG999 .W64 2001
   332.4′1′094309042—dc21

                                   00-064772

Manufactured in the United States of America

09   08   07   06   05   04   03   02   01   00

10   9   8   7   6   5   4   3   2   1

For Nadine

Contents

Illustrations

Tables

Acknowledgments

I am grateful to the many colleagues and friends who have accompanied me through the different stages of writing this book. Their intellectual curiosity, their scholarly expertise, and their constructive criticism helped me to clarify my ideas and sharpen my arguments. Their personal encouragement was essential at times when my writing on inflation seemed to become almost as overwhelming as the phenomenon that I was investigating. Therefore, I would like to express my gratitude to Christoph Asendorf, Sigrid Berka, Russell Berman, Klaus Michael Bogdal, Bettina Brandt, Peter Burgard, Michel Chaouli, John Czaplicka, Marie Deer, Peter Fritzsche, Martin Geyer, Peter Jelavich, Jennifer Jenkins, Melissa Johnson, Anton Kaes, Stephen Kalberg, Thomas Kniesche, Charles Maier, Eric Rentschler, Christian Rogowski, Johannes Rohbeck, Adelheid Scholten, Erhard Schütz, Maria Tatar, Peter Temin, and Edward Turk.

Particular thanks to Dan Reynolds, who helped me during the early stages of my research, and to Lisa Schuhmann-Harris, whose careful reading of all my drafts resulted in many suggestions that improved the coherence and structure of my manuscript immensely. I would also like to thank Suzanne Berger for her professional encouragement and support.

It has always been a privilege to work with my wonderful colleagues and friends in the German Group at MIT: Ellen Crocker, Kurt Fendt, and Monika Totten. I have enjoyed their never-ending enthusiasm, exemplary professionalism, and great humor.

I am grateful to the Massachusetts Institute of Technology, which helped me in many ways to complete this project. The Class of 1958 Career Development Chair and the 1997 Levitan Prize for Innovative Scholarship in the Humanities provided me with generous sources of funding. I received valuable grants for my research from the National Endowment for the Humanities and the American Council of Learned Societies. As an affiliate of the Minda de Gunzburg Center for European Studies at Harvard University, I have profited from the center as a stimulating forum for intellectual exchange, and I am also grateful for several travel grants from the center that allowed me to conduct research in Germany.

Many thanks to Sheila Levine and Juliane Brand at the University of California Press for their splendid work.

Throughout the work on this manuscript, my daughters, Juliane and Héloïse, have given me much joy, along with the sense of perspective so much needed in scholarly projects.

Finally, I dedicate this book to my wife and dearest friend, Nadine Bérenguier, whose strength, serenity, and humor have been invaluable.

Introduction

CHAPTER ONE

Money Matters

Culture and Inflation

I.

When this book reaches publication, few eyewitnesses will be left to remember World War I and its aftermath in Europe. Soon the last veteran of the war that brought the European world of the nineteenth century to such an abrupt and violent end will have died; and in only a few years those who remember the great inflations that rocked Germany and Austria after the war will also have disappeared. Nothing had prepared people for the uncanny power of the inflation that reached its peak in Germany in 1923. The ever-faster-swelling stream of money betrayed long-held persuasions, swept away economic livelihoods, and destroyed the trust and confidence of a whole generation.

When I was a young boy, my grandfather, born in 1896, took me on long walks through the proverbial German forest. He would tell me about matters he thought important for me to know so that I could get a sense of the world. As a good Catholic from the Rhineland, he informed me that, next to God, we had to thank then-Chancellor Adenauer for the astounding resurrection of Germany, for the *Wirtschaftswunder,* the economic miracle that followed World War II. In addition to Adenauer's achievements, the general course of German history was a frequent topic for our Saturday afternoon conversations. My grandfather's recollections of the two world wars he fought in as a soldier were without doubt selective and geared toward his young listener. Even though his memories of World War I were much older, they had by no means faded. On the contrary, they seemed to have a vivid urgency that was lacking from the stories of his service in Norway and Russia during World War II. Again and again he told me of the two-week furlough he had gotten from the trenches in Flanders in 1917. By the time he had returned to his platoon, they all, except one, had been killed in a single attack, just a day after his departure.

And then there was the story about the wheelbarrow. "Inflation"—in the dark shade of the beech forests that the two of us traversed he uttered this word as if it were a mental illness. "In the summer of 1923," he told me, "money was worth so little that we had to fill up a whole wheelbarrow with banknotes when we went to town and tried to buy groceries." Instinctively I held the fifty-pfennig coin my grandmother gave me every Saturday before our outing tightly in my pocket. I remember how deeply the story confused me. And however often I asked the simple "why" and "how," he could not really explain inflation to me; it had just happened, and it had been terrible.

"Inflation" wasn't just the wheelbarrow full of banknotes. Sometimes I got permission to go into the attic and explore the huge trunk that stored all kinds of memorabilia—my grandparents' own private museum of German history. A photo collection entitled *Neger in Deutsch-Südwest Afrika* reported on the happy fate of different African tribes under German colonialism. It contained several pictures of young naked black women—a confusing and enticing inconsistency in my grandparents' otherwise strictly Catholic world that initiated an early sense of wonder in me about the relationship of race, gender, and national identity. Under a few more books I found the neatly corded-up stack of postcards from my great-uncle Peter, whom I had never met. He was "the poet" in the family; he had written a novel that, alas, was never published. Uncle Peter was my grandmother's brother, and every day during World War I he had sent a postcard to his sister from the front in France. His last postcard, dated September 14, 1915, does not indicate that he would be dead the next day, killed in action somewhere near the river Marne. Next to the stack of postcards, in a flat wooden cigar box, lay the *Inflationsgeld*, banknotes that promised the value of 500,000,000,000 marks to its bearer. My numerical universe had not expanded beyond the notion of billions. Now I learned about trillions, numbers with endless tails of zeros. Yet one had to have a whole wheelbarrow full of this money to buy anything. My boyish belief that a bigger number always indicated more and better experienced its first challenge in view of the paradox of this

Figure 1. "The Reichsbank has to print new money." Photo by Gircke, Berlin, in Ostwald, *Sittengeschichte der Inflation,* 116.

money. The box also contained *Notgeld,* emergency money, which my grandfather's company had printed to pay its employees. As money, it seemed to me a joke: it was overly decorative, with a medieval painting and a poem on it.

I heard the story of the wheelbarrow full of inflationary money told so often by older Germans that there must have been a corresponding inflationary rise in the number of these vehicles in Germany around 1923. There were many variations on the theme: one of my grandfather's friends, for example, told me that his wheelbarrow got stolen, and the thief left the money in it behind. The legend of the wheelbarrow must have captured something essential about the inflation, because it entered German popular memory so thoroughly. It became an allegory for depicting inflation. It might have been the striking contrast between the archaic, primitive vehicle and its peculiar freight of money, those piles of banknotes, the stuff elegant bankers and businesspeople usually work with. And doesn't the wheelbarrow indicate the hurry that inflation would impose on people's lives, causing them to rush and buy something before their money lost even more value? The legend also addressed a bitter paradox: a wheelbarrow full of money invokes peasant fantasies of wealth and prosperity as if in a painting by Pieter Brueghel, and yet this inflated money would by no means buy a wheelbarrowful of precious goods. And it may suggest a specific mutation of the spheres of work and consumption that occurred during the inflation. The wheelbarrow, the quintessential tool for farming and construction, acquires a new, rather strange function as the carrier of piles of money. During inflation money became so overwhelmingly central that it invaded all spheres of society, everywhere displacing objects from their traditional contexts.

II.

For many years, my childhood questions of the why and how of inflation lay dormant. The Weimar period was not one of my history teacher's favorite subjects in the humanistic gymnasium I attended in the 1970s. Thus, the topic of inflation did not reappear until I studied economics at the university. The why and how were transformed into elaborate schemes of mathematical graphs and equations. They explained a lot, yet these formulas did not address the "craziness" my grandfather had emphasized so much in his talks with me. A course in modern German politics mentioned the inflation as one of the factors that contributed to the rise of National Socialism in the Weimar Republic. This time the word *trauma* was added to the list of characterizations highlighting the enormous dispossession of the German middle class.

Later on, I added German literature to my course of studies. Yet inflation, this traumatic experience that had shaped the collective cultural memory of a whole generation of Germans, simply did not fit within the bounds of a traditional conception of Germanistik. And why should inflation have anything to do with the course of modern German literature and high culture? None of the canonical texts of classic modernism covered the subject. Yes, Thomas Mann had captured the atmosphere of the early 1920s in his novella *Unordnung und frühes Leid (Disorder and Early Sorrow)* and Hans Fallada had addressed the topic in his successful middlebrow novel *Wolf unter Wölfen (Wolf among Wolves)*, but inflation was simply not regarded as a subject that fell within the scope of Germanistik. It was thought to be a strictly economic issue and therefore properly dealt with only by economists and historians.

The suggestive power of the word *inflation* did not fade over time. Often used in the political rhetoric of post–World War II Germany, it can still invoke vivid scenarios of social chaos and economic misery in the minds of Germans. In a way, the wheelbarrow image from my grandfather's generation continues to lurk in the background of the debates on the stability of the German mark and, more recently, of the Euro. Politicians and officials of the Deutsche Bundesbank, Germany's federal reserve, have been legitimizing their restrictive monetary policies by pointing to the German past. They argue that the great inflation following World War I and, to a lesser degree, the inflation after World War II left such a traumatic imprint on the German collective psyche that tight control of inflationary tendencies would always find broad popular support. Germans would stand behind the tough anti-inflationary policies of the Bundesbank, even if it required sacrifices in consumer spending and put Germany into considerable conflict with other European partners.

Were these politicians and bankers conveniently invoking a mere cultural myth for their defense of high interest rates and restrictive monetary circulation? Certainly not. Many biographies, diaries, and newspaper accounts illustrate what my grandfather termed simply the godless times of inflation. Many variations of what he meant are captured in Hans Ostwald's *Sittengeschichte der Inflation: Ein Kulturdokument aus den Jahren des Marktsturzes (Moral History of the Inflation Period)* from 1931. Ostwald begins his collection of historical anecdotes and vignettes of everyday life during the early 1920s with a long list: "Looking back at the years of inflation the crazy image of a hellish carnival comes to mind: Plunderings and riots, . . . painful hunger and wild gluttony, rapid pauperization and sudden enrichment, excessive dancing and horrible misery of children, nude dancing, currency conjurers, hoarding of material assets, . . . occultism and psychics—gambling passion, speculation, a divorce epidemic, emancipation of women, early maturity of youth, Quaker-food kitchen, . . . police raids and racketeering, jazz and drugs" (7–8). For Ostwald the period of inflation marks the time of a radical transvaluation that affected all spheres of society and culture. "Someone who once was rich and could afford all luxuries suddenly had to be happy if caring people gave him a bowl of soup. Little apprentices in banks turned overnight into 'bank directors' with endless supplies of money. Poor foreign pensioners could come to Germany and live on their valuta like princes" (7). Everything suddenly had turned around, and for Ostwald, whose social codes were rooted in imperial Germany, the sudden transgressions of established gender roles were particularly threatening.[1] He saw family structures falling apart, "an erotic ecstasy jumbling up the world" (ibid.), and women becoming more demanding, especially in erotic matters. "We experienced a peculiar rejuvenation in women. Grandma with bobbed hair danced in a short skirt with young men in

Figure 2. "Ash Wednesday: 'Have a lot of fun before it's all over.'" Artist unidentified; illustration in *Beilage zum Wahren Jakob* 40(February 16, 1923).

the foyer, in a hotel, a coffee-house: wherever she found an opportunity. Mama danced with friends. The nanny took the opportunity and danced as well—and the children at home were all alone" (8).

Inflation as a bizarre carnival is a standard image in many descriptions that try to capture the atmosphere of that time. It was an uncanny mixture of violence, frantic exuberance, and misery. The two caricatures in Figures 2 and 3 highlight this atmosphere. They are taken from two of the leading satirical journals of the time, the social-democratic *Der Wahre Jakob* and the famous *Simplicissimus,* whose political position spanned

Figure 3. "The Dance around the Golden Calf." Illustration by
Wilhelm Schulz, in *Simplicissimus* 24 (December 3, 1919).

the conservative and liberal spectrum. Both drawings depict a carnivalesque mood through frantic dances and wild entertainment. Figure 2
concentrates on the profiteers and speculators who amassed sudden
wealth during the inflation and often spent their money as fast as they
won it in the stock market. Money has long lost its serious, valuable quality. The man on the right decorates his hat with it and evokes the German
idiom *sich etwas an den Hut stecken,* a sarcastic way of saying, "Forget
about it, it's of no value anymore." Sadly, the illustrator fell prey to the
undercurrents of anti-Semitism and obviously saw the need to draw the
rich profiteer in the center with a stereotypical "Jewish" nose. The two
women on the left symbolize both the loosening of sexual mores and
greed as they try to steal money from the man's jacket. In the background,
disguised in a carnival costume, lurks the grim reaper evoking the imminent collapse of the economy and the actual misery of the times.

Figure 3 obviously alludes to the biblical story about the worship of false idolatry. "And they didn't notice that it was made out of paper," reads the subtext. The moral decadence of a society in the grip of inflation is represented through the worshiping of a strictly material object. Yet the calf of inflation is not even golden. Inflationary money betrays its worthlessness in this scene. It is not secured by gold, because once it peels off from the calf we see nothing but a barren skeleton.

The carnivalesque atmosphere indicates, albeit with differing shades of ambivalence, a momentary freedom from rigorous cultural norms, the breakdown of class and gender lines, and the transgression of moral standards. This frenzy and strange mood of a sudden and momentary liberation shines through in Stefan Zweig's otherwise dark and alarming autobiographical notes on the inflation that he witnessed in Austria: "The very fact that what once represented the greatest stability—money—was dwindling in value daily caused people to assess the true values of life: work, love, friendships, art, and Nature the more highly, and the whole nation lived more intensively, more buoyantly than ever despite the catastrophe; . . . I don't think that I ever lived and worked with greater zest than in those years" (*World of Yesterday* 225). As carnival finds its end at midnight before Ash Wednesday, so the hyperinflation was abruptly put to an end by the currency reform on November 15, 1923, with the introduction of the *Rentenmark*. The fact that the inflation ended almost overnight, like a dream or a collective hallucination, only reinforced its unreal, phantasmagoric quality. "The spook suddenly disappeared," remarks Ostwald (8).

An almost deterministic connection between the experience of inflation and the rise of National Socialism culminating in the twelve years of the Third Reich has often been made. It appears with special prominence in accounts of observers who reflect in exile or immediately after World War II on the causes of the rise of German fascism. Thomas Mann, for example, told his audience in a lecture he gave at Princeton in August 1942:

A straight line runs from the madness of the German inflation to the madness of the Third Reich. . . . The market woman who demanded in a dry tone "one hundred billion" mark for a single egg, had lost during inflation her ability to be amazed at anything anymore. Since that time nothing was so mad or so atrocious that it could have caused any awe in people anymore. . . .

They learned to look on life as a wild adventure, the outcome of which depended not on their own effort but on sinister, mysterious forces. The millions who were then robbed of their wages and savings became the masses with whom Dr. Goebbels was to operate. . . . Having been robbed, the Germans became a nation of robbers.[2]

Interestingly, Mann's linking of the inflation to the Third Reich challenges the commonly held consensus that the Germans chose National Socialist dictatorship out of their longing for order and stability. Instead, he argues that the madness and irrationality of the inflation left a deep imprint in people's minds. For Mann, people's longing for irrational revenge and for adventures beyond the codes of a civilized society was born during the inflation and could later be lived out without any reprisal during the Nazi period. He himself never forgot the horrific gap between the price and the value of the egg. Yet what seems to stick especially painfully in his mind is the "dry," demanding voice of the market woman expressing a mixture of cynicism and impudence, foreshadowing for him the National Socialists' callous disregard for civility and human decency.

Historians are understandably hesitant to draw such straight lines. Gerald Feldman, in the epilogue to his monumental historical study on the German inflation, *The Great Disorder: Politics, Economics, and Society in the German Inflation, 1914–1924*, remarks that the "horrendous unemployment, wage cuts, and general impoverishment of the Great Depression proved a far greater danger to German democracy than inflation ever had" (854). Yet there is hardly any disagreement among historians regarding the indirect, subterranean effects of the inflation on the demise of democracy and civil society in Germany. Inflation was one of the greatest mortgages imposed on the young democracy after the end of the Wilhelminian empire because it "caused the Republic to be identified with the trauma of all those who had lost out and with the shameful practices and violations of law, equity, and good faith that characterized the period." And Feldman continues, "No less offensive than the misappropriation of money and goods, however, was the sense that there had been a misappropriation of spiritual values and a soiling of what the *Bürgertum*—above all, the *Bildungsbürgertum*—held to be holy" (858).

Repeated references to these traumatic sociopsychological aspects of inflation should give us reason to look beyond the economic and political unfolding of the German inflation. It is precisely this somewhat hidden, yet highly consequential, impact of inflation on German culture and society that I address in this study. "The soiling of what has been held holy," the shattering of deeply embedded values, the reactions of mistrust, cynicism, and the feeling of betrayal left marks on German culture and on individual biographies that cut much deeper than the measurable economic consequences of inflation. Many historians argue that, from a strictly economic point of view, the rapid currency devaluation after the lost war had a whole range of positive effects on the economic reconstruction in postwar Germany. The inflationary economy, for example, ensured relatively high employment and eased the complicated process of reintegrating the millions of returning soldiers into the postwar economy.[3] To relativize things even further, Germany experienced a period of political stabilization after 1924, especially as a result of Gustav Stresemann's foreign policy initiatives. And who knows what would have happened to the course of German history if the depression of the late 1920s had not occurred. Thus, the real long-term consequences of the inflation are much more of a psychological than a strictly political and economic nature. They may indeed have more to do with questions of collective memory and trauma, with popular and fictional narratives, with visualizations and reenactments, with attitudes toward the medium of money, and with fostering certain ideologies of resentment that in the end helped pave the way for National Socialism.

III.

Any inquiry into the cultural and psychological dimensions of inflation that derives its methodological perspectives from literary and cultural studies stands in the shadow of an impressive, potentially overwhelming array of economic and historical scholarly works. Ever since the inflation in Germany after World War I shocked the world, economists of all schools and persuasions have taken seriously John Maynard Keynes's prophetic warning expressed in his short essay "Inflation" as early as 1919: "There is no subtler, no surer means of overturning the existing basis of Society than to debauch the currency. The process engages all the hidden forces of economic law on the side of destruction, and does it in a manner which not one man in a million is able to diagnose" (78). Indeed, as I will later explain in more detail, most people did not understand the exact mechanisms of the rapid currency devaluation during the early 1920s.[4] Yet Keynes's (quite inflationary) assertion that "not one man in a million" could diagnose the mechanism of inflation did spur many of his fellow economists to take up the challenge.

The first in-depth economic study of the German inflation emerged in the early 1930s, with the famous treatise *The Economics of Inflation: A Study of Currency Depreciation in Post-War Germany, 1914–1923* by the financial expert Costantino Bresciani-Turroni, published in its original Italian in 1931 and in English in 1937. Bresciani-Turroni was a widely respected member of the reparations commission. His study concluded that German financial and monetary policies were to be held responsible for the fall of the mark to a much greater extent than the Allies' reparation demands. While other works followed that investigated the specificities of the German inflation, economists were also concerned with developing a general theory of inflation. Their basic perspectives coincide roughly with a polarity that has been characteristic for the entire field of economic theory during the past fifty years.[5] While monetarists such as Milton Friedman and other economists of the Chicago school regard inflation predominantly with respect to the control of the circulation and quantity of money, theorists in the tradition of John Maynard Keynes base their explanations largely on paradigms such as the relationship between consumption and investment, weak supply structures, spiraling wages, and the possibility of state intervention into the structure of supply and demand.[6] The study and control of inflationary tendencies with sophisticated systems of monetary policies have become a major field of economic research and professional policy advising. Thus, Keynes's dire prediction has been turned aside: by now there are probably a million experts all over the world who constantly diagnose, analyze, and ultimately try to prevent the rapid and uncontrolled devaluation of currencies.

There are as many concepts of inflation as there are theories to explain it. Carl-Ludwig Holtfrerich offers a short and useful definition, describing it as "the process of continuously rising prices, and of the currency's persistent loss of external and internal purchasing power." In addition to this modern economic definition, he mentions "the process of monetary expansion itself—which was more central to the original and contemporary usage of the word" (6). The increased volume of circulating money loses its value if it is not met by a parallel increase in production and trade.

John Maynard Keynes was less detached and neutral in his description of inflation when he wrote in 1919 about its social and political effects:

> By a continuing process of inflation, Governments can confiscate, secretly and unobserved, an important part of the wealth of their citizens. By this method they not only confiscate, but they confiscate *arbitrarily;* and, while the process impoverishes many, it actually enriches some. . . . Those to whom the system brings windfalls . . . become "profiteers," who are the object of the hatred of the bourgeoisie, whom the inflationism has impoverished, not less than of the proletariat. As the inflation proceeds and the real value of the currency fluc-

tuates wildly from month to month, all permanent relations between debtors and creditors, which form the ultimate foundation of capitalism, become so utterly disordered as to be almost meaningless; and the process of wealth-getting degenerates into a gamble and a lottery. (*Essays in Persuasion* 77–78)

Keynes emphasizes here the properties of money and the monetary system as a constitutive social medium for modern capitalist societies. It is often forgotten that money creates a unique link between citizens and their government, which holds the exclusive right to print money. The blatant abuse of this powerful right by many governments accompanies the story of many inflations throughout history. Nowadays, the Bundesbank, the German Federal Reserve Bank, and many other federal reserves have gained considerable independence from political pressures in their task to regulate the flow of money.

Keynes also addresses other characteristics that will emerge at different points throughout this book. Inflation leads to an enormous redistribution of wealth that is not directly linked to specific classes or milieus but proceeds rather arbitrarily. I will also investigate the relationship between debtor and creditor that is turned upside down during an inflation. The rapid devaluation of money causes the debtor to have considerable power over the creditor, and all too often large loans are paid back with a bundle of worthless yet valid banknotes. Keynes concludes his remarks with a social scenario in which economic activity "degenerates into a gamble"—a world that finds its artistic expression in Fritz Lang's film *Dr. Mabuse, the Gambler.*

Inflations come in different shapes and sizes. Charles Maier distinguishes between so-called creeping inflations, with price increases of up to 10 percent per year; "Latin inflations," with rates between 10 and 1,000 percent per year; and hyperinflations, with price increases above 1,000 percent per year (*In Search of Stability* 196). The next chapter will introduce specific historical details about the German inflation, but a few numbers will illustrate the size and magnitude of the German inflation in view of Maier's classification (see Table 1).

Especially during the last twenty years, economic and social historians have given the German inflation the attention it deserves as one of the defining events in modern German history. Charles Maier, Knut Borchardt, and Carl Ludwig Holtfrerich, among others, have written excellent studies about the interplay between the economic unfolding of the German inflation and issues of public policy. Besides illustrating the social and economic turmoil of the time, these authors also stress the sta-

TABLE I
INTERNAL PRICE INCREASES,
1914–1923

Year	Increase (%)
1914–1918	140
1919	223
1920	67
1921	144
1922	5,470
1923	75,000,000,000 (75 × 10^9)

SOURCE: Maier, *In Search of Stability,* 198.

bilizing effect the inflation had in the early years of the Weimar Republic by stimulating the economy and allowing the implementation of numerous social programs. Martin Geyer's recently published excellent study *Verkehrte Welt: Revolution, Inflation, und Moderne: München, 1914– 1924* investigates the local impact of the inflation, while Georg Horsman's *Inflation in the Twentieth Century* reminds us of the whole series of inflationary episodes in Europe after World War I. The most comprehensive and detailed historical study is Gerald Feldman's *The Great Disorder: Politics, Economics, and Society in the German Inflation, 1914– 1924,* published in 1993. Feldman's book represents his lifelong scholarly involvement in the subject and is unsurpassed in its thorough historical research.[7]

My own study is much indebted to the richness of the historical sources these works contain, as well as to their persuasive analysis of the chronological unfolding of the German inflation that had already begun during World War I and that ended in November 1923. After all, there were many players involved in the process of German currency devaluation; different political interests were at stake, and inflation was not a god-given event. Feldman and other historians have meticulously disentangled the complex net of decisions that led to the increasingly rapid devaluation of the mark. I will show in a short historical account in the next chapter that the inflation, seemingly irrational, was based on a whole range of political and monetary decisions that in themselves made sense given the concrete historical circumstances. Yet representing inflation only as the result of a complex chain of political decisions or economic constellations unavoidably distorts the event. It emphasizes the perspective of those who were connected to the inflation through some position of power. It pushes into the background the fact that in the face of inflation the vast majority of Germans experienced an overwhelming feeling of powerlessness and helplessness.

All of these accounts stop short of linking inflation to the cultural "underbelly" of German society. Feldman calls the year 1922 "the year of Dr. Mabuse," yet Fritz Lang's film itself is mentioned only briefly (513). None of the historical studies, with the exception of Martin Geyer's study, investigate the phenomenon of inflation with respect to a theoretical discourse of modernity. None of them reflect sufficiently on their characterization of inflation as trauma and address the question of how to represent such a trauma, how to give it expression within a larger cultural narrative. Or, to present the link between inflation and culture in the broadest terms, we may ask: When we consider that, next to language, money is the most important medium through which a modern society communicates, what happens when this medium does not function properly anymore, when it loses its trustworthiness and ultimately wreaks havoc? What kinds of anxieties are created by such an event; what hidden energies are set free? How does a culture affected by the increasing breakdown of monetary functions try to conceptualize a reality that seems increasingly bizarre and beyond rational comprehension? In other words, while other works have focused on the economics of inflation, this study will explore the cultural semiotics of inflation.

IV.

As pressing as the relations between culture and inflation are, reflections on these questions by cultural or literary critics are almost nonexistent. In his 1989 article "Die ökonomische Dimension der Literatur: Zum Strukturwandel der Institution Literatur in der Inflationszeit (1918–1923)," Anton Kaes observes that "the close interweaving between economic and intellectual interests during the inflation is completely unexplored"; this remains, by and large, still true (307). Kaes lays important groundwork for my study by persuasively arguing that "the inflationary period after World War I marks a radical cultural rupture. By rejecting the nineteenth-century notion of culture of the educated bourgeoisie, a new economically based modern mass- and media culture constituted itself" (308). Kaes's article stands out as one of the very few contributions that not only conceptualizes the impact of inflation on the relationship of the changing loyalties of audiences to cultural productions such as literature, theater, and film but also reflects on inflation's impact on the most basic structures of symbolic communication: "To the degree that the symbolic power of the 'billions' and 'trillions' of paper money increasingly vanishes, the symbolic power of mass-produced cultural signs decreases accordingly. . . . Catchwords such as 'massification of literature,' 'commercialization,' and 'leveling,' 'culture-business,' and 'cultural egalitarianism' are indices of the anxiety of a widening cultural devaluation through inflationary massification" (323). By addressing the cultural side of inflation, I will enter a territory that many historians have avoided. Certainly the question of evidence and the status of fictional texts as historical sources will continue to be bones of contention between historians and proponents of cultural studies. As much as I respect the caution of historians, their attempt to restrict inflation to the narratives of either the economic or the macropolitical ultimately does not do justice to the phenomenon.

Elias Canetti writes that the runaway inflation "reached people down to their most private nooks and crannies" (*Torch in My Ear* 51–52); it influenced every aspect of cultural practice. Therefore, it is necessary to operate in this study with a terminology of "culture" that is as wide as possible, signifying both "a way of life—encompassing ideas, attitudes, languages, practices, institutions, and structures of power—and a whole range of cultural practices: artistic forms, texts, canons, architecture, mass-produced commodities, and so on" (Nelson, Treichler, and Grossberg 5).

Accordingly, this study will illuminate the phenomenon of inflation through canonical literature and films as well as through often unexplored cultural material. I found two sources of visual material especially helpful. The unfolding of the inflation was captured by hundreds of press photos, of which a thematically representative sample reappears in Ostwald's *Sittengeschichte der Inflation*. These photos rarely have a mere documentary character: they often directly or indirectly comment on the inflation. As such, they proved to be a rich interpretative resource and helped me to give my arguments an additional vividness and clarity. My second main source for visual representations was the famous satirical magazine *Simplicissimus*. The many caricatures through which the magazine commented on the everyday effects and consequences of the inflation turned out to be a true gold mine for my cultural analysis of the inflation. More than other artistic visual genres, caricatures incorporate the imagery, rhetorical fragments, and ideological positions of a contemporary public discourse. The satirical illustrations of *Simplicissimus* contain a wide spectrum of the cultural iconography of inflation, and the contributions of artists such as Thomas Theodor Heine, Olaf Gulbransson, and Eduard Thöny to *Simplicissimus* are masterpieces of poignant social criticism. Throughout the 1920s *Simplicissimus* addressed a predominantly liberal, bourgeois, and nationally oriented public.[8] Thus, the journal's visual commentaries on the social injustice of inflation give excellent insight into the fears and anxieties of a struggling middle class. At the same time, I have to stress that these illustrations are imbedded in and respond to the cultural archive of this specific segment of German society.

The choice of material for this study was naturally part of much larger methodological questions: How should this book differ from existing scholarship on the German inflation in history and economics? From what perspective should I approach the phenomenon of inflation? How should this book be structured? A recent methodological discussion in German cultural anthropology has helped me reflect on some methodological questions regarding my own work.

To elucidate opposing methodological positions in this field, Thomas Macho and Helmut Lethen have invoked the dichotomy between "hunters" and "gatherers" (in Lethen's "Kracauer's Pendulum," 37–38). Both authors refer to the anthropologist Peter Dürr's disputation of Norbert Elias's model of long-term structural change in *Über den Prozeß der Zivilisation*. Dürr has collected all kinds of cultural fragments and presents them in more than two thousand pages in his *Obzönität und Gewalt: Der Mythos vom Zivilisationsprozeß* to counter Elias's teleological model and to argue that we are no more civilized today than a thousand years ago. I am less interested here in the actual debate than in the suggestive typology of the "hunter" and "gatherer."

At stake in the discussion were not only Dürr's and Elias's conflicting views on the process of civilization, but equally important were their very different methodologies and scholarly practices. Elias, "the hunter," was, as a generalist, "symptomatically inattentive to detail, but extremely charismatic in his interest in grand themes and theories" (quoted in Lethen, "Kracauer's Pendulum," 37). Dürr, on the other hand, is an almost manic "gatherer," interested in the most minute and seemingly odd details, refusing to take any preestablished path in his efforts to gather what seems noteworthy to him. While "hunters" are accused of overlooking the actual richness and variety of the cultural landscape in their strategy of hunting down the big beasts of history, "gatherers" are criticized for losing themselves in details, for neglecting or even refusing a coherent interpretative agenda, for fixating too much on the muddy grounds of history in their search for ever-new glittering pieces of amber in which historical forces may have become ossified.

As an allegory for a critical perspective that originates in grand theoretical narratives, the term *hunter* incorporates much of the postmodern skepticism about the totalizing tendency of modern theorists, about their single-mindedness in pursuing a one-dimensional perspective. Often organized in groups, each member follows the directive of a master strategist. Their activity is interpreted as violence toward their object, as a form of conquest and a peculiar love/hate relationship that binds them to their prey. One can detect a gender component in this type linking the practice of hunting to a genuine patriarchal and male-dominated sphere that largely excludes women.

The term *gatherer,* on the other hand, somewhat romantically connotes a certain love and care for the researcher's surroundings, an archaic and mystical knowledge of things that predates the specialized, focused, and abstract knowledge of the "hunter." Subconscious, open for a spontaneous discovery in the next moment, present-minded, nomadic, interested in the contingent, the half-hidden—such adjectives describe the practice of the "gatherer." The gatherer's social position is that of a solitary, yet not lonely, socially unattached and independent figure whose roaming does not follow the order of an authority.

The "hunter" versus "gatherer" typology evokes differences in perspective that are at the core of discussions on methodology in many fields of the humanities and social sciences. It reappears, for example, in social history in the debate between *historische Sozialwissenschaft* and *Alltagsgeschichte.* The former, which takes a macrohistorical approach and emphasizes structure and a general model of modernization, is still the dominant tradition in Germany. The latter refers to oral and local history, "history from below," and other forms of microhistory. In the United States it manifests itself in the increasing importance of cultural anthropology—especially in the works of Clifford Geertz and James Clifford.

In literary studies the emergent methodology of New Historicism possibly marks the most interesting way of "gathering" cultural material. New Historicists are interested in a wide variety of texts and representations; they prefer the anecdotal over grand linear narratives and "eschew overarching hypothetical constructs in favor of surprising coincidences" (Veeser xii). They stray back and forth between high culture and popular culture. They call into question the traditional borders between text and historical context by arguing that works of art neither mimic social reality nor originate in the self of an individual artist; rather they emerge out of complex negotiations, including modes of exchange and circulation between different historical powers and discourse practices. New Historicism argues that the production of cultural artifacts does not take place in a privileged space outside the radius of social and political power. Rather, these forces run through the work of art. Therefore, the central notion of representation in New Historicism does not reflect, as it does in traditional forms of sociohistorical interpretations, a historical reality "out there," outside the text. Rather, it points to the manifold knots in the textual structure that weave this text into different historical discourses through different processes of translating, changing, and reformulation. New Historicism proposes a radical textualization of history wherein texts of all sorts are considered an integral part of history itself and are therefore to be historicized. New Historicists tend not to work with the teleological spear of hunters; instead they fill their baskets with a motley assortment of cultural artifacts, with the rare and precious stones of high culture next to ordinary bird feathers of everyday cultural practices.

Compared to the seemingly random gathering and somewhat intuitive practice of New Historicism's collecting, the methodology of traditional sociohistorical literary interpretation does not call into question the border between text and historical context. As an offspring of similar perspectives in history, such literary interpretations wish to participate in the illumination of grand parameters of historical understanding. They are sophisticated in marking the artistic representation of social forces in the work of art; yet these parameters of long-term historical structure predetermine to a considerable degree the interpretive activity. As Peter Uwe Hohendahl remarks, the contextualization of art or literature ends up as the reconstruction of its determining factors (78). The ontological status of history that is strictly separated from its representation, a totalizing and teleological concept of historical unfolding, and the belief in an intersubjective understanding of such a historical totality: these are some of the underlying parameters of sociohistorically informed interpretations of culture (ibid.). Obviously, scholars with an interest in *Ideologiekritik,* or literary history as social history, resemble hunters much more than playful gatherers.

The dichotomy between "hunters" and "gatherers" ultimately points to the old problem that each practice leaves something out. Friedrich Schlegel summarizes this paradox in his *Athenäum Fragmente:* "It is equally fatal for the mind to have a system and to have none. It will simply have to decide to combine the two" (24). Cultural interpretations oriented toward the grand parameters, the "master discourses" of

Marx, Weber, or Freud, are limiting because of the rigidity of their all-encompassing view. Playful, postmodern New Historicism sometimes lacks explanatory power and may ultimately fall prey to the subjective passions of individual "gatherers" who remain somewhat unconscious of their own interpretive interests. The "hunter/gatherer" opposition in its unmediated form is ultimately not very productive; yet its heuristic value helps us realize how both concepts are dialectically linked together. Every "hunter" is at the same time a "gatherer," and even the most innocent collecting of historical peculiarities, even the most associative, noncausal linking of cultural artifacts bears some hunting instinct. At stake are modes of aggression, the size and variety of the prey, and the social position of "hunters" and "gatherers."

Consequently, I have found for my own methodological approach most insightful and stimulating the works of those cultural critics that best display these subtle dialectics, writers such as Georg Simmel, Walter Benjamin, Elias Canetti, and to some degree, Pierre Bourdieu. All of them are exemplary in their way of mediating between a cultural artifact and its larger social reality, in their careful dialectic movement between "gathering" and "hunting" in order to minimize the pitfalls of either side. In addition, their conscious yet not deterministic linking of economic and cultural dynamics provided me with both a tradition of cultural studies and a theoretical framework to which I can relate my own work.

Thus, the present study attempts to move back and forth between the practices of "hunting" and "gathering" in the hope that the dialectical exchange between the two poles will bear some fruit. Both perspectives, therefore, inform this book. It responds, on the one hand, to an overarching theoretical discourse of modernity by presenting a general thesis about inflation and modern culture, a thesis that defines the way I conceptualize inflation as a cultural phenomenon. On the other hand, this thesis does not restrict the "gathering" of a multiplicity of voices, of themes, of artistic representations through which this phenomenon gained entrance and prominence in German cultural memory.

V.

In his short essay "Inflation and the Crowd" in *Crowds and Power,* Elias Canetti takes some basic argumentative steps that are central to my interest in inflation as a cultural phenomenon. He writes, "A man who has been accustomed to rely on it [the monetary unit of the mark] cannot help feeling its degradation as his own. He has identified himself with it for too long and his confidence in it has been like his confidence in himself. Not only is everything visibly shaken during an inflation, nothing remaining certain or unchanged even for an hour, but also each man, as a person, becomes less. Whatever he is or was, like the million he always wanted he becomes nothing" (186). Canetti's assertion that people felt themselves degraded as their money was devalued may not be a contested statement, yet it has profound consequences. It enables us to think about inflation not solely as a process of monetary devaluation but also as a grand metaphor that captures the enormous cultural and psychosocial dislocations and changes in attitudes and behavior in the wake of the inflation. It is one of the central arguments of my book that, despite all the different forms of reactions to the inflation, one can indeed assume this broad analogous structure: inflation did to its victims what it did to money. This does not mean that the inflationary process produced only losers. Throughout my book, I intend to show the confusing mixture of impoverishment for many and unabashed enjoyment of luxury, power, and moments of liberation for some.

I will distill the central characteristics of inflation as a cultural process by dissecting Canetti's answer to the question "What is it that happens in an inflation?" (185):

> The unit of money suddenly loses its identity. The crowd it is part of starts growing and, the larger it becomes, the smaller becomes the worth of each unit. The millions one always wanted are suddenly there in one's hand, but they are no longer millions in fact, but only in name. It is as though the process of sudden increase had deprived the thing which increases of all value. The movement has the character of a flight and, once it has started within a currency, there is no foreseeable end to it. . . . Here the growth negates itself; as the crowd grows, its units become weaker and weaker. What used to be one mark is first called 10,000, then 100,000, then a million. The identification of the individual with his mark is thus broken, for the latter is no longer fixed and stable, but changes from one moment to the next. It is no longer like a person; it has no continuity and it has less and less value. (185–86)

I argue, as Canetti does, that inflation consists of three interrelated dynamics that define in general terms the devaluation of money as an economic phenomenon while they also shed light on the triadic structure of the cultural trauma of inflation. Canetti describes inflation as a process of simultaneous, uncontrolled, and unpredictable massification and depreciation that takes place while the circulation of money increases at an ever faster pace. The notion of massification tries to capture the meaning of the German word *Vermassung,* the transformation of formerly distinct entities into larger and larger numbers that causes the single entity to lose its former value and its distinctiveness. Looking at the theoretical discourse of modernity, we realize that these three dynamic phenomena (circulation, massification, and depreciation), together with the centrality of money, hardly constitute new analytic terms. Already Marx saw them as central forces in the transformation of a bourgeois society into an increasingly antagonistic structure that would, he concluded, bring about a proletarian revolution. Of importance here is precisely the position of these terms as largely established defining forces for the discourse of modernity and the frequency with which they reappear in our theoretical understanding of modernity.

I argue in this book that inflation is an integral and essential part of modern culture, and that it intensifies and condenses the experience of modernity in a frightening, often traumatic way. The notion of a "crisis of modernity," often invoked to describe the cultural landscape of the early twentieth century in Germany, takes on an unsurpassed shrillness and clarity through the dramatic and dynamic forces of the currency devaluation. In short, inflation stands for a modernity "out of bounds." At the same time, the interrelated discourses that capture the dynamics of massification, of devaluation or transvaluation of individually and commonly held values, and of increasing circulation constitute the core of cultural debates during the 1920s—and they betray widely differing attitudes ranging from resentment, denial, or sober tolerance, to enthusiastic embracement. The experience of inflation resonates in all of these discourses, sometimes openly, sometimes as a half-hidden, threatening scenario lurking in the background. And sometimes it is reenacted on other, seemingly unrelated stages with new actors and different plots as the result of complete displacement.

The great German inflation achieved the subterranean power it would have for many years to come not because it represented some freak accident of monetary policy, but because it involved and expressed itself through these three central cultural dynamics of modernity that were already causing pain and social strains. I will present the blueprint of my main theoretical framework in more detail in chapter 3, on the works of Elias Canetti. There I will provide some examples that give these otherwise very general notions of massification, devaluation, and circulation greater historical concreteness.

Furthermore, inflation shakes the essential bearings of modern culture because, unlike any other event, it highlights the centrality of money.
All too often, concepts of modern culture, especially when linked to industrial and technological modernization, underestimate the role money
has played in the constitution of modern life. Georg Simmel's major
work *Philosophie des Geldes* and a few other essays lend my project a
tradition and perspective that highlight the intricate relationship between money and modern culture.

VI.

It is essential for any analysis of the inflation to stress its links to the war
experience. Walter Benjamin noted that the soldiers who returned from
the battlefields had "grown silent—not richer, but poorer in communicable experience."[9] He also applies this observation to the period after
the war and explains this period as a series of assaults that made it increasingly difficult to form any coherent structure of experience: "Never
has experience been contradicted more thoroughly than strategic experience by tactical warfare, economic experience by inflation, bodily experience by hunger and moral experience by those in power. A generation
that had still taken the horse-drawn tram to school found itself under the
open sky, in a landscape in which nothing remained unchanged but the
clouds—and in the middle, in a force field of destructive torrents and explosions, the tiny, fragile human body" (214). What Benjamin separates
into various categories of experience actually came together during both
the inflation and wartime: economic and social distress, the cynicism of
the powerful—be it the arrogance of the German General Staff or the unscrupulous speculations of the profiteers—and the painful experience of
seeing one's own life plans brutally dashed. Like war, inflation intervened
in the lives of individuals in unpredictable ways. During wartime, a sudden order to an embattled segment of the front lines could mean almost
certain death for some, while others sat out the horrors of war in a state
of stupefying boredom on the supply lines. Analogously, inflation robbed
some people of their entire fortunes, while lucky investments made others rich almost overnight. Furthermore, living up to such highly regarded
social mores as youthful bravery and bourgeois prudence could have
disastrous consequences during war or inflation. The daily erratic up
and down of the currency exchange and ruthless speculation did to the
world of a good Prussian household what the newly invented machine

gun and mustard gas did to the twenty-year-old German and French soldiers who jumped out of their trenches, eager to prove their heroism.

Of the numerous parallels between the world war and hyperinflation,
another example should be mentioned here. Both events affected the
rhythm and even the very notion of time. Soldiers' diaries speak of the
unbearable alternation between phases of complete temporal emptiness,
of waiting and boredom, and the sudden compression of time into extreme moments during combat when bare survival was at stake. This,
together with the unpredictable course of the war, led to a gradual disappearance of the temporal dimensions of past and present. The idea of
making plans for the future faded, and all that remained was the frequently dull, sometimes euphoric, and often terrifying present.[10] The inflation led as well to shifts in people's sense of time. Here the experience
was one of a fantastically heightened tempo, dragged along by the rising
speed of the circulation of money. Depreciation forced people to buy
quickly. Long-term economic planning collapsed because the inflation
did not progress along a linear path, but intermittently. Phases of rapid
depreciation were followed by moments of stabilization, which made
some people hope and others fear for their investments.[11]

The shame, humiliation, and silence that occur when events over-
stretch any framework of communicable experience—these reactions
were common both to war and to inflation. Only a naive perspective on
human experience and its translation into cultural representation assume that everything that happened can more or less smoothly enter into
a meaningful narration or at least a descriptive expression. Instead, we
recognize that events linked to pain, shame, and humiliation or, even
worse, events that violate all limits of moral categories resist narrative
integration.[12] Canetti observed that people wanted to conceal, to hush
up their experiences during inflation (*Crowds and Power* 183). Both the
experience of war and inflation are aptly described as traumatic. The et-
ymology of *trauma* goes back to the classical Greek word *wound*. In its
modern use it contains three meanings. In surgery, a trauma is a massive
internal injury that may not be apparent from the outside. In psychiatry,
the word means a psychic injury caused by an emotional shock that is
then repressed, and often results in a variety of behavioral disorders.
And third, as with many terms from individual psychology, *trauma* is often used figuratively and expansively to indicate the effects of an event
on groups of people or even on whole societies.

For many soldiers who survived the atrocious trench battles, the war was by no means over in 1918. Already during the conflict, all armies had to account not only for the dead and the physically wounded but also for victims of war neuroses or so-called shell shock.[13] Many of those continued to have nightmares and anxiety attacks and showed erratic forms of behavior after the war.[14] In her work on trauma, Cathy Caruth emphasizes certain observations that Freud made on war neuroses: traumatic dreams and flashbacks are of a "surprising literality and non-symbolic nature," and a period of latency lies between the traumatic event and the development of neurotic symptoms (5).

For our discussion these recurrent, nonsymbolic nightmares characteristic of survivors of extreme situations need to be separated from the figurative use of the word when it refers to the "trauma of inflation." Obviously, whole societies cannot be traumatized in the same way as an individual who suffers a concrete traumatic episode. Certainly, the figurative use of *trauma* includes some of the characteristics of the medical condition: a deep injury not directly visible, repeated memories of the event, and sometimes a latency between event and recollection. Yet the figurative nature of "inflation trauma" points beyond the strict limits of clinical psychology; rather, it addresses the impact on social mentalities and forms of shared memory. Considering inflation as trauma helps us to realize that much of the humiliation suffered during the inflation was repressed. We should also remember that representations of the inflation may be affected in the same way that shameful personal experiences are reformulated, displaced, and condensed by dreams. The methodological consequences of these realizations are twofold. First, the figurative use of *trauma* should lead us to investigate a wide range of symbolic representations and cultural reenactments of the inflation. Second, such an analysis is possible only if we have a firm idea of what made the inflation so traumatic. Jürgen von Kruedener summarizes its devastating social effects as a "three-pronged attack on social identity" (251) that left deep psychological wounds on its victims: a loss in social prestige or position, a loss in personal freedom as they were forced to adapt their daily lives to the frenzy of currency devaluation, and a loss in personal security (231). As a description of real social distress, these three categories are certainly correct. Yet in order to integrate inflation into a larger concept as a crisis of modernity, one has to stress the specific dynamics that in the end resulted in such a loss of status, freedom, and security. I argue that the triadic constellation of massification, depreciation, and accelerated circulation gives us not only a fuller perspective on the cultural and psychological circumstances of these traumatic losses, but it also leads us to the primary concern of this study, the question of how the "trauma of inflation" manifests itself in German culture.

VII.

Finally a word about the thematic content and the organizational structure of this book. Following the introduction, part 1, "History and Experience," recaptures the German inflation as a historical event from both a collective and an individual perspective. Chapter 2 describes the general historical unfolding of the inflation. Through some telling statistics and poignant eyewitness accounts, this chapter conveys the enormity of the currency depreciation.

Of all the towering intellectual observers and commentators of this century, Elias Canetti has given us the most profound insights into the interplay between culture and inflation. Chapter 3 explores the topic of inflation as it appears in a variety of literary genres in Canetti's oeuvre. He captured his personal experience of the currency devaluation in Germany in his autobiography *Die Fackel im Ohr (The Torch in My Ear)*. His essayistic writing on inflation in *Masse und Macht (Crowds and Power)* helped me to develop a theoretical framework for understanding the cultural impact of inflation. Finally, his novel *Die Blendung (Auto-da-fé)* includes a striking allegorization of the inflationary process.

Part 2 of *Culture and Inflation in Weimar Germany* is titled "Money." Canetti, in the tradition of Georg Simmel, emphasizes the fundamental role money plays in the constitution of a modern cultural and psychosocial identity. Money's crucial role as a medium of social interaction becomes especially apparent during inflation. In chapter 4 I ask in what ways the medium of money itself established a conceptual framework for the experience of the great German inflation. How did the hyperinflation damage the basic functions of money, and how were the daily lives of people affected by the increasing breakdown of money's functions? Another aspect of money's role in the inflation scenario concerns its actual physical appearance. The very image and sight of masses of paper money remain among inflation's most striking features. In the second part of chapter 4, I investigate these visual and semiotic dimensions of inflation money, especially the significance of the number zero, which is at the core of inflation's exploding numerical universe. Signifying nothing and at the same time suggesting enormous multiplying powers, the number zero captures the very essence of the inflationary process. After these functional and aesthetic aspects, I address the role of money within a larger context of cultural ideology. Oswald Spengler's *Der Untergang des Abendlandes* (*Decline of the West*, 1918–1922) was one of the most widely read and discussed books during the 1920s. I argue that Spengler's philosophical best-seller provided a cultural and intellectual framework that served to integrate the actual inflationary experience into a larger historical picture.

"Figures," part 3 of the book, features two larger-than-life individuals who are inextricably linked to the culture of inflation and who highlight specific aspects of the inflationary experience. Chapter 5 explores Fritz Lang's film *Dr. Mabuse, the Gambler* (1922), which was heralded by critics at the time as a cultural-historical document of the inflation. I investigate both the documentary character of the film and a psychosocial traumatic dimension that comes to the fore in the film's fascination with its protagonist, the megalomaniac and power-hungry Dr. Mabuse. Of special significance in this context is the figure of the gambler. Fritz Lang's film offers a fitting example of how the abstract dynamics of the inflation are transferred into an artistic, multilayered mode of representation, invoking both fear and fascination.

In contrast to the fictional Dr. Mabuse, who is linked to the anarchic side of inflation, the second figure is of equally mythical proportions, yet is by no means fictional. At the center of chapter 6 is the industrialist Hugo Stinnes (1870–1924), who became Europe's richest man during the inflation. The main emphasis of this chapter is on the enormous role the shy industrialist played in the popular imagination. Surprisingly, the one-dimensional portrait of Stinnes simply as a ruthless profiteer and power-hungry capitalist does not do justice to this figure. It is rather the complex connection between Stinnes as a cultural icon and the notions of work and production that make him so fascinating. During the inflation, the sphere of work, with its strong ideological halo, became a central cultural and ideological paradigm that served as a counterdiscourse, as an antidote to the rapid and destructive circulation of money. From among the many contemporary accounts, I have chosen three different texts that each illustrate the power of Hugo Stinnes as a cultural icon during the early 1920s: Heinrich Mann's 1925 novella, *Kobes,* is a barely disguised story about Hugo Stinnes and paints a nightmarish scenario of the abuse of economic power; Eugen Ortner's small volume, *Gott Stinnes: Ein Pamphlet gegen den vollkommenen Menschen* (*God Stinnes: A Pamphlet against the Universal Man*, 1922), represents the enthusiastic vision of "total production," with Germany as a giant *Weltfabrik;* and third, Fritz Lang's film *Metropolis* portrays a Stinnes-like figure in the character of Fredersen, the industrial emperor of the Metropolis.

Part 4 of the book, "Accounts," presents two case studies that explore specific aspects of the culture of inflation. Chapter 7 analyzes the discussion around the erosion of the status of writers, artists, professors, and scholars. The impact of inflation on a professorial, bourgeois household is the theme of one of the most sophisticated and subtle accounts of the inflation, Thomas Mann's novella *Unordnung und frühes Leid (Disorder and Early Sorrow)*. The textual analysis of this novella provides a background for a general discussion about the socioeconomic situation of intellectuals. Alfred Weber's influential speech *Die Not der geistigen Arbeiter (The Distress of the Intellectual Workers)* at the 1922 convention of the Verein für Sozialpolitik represents a programmatic document that addresses the inflation's threat to the economic livelihood of intellectuals and raises the fundamental question about the very survival of high culture in modern German society. I was struck by the many echoes between Weber's speech and the cultural sociology of Pierre Bourdieu. My interpretation of Weber's text through Bourdieu's concepts links the 1922 speech to modern cultural studies and at the same time tries to elucidate the historical specificity of Weber's remarks.

The second case study, detailed in chapter 8, addresses the fact that many symbolic and visual representations of the inflation are coded as feminine. In particular, the economic misery of inflation is often shown as feminine misery—for example, in the frequent photos of women waiting in line in front of grocery stores. Because the crisis of inflation predominantly takes place within the spheres of distribution and consumption, its representation is in general imbedded within the narratives of a "feminized modernity." This tradition, which is saturated with a feminine iconography that depicts women as demonic, irrational, or amoral forces, heavily influenced the imagery of the inflation. I analyze and contextualize three female figures that are particularly significant within the symbolic discourse of the inflation: the witch, the *Luxusfrau*, and the prostitute. In addition, I show how these figures are inscribed in G. W. Pabst's inflation film *Die Freudlose Gasse (The Joyless Street,* 1925*)*. The film vividly illustrates the interplay between monetary circulation, female identity, and the breakdown of family structures during the inflation.

My study closes with part 5, an epilogue that addresses the question of the "afterlife" of the German inflation. In many ways, the National Socialist vision of German culture represented the complete opposite of the culture of inflation. The fascist ideology of "blood and soil" can be read as a counterdiscourse against the unpredictable circulation of money during inflation, which was seen as part of a "Jewish modernity." In German fascism the threat of uncontrolled circulation is countered by the image of a predictable, seemingly natural circulation of "German blood" in a rigidly defined *Volkskörper*. Besides reflecting on the relationship between anti-Semitism, inflation, and National Socialist ideology, the epilogue also addresses the question of a specific "inflationary" rhetoric that was characteristic of National Socialism.

The collective memory of the inflation, as I pointed out at the beginning of this introduction, has continued to shape Germany's postwar society. At the close of this study, I briefly discuss the ambivalence many Germans feel at the prospect of the surrender of German monetary fiscal control to the new European Central Bank with the introduction of the Euro. While actual inflation has not been an issue for the German economy of the 1990s, the traumatic memories of the great German inflation still reverberate within the current German public discourse.

PART ONE

History and Experience

CHAPTER TWO

Flirting with Disaster

The German Inflation, 1914–1923

I.

For many American readers the German inflation of the 1920s may trigger much more recent personal recollections of life in the United States during the late 1970s and early 1980s, when a hapless President Jimmy Carter tried to fight the frightening climb of the Consumer Price Index, which had reached more than 13 percent in 1979 (Nocera 176). Meat prices rose by 85 percent in a single three-month period; teamsters would call for 30 percent wage hikes. Many remember that the prime interest rate rose by as much as 19 percent. To make matters even worse, OPEC decided at a meeting in June 1979 to nearly double the price of a barrel of oil, from $12.50 to $22. It was then that Carter gave his famous "malaise" speech, in which he "conveyed a sense of gloom and American helplessness" (ibid.). The stigma of Carter's inability to fight inflation paved the way for Ronald Reagan's victory over him in 1980. The inflation of the Carter years changed the way many Americans looked at the virtues of saving. As credit cards became more broadly accepted and people became disappointed by the meager interest their saving accounts accrued as a result of the spiraling inflation, the old lessons of the depression—which had taught the qualities of thrift and frugality—were replaced by new lessons appropriate to the rising inflation. Borrowing money now made more sense than saving it; going into debt became guilt-free and was considered financially savvy. The strategy of many Americans became a matter of "purchasing yesterday's less expensive goods with tomorrow's inflated dollars" (191).

For some years now, the volcano "inflation" has been quiet in most Western industrial nations.[1] While nobody knows the date or the force of the next eruption, the events of the late 1970s have made the American public quite inflation-sensitive. Nowadays, a global network of economic experts reports and forecasts inflationary tendencies on the international financial markets. Every move by the American Federal Reserve Board or the newly created European Central Bank to change short-term interest rates makes for immediate headlines. The slightest unexpected rise of the Consumer Price Index can let stock and bond prices tumble.

Although inflation rates of 12 or 13 percent in the late 1970s caused much worry, these price rises seem mere puffs of smoke when compared to the volcanic eruption of the German inflation, which stands out as the most devastating outburst in modern times. Yet this inflation itself needs to be put within the larger framework of European economic history. While I make the argument in this study that inflation captures and intensifies the crisis of modern culture in a unique way, it is important to point out that the phenomenon of currency devaluations has plagued societies since the introduction of money.[2] Prominent examples reach as far back as the Roman Empire, when the gold content in the widely circulating denarius was steadily reduced while at the same time the number of circulating coins was drastically increased. Between 1618 and 1623 many German principalities suffered from a currency devaluation that had similar causes. Valuable silver and gold coins were melted and mixed with less valuable metals. Mint shops then produced masses of cheap coins of smaller denominations.

France witnessed two currency devaluations during the eighteenth century. These are significant because they were the first to exhibit many characteristics of modern inflations. The first of these devaluations is closely connected to John Law (1671–1729), the Scottish banker and financial adviser to the French court. Law had the revolutionary idea to issue money not as coins but as banknotes, as *billets,* that were printed on paper. In several letters to the French crown, he argued the advantages of such paper banknotes. As long as the public trusted the promise that the notes were backed by gold and silver, Law insisted, they would be superior to coins, because they simplified monetary transactions and were easy to transport.

In his *Mémoire sur les banques* from 1715, he compared the importance of the proper flow of money to all regions of the country with the natural circulation of blood in the human body (Gaettens 106). As a mercantilist, he believed that money was an important force in stimulating the economy, which would then lead to an increase of national power. Law finally gained the support of the French crown under Philip of Orleans, and in July 1716 he was allowed to open his Banque Generale with the right to issue banknotes. The enterprise turned out to be a great success, yet Law's plans were much bigger. He speculated in the development of the French colonies and became involved in the Compagnie d'Occident and the Compagnie des Indes. Law consolidated his bank with these ventures and raised enormous sums of capital for his colonial projects in Louisiana and Canada by issuing stocks to the general public. Soon these stocks became the object of frantic speculation: within a few months their value had risen from 500 livres to over 10,000 livres. Law issued several new emissions of 100,000 stocks each to meet the insatiable demand of both the public and the court. Accounts contemporary to the time describe Paris in the fall of 1719 as a frantic gambling casino that attracted people from all over Europe.[3]

In January of 1720 the stock prices began to fall, and clever speculators realized the market was about to crash. Soon stocks were sold on a massive scale, and the volume of circulating banknotes increased rapidly. Between December 1719 and February 1720 the collective face value of banknotes in circulation rose from 600 million to over 1 billion livres; in March it reached 2 billion livres. People's desperate attempts to exchange these banknotes for gold and silver coins were soon prohibited. The value of the individual stocks continued to fall to an abysmal 600 livres in May of 1720. What had started as an inflation of stocks turned into an inflation of banknotes when these stocks were sold. In the end, Law's bank promised to exchange small amounts of banknotes into hard coins. The rush on the counters created unbelievable chaos. On July 16, 1720, fifteen people were trampled to death. Law had to flee the country, and he died a poor man in Venice in 1729.

The second important inflation in France coincided with the Revolution. During the entire eighteenth century, the French state had been amassing a huge financial debt. In 1786, the yearly deficit had reached 200 million livres, with an annual tax revenue of only 357 million livres. The desperation over the royal finances led to the convocation and consultation of the General Estates on May 5, 1789—a date that would later mark the beginning of the French Revolution. Once the national assembly was in power, members tried to solve the problem of state debt through assignats, government bonds and securities that were backed by

the confiscated church estates. These bonds, most of them printed in
1790, were soon circulating and used as regular money. However, these
steps did not alleviate the financial malaise the revolutionaries had inherited from the ancien régime. New bonds were issued, and in February of 1793 the volume of assignats had reached a total value of 3.1 billion livres. In July of 1795 the volume of assignats was valued at 12.3
billion livres; finally, in January of 1796, the staggering sum of 27.5 billion. When in February 1796 the printing of assignats was stopped, the
monetary system in France had collapsed. By the end of the year, recovery had begun and metal coins became again the predominant mode of
money. Gaettens argues that the assignat inflation between 1790 and
1796 resulted in a more drastic destruction of the wealth of the proper-
tied classes than any of the revolutionary confiscations.

These few examples indicate that throughout history the occurrence
of inflation was intimately linked to the financing of expansionist political endeavors and usually coincided with political instabilities and revolutions. The story of the great German inflation between 1914 and
1923 starts where so many other inflations had their origins: in the
financing of a war that would devour an enormous amount of economic
resources.

II.

Shabbily dressed women setting off to go shopping with large baskets
full of money, children building paper airplanes out of banknotes, speculators showing off their expensive clothing on the boulevards of big
cities—these are popular images of the inflation that for generations
have been branded into the collective memory of Germans. Yet these images originate mostly from the time between the summer of 1922 and
the fall of 1923, when the inflation had turned into a hyperinflation.

Although that period in particular constituted a traumatic experience
for many Germans, the devaluation of money in Germany actually
spanned from 1914 to the end of 1923. The loss of purchasing power
and the weakening of the German mark relative to foreign currencies
during this decade did not progress in linear fashion but rather in unpredictable waves and intermittent episodes.[4] The overall unfolding of
the inflation becomes apparent upon looking at the dollar exchange rate
(see Table 2). Before World War 1 the exchange rate of the dollar was
already considered an important measuring stick for the value of the
mark. Yet during the years of inflation, its importance became even more

TABLE 2

PAPER MARK EXCHANGE RATE AGAINST U.S. DOLLAR IN BERLIN, 1914–1923 (MONTHLY AVERAGE)

	1914	1915	1916	1917	1918	1919	1920	1921	1922	1923
January	4.21	4.61	5.35	5.79	5.21	8.20	64.80	64.91	191.81	17,972
February	4.20	4.71	5.38	5.87	5.27	9.13	99.11	61.31	207.82	27,918
March	4.20	4.82	5.55	5.82	5.21	10.39	83.89	62.45	284.19	21,190
April	4.20	4.86	5.45	6.48	5.11	12.61	59.64	63.53	291.00	24,475
May	4.20	4.84	5.22	6.55	5.14	12.85	46.48	62.30	290.11	47,670
June	4.19	4.88	5.31	7.11	5.36	14.01	39.13	69.36	317.14	109,966
July	4.20	4.91	5.49	7.14	5.79	15.08	39.48	76.67	493.22	353,412
August	4.19	4.92	5.57	7.14	6.10	18.83	47.74	84.31	1,134.56	4,620,455
September	4.17	4.85	5.74	7.21	6.59	24.05	57.98	104.91	1,465.87	98,860,000
October	4.38	4.85	5.70	7.29	6.61	26.83	68.17	150.20	3,180.96	25.2 billion
November	4.61	4.95	5.78	6.64	7.43	38.31	77.24	262.96	7,183.10	2.1 trillion
December	4.50	5.16	5.72	5.67	8.28	46.77	73.00	191.93	7,589.27	4.2 trillion

SOURCE: Statistisches Reichsamt, Zahlen zur Geldentwertung in Deutschland 1914 bis 1923, Sonderheft 1 zu Wirtschaft und Statistik, vol. 5 (Berlin: n.p., 1925), 10.

Figure 4. "So many thousand-mark notes for just one dollar?"
Photo by Presse-Photo, Berlin, in Ostwald, *Sittengeschichte
der Inflation,* 215.

central. Often people's first glance in the morning newspaper was at the latest quote of the dollar, which gave an indication of possible new price hikes. Only with that information at hand could people estimate how much they could buy with their money. In the opening chapter of his novel *Der schwarze Obelisk,* Remarque reminds his readers of this daily routine. Georg, one of the protagonists, sighs, "Thank God that it's Sunday tomorrow, . . . there are no rates of exchange for the dollar. Inflation stops for one day in the week. That was surely not God's intention when he created Sunday" (12).

Before the war, the exchange rate for the dollar was 4.2 marks. The table shows that the mark's loss of value relative to the dollar began comparatively slowly during World War 1 and increased rapidly in the fall of 1919. In December of 1919, the mark had only one-tenth the value it had held in 1914. Despite several ups and downs, the situation stabilized somewhat between the spring of 1920 and the spring of 1921, when one had to pay between 50 and 70 marks for 1 dollar.

The beginning of the hyperinflation is quite clearly marked by the jump of the dollar exchange rate from 493 marks in July to 1,134 marks in August 1922. Yet even during its last step into monetary disaster, the German currency saw occasional and deceiving downward moves. In March of 1923, for example, the dollar briefly fell from 27,918 to 21,190 marks. Finally, in December, 1 dollar sold for the astronomical sum of 4.2 trillion marks.

The uneven and sometimes erratic course of the inflation can be explained by a number of political events and economic decisions that either strengthened or weakened trust in the German economy and the young republic. From the viewpoint of historical analysis, inflation was only one possible financial reaction to a whole range of political problems. During its ten-year course, the inflation was part of different political strategies and changing interests. Political and financial leaders were not completely uninformed about the dangers of currency devaluation, yet they downplayed or even denied the potential for a complete meltdown of the financial system. It was a flirtation with disaster, a risky political course of action that provided many remedies for the immediate present and that was justified by the unspoken assumption "In the end, even if disaster strikes, what do we have to lose?"

In view of the changing political circumstances, German inflation can be structured into three different phases: a first phase during the war between 1914 and 1918; a second phase related to demobilization in Germany between 1919 and 1922; and a third phase of runaway hyperinflation between the summer of 1922 and November or December of 1923, which coincided with, among other events, increasing tensions over reparation payments (Peukert 71).

The first phase of the German inflation started with the beginning of World War 1. Germany did not try to finance the war through taxation, but rather by issuing war bonds and by simply printing more money. With the outbreak of the war in August 1914, the Reichsbank suspended the convertibility of its banknotes into gold. The population was urged to exchange popular gold coins, such as the *Goldmark*, for paper money as an act of patriotic duty, to give the government enough gold reserves for its international trading.[5] In the following years coins were minted with increasingly cheaper material, and then they gradually disappeared. Remaining copper or nickel coins were hoarded. The *Papiermark* became the most widespread form of money. Between 1913 and 1918 the volume of banknotes rose from 2.6 billion marks to 22.2 billion marks (Sprenger 206–7). Such an expansion of the money volume was obviously not met by similar increases in production, and therefore led to price increases. The Consumer Price Index rose from 100 in 1914 to 310 in 1918, with annual price increases from 1915 on of about 30 percent (ibid. 207). The state tried to dampen these price increases by setting strict price controls on many goods. This first phase of the inflation was certainly still moderate compared to later phases. Nevertheless, someone who in 1914 had put money aside in a savings account with the plan to live on the interest after the war had to deal with the fact that this money had lost half its purchasing power in 1918.

Although the currency's loss of value was devastating to many, people suffered much more from the general scarcity of food and other basic goods toward the end of the war. During 1917 and 1918 food was strictly rationed. The daily dietary intake of the civilian population had fallen to half the prewar level (Holtfrerich 84–86). Many complained about the bad quality of food. The miserable food supply for the civilian population and most parts of the army, together with the hopeless situation on the Western Front, caused rapid deterioration of morale. In early November 1918 mutinies broke out among sailors in the German navy. Open revolt spread quickly all over the country. On November 9, 1918, Kaiser Wilhelm II abdicated and fled to Holland. On the same day, the Social Democrat Philip Scheidemann declared Germany a republic. General elections were held in January of 1919.

The first German democracy faced a mountain of almost unsolvable financial problems. The old regime had abandoned the scene and left the young republic with the daunting aftereffects of the lost war. To have any chance of survival, the government under Reichspräsident Friedrich Ebert had to act quickly and decisively. First of all, millions of returning soldiers had to be integrated back into a regular work environment. Therefore, the depleted economy had to be jump-started as quickly as possible. Second, the new government needed the loyalty of civil servants to maintain a well-functioning state bureaucracy. A prerequisite for such loyalty was the assurance of regular pay. Yet the initial tax revenues were minimal, and any rigorous tax hike in the immediate postwar period would not have found the support it needed from the population. Third, the Social Democrats, who were the leading force in the first coalition government, had promised ambitious social programs that would ease the enormous burden of the war. The Weimar constitution, enacted in 1919, contained the principle of state responsibility for social welfare. The Social Democrats wanted to extend the system of social security and public health. War widows and disabled soldiers were assured financial support. All these programs were obviously costly. Fourth, the new government inherited a huge state debt that had accumulated during the war, increasing between 1913 and 1919 from a few billion marks to about 175 billion marks (Holtfrerich 126). And last but not least, politicians had to confront the economic and psychological effects of the Versailles treaty.

On June 28, 1919, the German government had signed this treaty under great pressure from the Allies, who had threatened to march into German territory. After the surrender in 1918, German leaders had expected both to lose some territory and pay reparations of about 30 billion *Goldmarks* (Holtfrerich 141). Yet the victorious powers took the position that Germany should not only pay for immediate war damages but in addition make reparations for all costs related to the war, such as pensions for disabled Allied veterans and war widows. In January 1921 the bill for the war was presented to Germany: the Allies demanded 269 billion *Goldmarks* in total reparations, at the time a barely conceivable sum of money. After several rounds of negotiations later that year, the Allies drafted the London Ultimatum, which reduced the reparation payments to 132 billion *Goldmarks*. This sum was to be paid in yearly installments of 3 billion *Goldmarks* or the equivalent in gold or foreign currency (ibid.).

Faced with such daunting problems, the German government decided on a strategy that in hindsight is not only understandable but also may have been the right course of action, as some economic historians argue

TABLE 3
PRICES AND DOLLAR EXCHANGE RATE, 1918–1923

Monthly Average	Prices		U.S. Dollar Exchange Rate	
	Cost-of-Living Index 1913 = 1	Wholesale Price Index 1913 = 1	Exchange Rate Index 1913 = 1	Mark per Dollar 1913 = 4.20
Dec. 1918	—	2.5	2	8.25
Dec. 1919	—	8	11	48
Dec. 1920	12	14	17	73
Dec. 1921	19	35	46	192
Dec. 1922	685	1,480	1,810	7,590
June 1923	7,650	19,400	26,200	110,000
Sept. 1923	15,000,000	23,900,000	23,500,000	99,000,000
Oct. 1923	3.7 billion	7.1 billion	6.0 billion	25 billion
Nov. 1923	657 billion	726 billion	522 billion	2,160 billion
Dec. 1923	1,247 billion	1,262 billion	1,000 billion	4,200 billion

SOURCE: Sprenger, *Das Geld der Deutschen*, 213.

today. The government pursued a "policy of easy money" (Peukert 72). New money was printed, credit was available without any adjustment to inflation, and interest rates remained unchanged for quite some time. Soon, more than half of state expenditures were financed through the printing of new money (Sprenger 211). The excessive creation of new money led to rapid price increases and devaluation relative to the dollar, as Table 3 shows. By the end of 1921, consumer prices were nineteen times as high as in 1913, and the dollar stood at 192 marks. But this inflationary spiral helped the government solve its most pressing problems. Many improvements to the social security system were implemented. On the foreign policy front, German reparation payments were delayed several times; the government was obviously interested in pushing the thorny issue of reparations back as far as possible. The economy grew rapidly and resulted in almost full employment. While France and England suffered severely from a worldwide recession in 1920 and 1921, Germany was by and large unaffected. Export industries in particular were booming as they took advantage of the decreased value of the German mark abroad.[6] Table 4 helps to evaluate the German economy in international perspective. As this table illustrates, World War 1 had inflationary effects in other countries as well. Immediately after the war, there were not even exaggerated price increases in Germany. Yet by

TABLE 4
PRICES AND INDUSTRIAL PRODUCTION
OF SELECTED COUNTRIES

Year	Germany	Great Britain	France	Italy	United States
	Index of Wholesale Prices (1913 = 100)				
1918	217	226	339	409	194
1919	415	242	356	366	206
1920	1,486	295	509	624	226
1921	1,911	182	345	578	147
1922	34,200	152	419	575	154
	Change in Industrial Production (%)				
1920	+45	—	+8	+1	+3
1921	+20	−31	−12	+3	−22
1922	+7	+19	+41	+9	+26
1923	−34	+9	+13	+7	+19
1924	+50	+3	+23	+13	−6

SOURCE: Czada, "Ursachen und Folgen der großen Inflation," 41.

the end of 1920, the German economy was developing quite differently and price increases were becoming disproportionate.

The successful defense against a right-wing coup, the Kapp-Putsch, and a new round of negotiations concerning reparation payments in Spa, Belgium, in July 1920 led to a currency stabilization for a short period during the spring and summer of 1920. Soon, however, events at home and the continued tension over reparation payments created new problems that would accelerate the complete collapse of the German monetary system. On June 24, 1922, German foreign minister Walter Rathenau was killed by members of the radical right-wing Freikorps. For a short time, the shock and horror felt by many in reaction to the assassination united a majority of the German population. Yet the inner stability of the Weimar Republic had received another devastating blow.

After July 1922 the inflation turned into a hyperinflation of hitherto unknown dimensions. We may wonder why the officials in charge of the German monetary system did not try harder to stop this explosion of the money supply. One of the key figures of the German financial system, Dr. Rudolf Havenstein (1857–1923), president of the Reichsbank from 1908 to 1923, held views on the monetary system that may seem peculiar today yet were exemplary for the times. His positions only underscore how underdeveloped and inexact knowledge of the disastrous effects of inflation was even among high-ranking bankers. Even during the days of hyperinflation, he "held firmly to his view that money supply was unconnected with either price levels or exchange rates; saw his duty as having to supply to the limit of his ability the medium of exchange for which, because of the mark's ever-tumbling purchasing power, his countrymen were crying out" (Fergusson 168). A speech he gave on August 17, 1922, illustrates his position: "The Reichsbank ... today issues 20,000 billion marks of new money daily, of which 5,000 billion are in large denominations. Next week the bank will have increased this to 46,000 billion daily, of which 18,000 billion will be in large denominations. . . . In a few days we shall therefore be able to issue in one day two-thirds of the total circulation" (quoted in Fergusson 169; translation slightly altered). Within forty-eight hours after Havenstein's speech the value of the mark dropped from 3 million to 5.2 million to the dollar.

The essayist Friedrich Kroner represents the many contemporary voices that captured the everyday craziness of the hyperinflation. In his piece "Überreizte Nerven" ("Overwrought Nerves") he observes:

> It pounds daily on the nerves: the insanity of numbers, the uncertain future, today, and tomorrow become doubtful once more overnight. An epidemic of fear, naked need: lines of shoppers, long since an unaccustomed sight, once more form in front of shops, first in front of one, then in front of all. . . . Rice, 80,000 marks a pound yesterday, costs 160,000 marks today, and tomorrow perhaps twice as much; . . . The piece of paper, the spanking brand-new banknote, still moist from the printers, paid out today as a weekly wage, shrinks in value on the way to the grocer's shop. The zeros, the multiplying zeros! . . .
> They rise with the dollar, hate, desperation, and need—daily emotions like daily rates of exchange. The rising dollar brings mockery and laughter: "Cheaper butter! Instead of 1,600,000 marks, just 1,400,000 marks." This is no joke; this is reality written seriously with a pencil, hung in the shop window, and seriously read.[7]

In January 1923, the conflict with France over outstanding reparation payments escalated. The German and French positions had hardened and no compromise was in sight. On January 11, French troops marched into the Ruhrgebiet, Germany's most important industrial area. Reich chancellor Cuno called for the passive resistance of the civilian population and promised to support such resistance in any financial way possible. Psychologically, this policy against France may have resulted in a renewed feeling of unity among the heavily splintered political parties in the Reichstag; from an economic point of view the action was a complete disaster. The costs of funding the civilian passive resistance were much higher than what the French demanded in reparations. The paralysis of the steel and coal industry in the Ruhrgebiet over a period of several months had drastic ramifications for all industrial production in the German Reich. The government's money-printing machines ran continuously to finance the general strike and public resistance. Trust in the German economy and in the value of the German mark dwindled more and more. While in 1920 foreigners held about 36 percent of German bank accounts, this dropped to 11 percent in 1921 and to 2 percent in 1923 (Feldman, *Disorder*, 838).

Prices doubled now at shorter and shorter intervals. The Reichsbank increased the volume of circulating money as fast as it could, yet it still could not fulfill the demand created by the rapid price rises. In the fall of 1923, at the high point of the inflation, 30 paper mills and over 130 printing companies were under contract to produce the enormous quantities of money (Gaettens 268). In January 1922, the 10,000-mark banknote was introduced; a year later the first 100,000-mark note; in July 1923 banknotes of 10 million, 20 million, and 50 million began to circulate. In November of 1923, one could make payments with a 1-trillion (1,000-billion) mark banknote. Banks had to hire scores of employees who were busy counting money. A bank clerk recounts the bizarre experience: "Writing all those noughts made work much slower and I lost any feeling of relationship to the money I was handling so much of. It had no reality at all, it was just paper. We had to sort so many different kinds of notes and count them. And if it didn't come out right we had to stay on at night and count and count again. It might be a million that was missing, but after all it was worth nothing" (Guttmann and Meehan 46–47).

Many towns and companies began to issue their own money, so-called *Notgeld*, emergency money. *Notgeld* actually retained its value quite well but caused additional confusion because the state had lost its exclusive position of controlling the volume of money. Employees received their pay at ever shorter intervals; at the height of the inflation many people were paid daily. As soon as they had received their bundle of money, everybody rushed out and tried to buy something before the next price hike made the money worthless. Table 5 gives some examples of the incredible price increases during the hyperinflation. Hyperinflation created many grotesque situations. Often banknotes came so fresh from the printing presses that whole bundles of money were stuck together, and single banknotes could not be separated from each other (Guttmann and Meehan 47–48). During the peak of the hyperinflation, the value of the mark in relation to the dollar changed several times a

TABLE 5
RETAIL PRICES (MARKS), BERLIN, 1923

Date	Rye Bread (1 kg)	Beef (1 kg)	Pressed Coal (50 kg)
Jan. 3	163	1,800	1,865
July 4	1,895	40,000	28,000
Aug. 6	8,421	440,000	227,000
Sept. 3	273,684	4,000,000	3,314,000
Oct. 1	9,474,000	80,000,000	82,430,000
Oct. 22	1 billion, 389 million	10 billion	4 billion, 344 million
Nov. 5	78 billion	240 billion	198 billion, 100 million
Nov. 19	233 billion	4 trillion, 800 billion	1 trillion, 372 billion

SOURCE: Blaich, *Der Schwarze Freitag*, 31.

day. A cup of coffee in a café might cost 5,000 marks when it was ordered. After one hour of sitting and contemplating the insane situation, the customer could discover that the price had risen to 8,000 marks (Blaich 14).

Saving accounts lost most of their value. Before the war, an account of 50,000 marks offered enough interest to live on. In August 1923 this amount could barely buy a daily newspaper. During these months many stores stopped selling goods for money. Barter trading supplemented, or even displaced, money exchange. Many farmers refused to sell any produce, milk, or meat in exchange for money. Their hoarding of food aroused considerable anger, especially among the starving urban population. At the same time, foreign currency would buy everything. Tourists who visited from abroad could live luxuriously on a few dollars.[8] Ernest Hemingway, as a young reporter on assignment for a Canadian newspaper, remembers entering Germany from France: "For 10 francs I received 610 marks. Ten francs amounted to about 90 cents in Canadian money. That 90 cents lasted Mrs. Hemingway and me for a day of heavy spending and at the end of the day we had 120 marks left. . . . Our first purchase was from a fruit stand. . . . We picked out five very good looking apples and gave the old woman a 50-mark note. She gave us back 38 marks in change" (Fergusson 92).

Yet as Table 6 shows, price increases during inflation did not affect all expenditures to the same degree. Even though this table cannot tell us how individual families or persons reacted to price hikes, two numbers are certainly striking.[9] At the peak of the inflation, 91.6 percent of a family's budget was used to purchase food. This indicates the breakdown of the food supply, especially after many farmers refused to sell their prod-

TABLE 6

EXPENDITURES OF A THREE-PERSON HOUSEHOLD (MIDDLE-RANKED SALARIED EMPLOYEES), FROM 1912–1913 TO 1923 (%)

	Rent	Food	Heating and Lighting	Other Outlays
1912–13	30.2	30.3	4.8	34.7
1913–14	27.1	30.7	6.8	35.4
1914–15	22.4	34.2	4.7	38.7
1915–16	21.4	42.5	4.4	32.0
1916–17	18.1	48.6	2.1	31.2
1917–18	17.7	42.7	5.5	34.1
1918–19	13.1	55.5	4.9	26.5
1919–20	6.8	58.1	11.6	23.5
1920–21	4.3	47.8	8.8	39.1
1921–22	2.3	59.3	10.8	27.6
I/1922	3.8	55.2	4.3	36.7
II/1922	2.6	47.2	21.5	28.7
III/1922	1.2	69.3	9.3	20.2
IV/1922	0.4	64.7	15.7	19.2
I/1923	0.5	53.6	13.1	32.7
II/1923	4.6	35.7	6.1	53.6
III/1923	0.2	91.6	3.6	4.6

SOURCE: *Wirtschaftskurve* 2, no. 1 (1923): 29; no. 4 (1923): 21. Quoted in Holtfrerich, *The German Inflation, 1914–1923*, 261.

ucts on the urban markets. On the other hand, rent became an almost negligible outlay for many households due to strict rent-control regulations after the war. Yet for those who depended on rental income this development often meant a financial catastrophe.

In the end, any kind of economic planning that exceeded a few days or one month had become impossible because money no longer fulfilled its function. It had long lost its capacity to store value; its function of measuring and its exchange value had disintegrated as well. Thus, the inflation that had jump-started the paralyzed economy after the war had become a destructive force that was about to devour the entire German economy. In 1923, industrial production decreased by 23 percent. Unemployment spread rapidly and caused dangerous social tensions. In view of the disastrous economic situation, and fearing that a hunger epidemic would spread throughout Germany, the German government decided to make a radical break and implement a new currency.

On November 15, 1923, the *Rentenmark*, a provisional currency, was introduced. Within a few weeks, the hyperinflation had disappeared as

quickly as it had arrived a year and a half before. A strict interest-rate policy and the limiting of the money supply to not more than 3.2 billion
Rentenmark were powerful instruments in protecting this new currency
against another inflationary whirlpool. One *Rentenmark* was worth
1 trillion *Papiermark*. The exchange rate to the dollar was fixed at
4.2 *Rentenmark,* the rate used in 1914. On August 30, 1924, the new
Reichsmark replaced the provisional *Rentenmark*. The Reichsbank had
to provide a backing in gold or foreign currency for up to 40 percent of
the circulating money. The old *Papiermark* could still be exchanged
until July 1925, with an exchange rate of 1 trillion *Papiermark* for 1
Reichsmark.

I will conclude this historical account with a few remarks on inflationary events in postwar Austria, because some of the most interesting cultural manifestations of inflation, such as *Joyless Street,* G. W.
Pabst's silent film from 1925, deal with the economic and social hard-
ships after the war in Austria.[10] After World War I, Austria faced many
of the same challenges that Germany did. Emperor Karl I abdicated the
throne in November 1918, and a Republican government came to
power. Yet while Germany lost only some territory as the result of the
Versailles treaty, the once huge Austro-Hungarian Empire of the Habsburg dynasty was radically dismantled through the treaties of St. Ger-
main and Trianon.[11] Vienna, once a great imperial capital, lost much of
its hinterland. The new Austrian Republic comprised only one-quarter
of the old empire and only 23 percent of its population. Almost one-
third of the entire population was then living in Vienna, creating massive food supply problems (Horsman 38). Hunger riots broke out, and
the city tried to alleviate the shortages by setting up soup kitchens and
other relief actions. Faced with a situation similar to the one in Germany, the Austrian government had incurred a substantial budget deficit
that it financed by printing new money. In addition, Austria had a severe
import deficit and was burdened by reparation payments. Consequently,
the country was forced to borrow large amounts of money at home and
abroad, which led to a steep decline of the Austrian currency, the crown.
The resulting Austrian inflation was, however, by no means as dramatic
as its German counterpart. As Horsman observes, "The cost of living
[index] (including housing) rose from a base of 100 in July 1914 to 1326
in November 1918. Thereafter for nearly four years prices rose continually, accelerating dramatically in the course of late 1921 and especially
in 1922, to a peak of 11,271 in September 1922" (40). In comparison,
while prices in Austria rose by a factor of about 11,000, they rose in

Germany by a factor of 1 trillion, that is 1 million millions (ibid. 54). Nevertheless, Austria experienced a hyperinflation for most of 1922. Remedy for the failing Austrian economy finally came through a financial aid package from the League of Nations at the end of 1922. This foreign aid helped to stabilize prices after a while, and by the end of 1924, a new currency unit, the shilling, was introduced at a value of 10,000 paper crowns. The stabilization of the Austrian currency resulted in a positive economic outlook that led to a short-lived stock market boom between January and March of 1924. When Austrian economic problems began to be looked at more soberly, this euphoria was quickly followed by a dramatic fall of the stock market index and resulted in many bank failures during the mid-1920s.

Stefan Zweig's autobiography paints a vivid picture of Austria during the inflation that paralleled the frenzied inflation in the young Weimar Republic: "An economist who knew how to describe graphically all the phases of the inflation which spread from Austria to Germany would find it unsurpassed material for an exciting novel, for the chaos took on ever more fantastic forms. . . . A man who had been saving for forty years and who, furthermore, had patriotically invested his all in war bonds, became a beggar. A man who had debts became free of them. . . . Standards and values disappeared during this melting and evaporation of money; there was but one merit: to be clever, shrewd, unscrupulous, and to mount the racing horse instead of be[ing] trampled by it" (*World of Yesterday* 222–23).

III.

Inflation did not lead to an atmosphere of solidarity among those who suffered from its consequences; rather, it created an atomized society of survivor types who tried desperately, as Zweig remembers, to ride the wild horse of inflation. Carl-Ludwig Holtfrerich writes, "Under inflation, financial proficiency matters more than status or long established fortune, and the state's power to exact taxation is partially abdicated to its citizens, the most expert of whom turn to profit and subsidy what others experience as severe expropriation" (121). The relationship between the individual and the state, Holtfrerich continues, was characterized by a laissez-faire atmosphere that rewarded personal survival skills more than loyalties to social institutions or norms. During the German inflation, very different social groups were confronted with similar problems. Yet the reactions to these challenges varied widely and could lead to fortune or ruin. An early exchange of savings into a foreign currency, or helpful relatives in the countryside willing to send some food, could make the difference between misery and keeping one's social and financial status. From this often highly personal impact of the inflation, Knut Borchardt concludes: "It is because the manifold distributive effects are so diffuse and unclarified that inflation can be allowed to go on so long without becoming an acute scandal. The effects do not spring forth in a manner visible to every person, as is the case with unemployment, where no scientific investigation is needed to determine who is unemployed" (quoted in Feldman, *Disorder,* 5).

Bearing these cautionary remarks in mind, it is nonetheless possible to generalize about the winners and losers of the inflation. All those in debt, all those who knew how to speculate on the stock exchange, and all those who possessed foreign currency and could transfer money into *Sachwerte,* or material assets, had a good chance to profit from the inflation. The biggest debtor after the war was the German state. There is no doubt that the state used inflation as a means to rid itself of the enormous war debt it had accumulated. By the end of the war, in 1918, the German state owed 154 billion *Reichsmark* to its creditors. When inflation ended on November 15, 1923, this enormous sum, measured against the purchasing power of 1914, was worth merely 15.4 pfennig (Henning 69).

Because the state was interested in inflation as a means of shifting the cost of war to the general public, it had little interest in changing the legal framework by which the liquidation of indebtedness functioned. That framework was based on the "mark = mark principle" that during times of monetary stability was fully justified. A regular loan contract states that the debtor receives a certain amount of money, for example 50,000 marks, which must be paid back, usually with interest, within a certain amount of time. Yet what happens when the value of this money, its real purchasing power, is suddenly reduced to a small fraction of its former value? What if, as during inflation, one could earn 50,000 marks within a few hours? The "mark = mark" principle, upheld during most of the inflation, allowed debtors to pay back large amounts of debt with money that had actually lost most of its value. Several attempts were made during the inflation years to legally require inflation adjustment in all credit or mortgage contracts (Pfleiderer 69–82). Yet it was not until 1925, two years after the end of inflation, that an agreement was reached. Among other regulations, mortgages were reevaluated at 25 percent of their prewar value; war bonds were reassessed as well. In 1925, a bond valued at 1,000 *Reichsmark* could be redeemed for 25 *Reichsmark* (Sprenger 226–27). The German state was probably the biggest winner of the inflation, since all those who had loaned their money out of patriotic duty received only a fraction of their investment back.

Large segments of German industry were also winners in the inflation. Loans were cheap, and many big companies swallowed smaller firms that had run into financial trouble. Through clever investment and ruthless speculation, a handful of businessmen and profiteers created giant industrial conglomerates within only a few years. An observer at the time called these men appropriately the "kings of inflation": legendary figures such as Otto Wolff, Friedrich Flick, Hugo Herzfeld, Alfred Hugenberg, and the most successful of them all, Hugo Stinnes.[12] After the inflation the number of small- and midsized companies dropped considerably, while these huge conglomerates increased their power. Operating on a much smaller level were the *Raffkes* and *Schieber,* the profiteers and racketeers, people who got rich quickly through their deals on the black market. For most of the early 1920s, farmers also profited from the inflation. Many of them quickly paid off their mortgages and gained considerable wealth through bartering. The portly farmer who cruised the streets in his new car unabashedly displaying his new wealth was not an uncommon scene and caused much resentment among urbanites.

The effect inflation had on the millions of blue- and white-collar workers is difficult to measure. Inflation resulted in a massive redistribution of income and wealth. It worked as an equalizing force on German society insofar as lower-income groups suffered less from the inflation than did higher-ranking civil servants or professionals. Table 7 illustrates this tendency. "Real weekly wages" means that the nominal weekly wages are deflated by the cost-of-living index. These numbers give some indication about the real purchasing power of employees. Immediately after the war a modest rise can be observed, especially for low-income groups. From 1920 on, real wages began to sink and in 1923 were only half as high as in 1913. While higher-ranking civil servants suffered considerably from inflation and in 1922 had only a third of the real wages of 1913, lower-ranking civil servants maintained about three-quarters of their standard of living.

The biggest losers in the inflation were those who had saved money or who depended on entitlement programs from the state. Inflation made these entitlements, which were not adjusted often enough to the general price increases, almost worthless. Many of the victims of inflation were

TABLE 7

INDEXES OF AVERAGE REAL WEEKLY WAGES
OF RAILWAY WORKERS, PRINTERS, AND RUHR MINERS
AS PER COLLECTIVE AGREEMENTS, 1913–1923

(1913 = 100)

Year	Skilled Railway Workers	Unskilled Railway Workers	Printers	Hewers and Haulers in Mining	Higher-Ranked Civil Servant	Middle-Ranked Civil Servant	Lower-Ranked Civil Servant
1914	97.2	97.2	97.2	93.3	97.2	97.2	97.2
1915	79.7	80.8	77.3	81.3	77.3	77.3	77.3
1916	69.2	73.8	60.6	74.4	58.9	58.9	58.9
1917	63.9	74.2	49.4	62.7	42.9	48.6	53.6
1918	83.3	99.8	54.1	63.7	46.8	55.0	69.6
1919	92.2	119.8	72.3	82.4	40.2	54.8	89.3
1920	66.7	89.1	60.8	77.6	31.7	44.0	71.3
1921	74.5	100.0	68.9	89.1	39.3	52.2	82.3
1922	64.2	87.6	60.9	69.9	35.6	46.4	72.9
1923	50.9	69.1	54.2	70.1	38.0	49.5	69.9

SOURCE: Statistisches Reichsamt, *Zahlen zur Geldentwertung,* 41. Quoted in Holtfrerich, *The German Inflation, 1914–1923,* 233–34.

pensioners, but professionals who had saved money for their retirement and those who depended on rental income suffered as well due to the tight rent-control regulations, which insufficiently adjusted rents to the inflationary price hikes.

Although we can analyze these effects endlessly, we should not forget that all such assessments are made in hindsight. It is certainly possible for us to determine that the inflation was the best available strategy to jump-start a depleted economy. Yet for the vast majority of Germans— and Austrians, too—who lived through the inflation it was a time of social and personal humiliation. Values such as frugality and saving money were demolished as the inflation unfolded, and trust in the state was shattered. Inflation forced people to concentrate on their own fate. The result was a dog-eat-dog society that reversed many traditional values. Inflation entered into collective memory as a multifaceted trauma, whose many cultural representations this book will now explore.

CHAPTER THREE

Daily Explosions

Canetti's Inflation

I.

Elias Canetti is, in many respects, a key witness for this study on culture and inflation.[1] He is one of the few great intellectual observers of this century who have given inflation a place in their work commensurate with its impact on modern society. His personal testimony on the inflation in his autobiography, *Die Fackel im Ohr (The Torch in My Ear),* and the dense and powerful essay "Inflation and the Crowd" in his cultural-anthropological study *Masse und Macht (Crowds and Power)* initially led me to pursue this subject further. In addition to his autobiographical and essayistic writings, his novel *Auto-da-fé (Die Blendung)* contains a dramatic and quite striking fictionalization of the inflationary process.

In this chapter I will explore the wealth of perspectives that comes through the prism of these three literary forms. Canetti's autobiographical writing combines astute observations of German everyday life during the inflation with reflections on how to represent the seemingly nonsensical outbursts of the currency depreciation. He understands himself as a witness of a historical period, and in his writing he succeeds in masterfully weaving together his subjective, personal experience with the conflicting and chaotic historical totality of Germany in the early 1920s.

Canetti's essayistic writing on inflation in *Crowds and Power* represents a unique attempt to develop a framework for understanding the cultural impact of inflation. It is grounded in the actual economic unfolding of currency devaluation, yet Canetti, in the tradition of Georg Simmel in his *Philosophy of Money,* highlights the active role money plays in the constitution of a modern cultural and psychosocial identity. Throughout this study, Canetti's theoretical writings have provided me with a heuristic framework. In the beginning of my book, I introduced some of the central notions of Canetti's interpretation of inflation, and I will further develop them in the third and fourth parts of this chapter. They are broad enough to lift the phenomenon of modern inflation out of its historical singularity, yet specific enough to allow for a dense interchange between interpretative work with texts and historical contextualization.

Finally, a look at Canetti's major novel *Auto-da-fé* reveals that the bizarre struggle between the protagonist of the novel, the world-famous sinologist Peter Kien, and his housekeeper, Therese, reenacts some of the terrifying and unpredictable moves of the inflation. While Canetti's essayistic writing impresses the reader with its somber and almost cold directness and assertiveness, his fictional account of the inflationary process in *Auto-da-fé* plays on multiple registers of emotion and is often bitterly sarcastic.

II.

The seventeen-year-old Canetti moved with his family from Zurich to Frankfurt in the fall of 1921. Unsure how long they would stay, the family took lodging in a boardinghouse, the Pension Charlotte. Canetti ended up staying almost three years in Frankfurt, a tumultuous time that he remembers in his autobiography in a chapter titled "Inflation and Impotence" (*Torch* 3–54). For the young Canetti, the move from Zurich to Frankfurt was a violent break, an expulsion from paradise. Switzerland had become home for him, an idyll, which he describes all the more longingly when "the pension," the boardinghouse in Frankfurt, becomes its exact opposite, the paradigm of modern, rootless society.

A motley assortment of people inhabit the Pension Charlotte. Their paths have crossed by chance, certainly not by mutual affection. Canetti represents them as a sort of shrill panopticum of German society after World War 1. Their mealtime conversation is biting, often openly aggressive; the general mood is quite different from the dignified and elegant atmosphere of the prewar dining room in the sanatorium of Thomas Mann's *Magic Mountain.* In the Pension Charlotte, slogans and opinions from the mass media dominate discussions. All the participants in the daily dinner routine seem to live in their own moral and cultural universe.

There is Fräulein Rahm, a slender young fashion model, who takes advantage of the turbulent times and her good looks by having one steady boyfriend and many lovers; and there is Herr Rebhuhn, a German-Jewish nationalist bank official, who still lives with the moral code of the nineteenth century. He frequently expresses his bitterness about the lost war and asserts the popular Dolchstoß legend, claiming that weak civilians and leftist saboteurs in the hinterland had caused the defeat of the German army. This in turn causes strong objections from Herr Schutt, a wounded veteran on crutches who eases his constant pain with heavy doses of morphine. Further down the table sit two unmarried women teachers whose views on cultural life coincide remarkably with the latest reviews in the *Frankfurter Zeitung,* and the Bembergs, a young married couple whose stock market speculations seem to bring in a tidy income. And between them all: Frau Canetti, who represents the old liberal educated bourgeoisie and seems like a fossil in their midst.

The young Canetti's disappointment at leaving Zurich turns into rage at his mother when he discovers that the German entrepreneur Hungerbach, a cross between an officer and an aggressive self-made man, had convinced her to move from Zurich to Frankfurt, because she could live in Germany more cheaply on her Swiss money. "The thought of leaving the place I loved more than anything in the world, leaving it just to live *more cheaply* somewhere else, was utterly humiliating," writes Canetti (20). Thus Canetti himself becomes a victim of the inflation, his life swept up in the currency depreciation, and he is forced to trade his home for a pension. With its dual meaning, signifying, on the one hand, a boardinghouse, and on the other, the financial support of a caste of retired civil servants, upper-level employees, and officers' widows, the word *pension* frames the precarious situation of an entire social stratum during the inflation. Frau Kupfer, the operator of the Pension Charlotte, a haggard, elderly lady, personifies this dual meaning: as a war widow she has a state pension yet is obliged to rent out rooms in her house because the payments have become increasingly worthless. In the early 1920s, living on and in a pension meant living in a state of instability and unpredictability behind the façade of a previously prosperous house, in constant fear of the effects of the next depreciation.

Canetti's snapshot of the transitory, uprooted existence of the middle class, the group hardest hit by the inflation, is varied enough to describe more than just its tragic aspects. He also depicts the Bembergs, who represent those who managed to successfully ride the waves of the inflation, whose flexibility and conscious lack of traditions made them the beneficiaries of the currency depreciation. Crazy about the latest American fashions, which they integrate into their dress, speech, and gestures, the Bembergs build their life around the pleasures of consumption and constant novelty: "You could tell she bought anything she felt like buying, but few things looked right on her; she went to art exhibits, was interested in women's clothing in paintings, admitted to having a weakness for Lucas Cranach, and explained that she liked his 'terrific' modernity, whereby the word 'explain' must sound too deep for her meager interjections" (9). Frau Bemberg represents a new social type of the emerging milieu of an *Angestelltenkultur,* a white-collar culture. Her disrespect for the traditional borders of high culture and her unabashed interest in art, not as a vehicle for aesthetic appreciation but rather as a way to get inspired for her next fashion statement, coincide with the breakdown of a prewar bourgeois concept of culture. The Bembergs look to the United States in search of a new cultural model, and Herr Bemberg tenderly calls his wife "Patti" after his first girlfriend, who apparently was American. In these vignettes Canetti typifies and condenses a major cultural break that came about with the inflation. As Anton Kaes puts it, "The inflationary period after World War 1 marks a radical cultural rupture. By rejecting a nineteenth-century notion of culture of the educated bourgeoisie a new economically based modern mass- and media culture constituted itself" ("Ökonomische Dimension" 308).

The disjointed, hectic, and transitory atmosphere in the Pension Charlotte is a microcosm of the overall atmosphere in Frankfurt during the early 1920s. Canetti, summarizing the daily impact of the hyperinflation, writes:

> This was the time when the inflation reached its high point; its daily jump, ultimately reaching one trillion, had extreme consequences, if not always the same, for all people. It was dreadful to watch. Everything that happened—and a great deal happened—depended on one thing, the breakneck devaluation of money. It was more than disorder that smashed over people, it was something like daily *explosions;* if anything survived one explosion, it got into another one the next day. . . .
> In order to stand my ground against the money-minded people in my own family, I had made it a rather cheap virtue to scorn money. I regarded money as something boring, monotonous, that yielded nothing intellectual, and that made the people devoted to it drier, more and more sterile. But now, I suddenly saw it from a different, an eerie side—a demon with a gigantic whip, lashing at everything and reaching people down to their most private nooks and crannies. (51–52)

This description of the inflation is reminiscent of the terror of the seemingly endless bombardments during the trench warfare in Flanders and elsewhere: daily explosions that transformed reality into a barely recognizable mash of bits and pieces once called "humans" or "nature." The term *disorder* does not do justice to the power of such explosions; it merely indicates a sporadic attack on order, a grenade crater in an otherwise intact landscape. What impresses Canetti are the daily explosions that transform order into atomized chaos. With such images, Canetti presses the reader to understand the unpredictable and all-encompassing character of the inflation. Precisely because money reaches into "the most private nooks and crannies" there is no escape. For Canetti, the inflation does not create another order. Instead, it brings with it the most intense isolation of individuals at the same time that class differences are dissolving into the great mass of inflation casualties. All of this happens with breathtaking yet unpredictable speed.

Canetti's surprise at the power of money was shared by many members of the educated middle class, the *Bildungsbürgertum*. Brought up in Wilhelminian Germany and having a worldview that combined lofty idealist rhetoric with a certain aristocratic contempt for money matters, this segment of German society thought it utterly shocking that money could be the source of such destruction. Having internalized the long tradition in German culture of playing off *"Geist"* against *"Geld,"* that is, the sphere of ideas and words against the material world and the sphere of numbers and commerce, Canetti cannot help but phrase his shock in a mythological language: the inflation is a demon with a gigantic whip that reaches people even in the most secret and private niches of their existence.

At the same time, though, Canetti writes that he felt freer during the Frankfurt years than he ever had before. His mother soon moved to Vienna, and the young Canetti, still finishing up school, stayed behind and took lodging with a family but was otherwise left to his own devices. He describes this time: "I often attended meetings, listening to the discussions that followed them on the streets at night; and I watched every opinion, every conviction, every faith clashing with others. The discussions were so passionate that they cracked and flared. . . . I still had no sense of the separateness of *languages* colliding here. . . . What I grasped was the separateness of *opinions,* the hard cores of convictions; it was a witches' cauldron, steaming and bubbling, but all the ingredients floating in it had their specific smell and could be recognized. . . . I have never experienced more disquiet in people than in those six months" (52). The image of an atomizing explosion is taken to its logical conclusion here. The explosions of inflation have torn people from their moorings, unleashing powerful forces, crackling and flickering with energy. Opinions, positions, and doctrines of salvation multiply during this period, colliding like atoms.[2] The increasing breakdown of money as a medium for social communication and exchange affects even language itself. Canetti registers the effect first of all on the performative and rhetorical side of language. Opinions and hard cores of convictions clash with one another; they are ossified fragments, nomads of expression that no longer allow for dialogue. He pushes the atomized structure of public discourse even further by assuming that the violence of inflation had exploded language itself and created many languages, many different systems of signification that were not compatible with each other.

Canetti is well aware of the difficulties in representing and expressing the experience of the great inflation. Certainly the notion of tragedy comes to mind if we search for a concept that describes the fate of many victims of the inflationary period. Yet as painful as the currency depreciation was for so many people, Canetti makes us aware that the characteristics of social chaos during inflation move beyond the boundaries of tragedy. Tragic discourse depends on a stark, clearly recognizable dislocation of moral or political order. Tragedy draws its power from the pain arising out of a wound created within order. Guilt may be associated with this injury; and even if such guilt is inevitable and a tragic conflict does not offer any possible alternative outcome, tragic action is always oriented toward the body of order. For Canetti, however, the old order is splintered by inflation into countless particles and beyond any structure. For him, the "daily explosions" of inflation could be grasped only through grotesque and anarchic comedy.

Intertwined with Canetti's account of the effects of inflation on his social surroundings are his reflections on the comedies of Aristophanes, which he read during the inflation years. Through these ancient comedies, Canetti came to recognize that the removal of a particular basic prerequisite of social organization could set off a chain reaction with enormous and incalculable consequences. Similarly, he realized that the frantic movement of money could equally tear a modern social order from its moorings. "It [inflation] was no brainstorm, it was reality; that's why it wasn't funny, it was horrible. But as a total structure, if one tried to see it as such, it resembled one of those comedies. One might say that the cruelty of Aristophanes's vision offered the sole possibility of holding together a world that was shivering into a thousand particles" (53).

After reading *The Torch in My Ear,* one wonders how deeply the process of inflation affected Canetti himself. It is striking that the dichotomy between money and intellect, which Canetti, as I will show later, exaggerates to grotesque proportions in *Auto-da-fé,* pervades all his memories of the 1920s. As subtly and sensitively as his autobiography captures the atmosphere of the time, it also reveals an undisguised hatred for everything connected with money: hatred of his mother when she adjusts too pragmatically to the world, hatred of that part of his family that had dedicated itself to money and was involved in banking, and hatred of Bertolt Brecht, who "writes for money" (276).

A remarkable episode that happened on July 24, 1925, the day before his twentieth birthday and more than a year after the currency reform, illustrates how the power of money during the inflation must have traumatized the young Canetti. He refers to this event laconically as a "blowup" and informs the reader, "I have never spoken of it since then and it is difficult for me to describe it" (131). For weeks, he had been planning a hiking trip through the Karwendel Mountains. He had spoken of it to his mother in detail and was certain he would receive her approval of his plans. Suddenly she informs him that he might as well forget the idea because "she had no money for such luxuries" (137). At that moment, the young Canetti went wild. He grabbed a writing block and

> covered page after page with gigantic capital letters: "MONEY, MONEY, AND MONEY AGAIN." The same words, line after line, until the page was full. Then I tore it off and began the next page with "MONEY, MONEY, AND MONEY AGAIN." Since my hand-writing was huge, such as it had never been, every page was soon filled; the torn-off pages lay scattered around me on the large table in the dining room. . . . The pad had a hundred sheets; I covered each single page with my writing. My brothers noticed that something unusual was going on, for I pronounced the words I wrote, not excessively loud, but clearly and audibly. . . . Then Nissim, the middle one, dashed over to Mother in the kitchen and said: "Elias has gone crazy. You've got to come!" (138)

Canetti reenacts his own private inflation here; he mimics the hectic process of devaluation that transforms a piece of paper into worthless banknotes. Only a physician called in by his mother is able stop him, with the assurance that he may embark on his planned expedition to the Karwendel Mountains. Still, money had become an obstacle that acted against all careful planning, one that destroyed hopes and did so with sudden, senseless force.

The horror of the enormous power of currency depreciation never left Canetti. In that sense, he is no neutral, detached observer. The vehemence with which he handles the subject of the inflation is connected to the deep-seated dichotomy between money and intellect that structured the experiences he describes in the memoirs of his youth. However, Canetti's negative stance toward money should not be confused with a kind of bohemian indifference. Rather, his writing conveys a fascinated, extremely productive reflection on money, and, despite his aversion, he accords money and the inflation a defining role in the course of modern history.

III.

Nowhere does this knowledge about the significance of inflation find better expression than in his short essay "Inflation and the Crowd" in his opus magnum, *Crowds and Power*. Canetti spent thirty-five years of his life writing this book, and for almost twenty-five years he invested all his energies exclusively in this project (M. Krüger 8). The deep impressions that both the inflation and the mass demonstrations of the 1920s made on Canetti mark the beginning of his lifelong thinking about the basic nature of masses and crowds and their relationship to power (Stieg 30). When the book finally appeared in 1960, it barely resonated. Yet Canetti's *Crowds and Power* is now slowly being acknowledged as one of this century's great studies on human culture (M. Krüger 7). Canetti's idiosyncratic reflections, which ignore established disciplinary boundaries, are somewhat difficult to integrate in current debates on the culture of modernity. Yet his arguments about inflation, precisely because they ignore the restrictive view on inflation as a strictly economic or sociohistorical phenomenon, help establish a conceptual framework for this study.

In *Crowds and Power,* Canetti forcefully argues inflation's significance for the course of modern history:

> The confusion it wreaks on the population of whole countries is by no means confined to the actual period of the inflation. One may say that, apart from wars and revolutions, there is nothing in our modern civilizations which compares in importance to it. The upheavals caused by inflations are so profound that people prefer to hush them up or conceal them. They may also hesitate to attribute to money—the value of which is, after all, artificially

fixed by man—an efficacy in forming crowds which is out of all proportion to its practical function, and which seems both contrary to reason and infinitely shaming. (183)

These opening lines of Canetti's essay imply a specific perspective on the phenomenon of inflation. At stake is not only the reconstruction of these upheavals, which many historians have succeeded in creating, but also a registration of the traumatic quality of inflation. Canetti offers a very convincing argument about why we should be cautious in our expectation to find a wealth of narrative accounts that master the experience of inflation. He emphasizes the long-term effects of inflation on society and culture, he points at the hidden, submerged, subconscious traces of memory, and he offers the first hints about why so many experienced the German inflation as traumatic.

First of all, he says, inflation pushes money into the center of existence. Under normal circumstances, we take for granted money as a medium to convey certain information as much as we do the language we use in our everyday conversations. Only when we examine language from a linguistic or philosophical standpoint are we amazed that human conversation through language actually succeeds most of the time. In the same manner, we trust money to fulfill its major functions as a medium of exchange, as a measurement of value, as a way to defer payments, or as a convenient form in which to store our wealth. As I will demonstrate in detail in the next chapter, inflation brings all these functions into everyone's consciousness because they can no longer be taken for granted. The artificiality of modern society, its reliance on the precarious calculations and preconditions of a monetary system, must, as Canetti points out, have shocked anyone who had dreamt of a modern society as a large, seemingly organic community of people.

Inflation works like the Brechtian theory of theater: it cuts through any illusionary identification on the part of the audience and instead lays bare the organizing structure of the piece called "modern life." Walter Benjamin describes this process in his collection of fragments called "Imperial Panorama—A Tour of German Inflation": "All close relationships are lit up by an almost intolerable, piercing clarity in which they are scarcely able to survive. For on the one hand, money stands ruinously at the centre of every vital interest, but on the other, this is the very barrier before which almost all relationships halt; so, more and more, in the natural as in the moral sphere, unreflecting trust, calm, and health are disappearing" (*One-Way Street* 55–56). Benjamin's fragment resonates with Marx's famous statement in *The Communist Manifesto* that with the development of capitalism and its "uninterrupted distur- bance of all social conditions, everlasting uncertainty and agitation . . . man is at last compelled to face with sober senses his real conditions of life and his relations with his kind" (Marx and Engels 13). For Ben- jamin, whose analysis is imbedded in a Marxist tradition, inflation in- tensifies fundamental truths about human relationships in a capitalist society to such a degree that they become hardly bearable. With "pierc- ing clarity" we have to recognize the power by which money structures human relationships. During inflation, however, this power becomes so unpredictable and overwhelming that people withdraw from each other and lose all trust.

Second, Canetti argues, inflation is experienced as a process that works contrary to common reason and knowledge. The manner in which wealth was redistributed, the bizarre situation that one could be- come wealthy by going into debt and putting off payments, was contrary to all Prussian ideals of good bookkeeping. The victims of currency de- preciation found the process of inflation absurd. Inflation took a very diffuse course and manifested itself in scarcely predictable fits and starts. As sociohistorical studies have frequently shown, people had a rather rudimentary knowledge of the circulation of money and of inflationary developments (Feldman, *Disorder,* 5). In the final analysis, most of them had no idea how the inflation came about, or how it might be halted. As Canetti saw it, grotesque comedy was the appropriate form to represent such a meaninglessness that defied all order.

Third, Canetti believed, inflation leaves a deep sense of shame in people. "When one is ashamed," writes Georg Simmel in his *Zur Psy- chologie der Scham (On the Psychology of Shame),* "one feels one's own self rendered conspicuous in the eyes of others while, at the same time, this conspicuousness is connected to the violation of some norm (mate- rial, moral, conventional, personal)" (141).

In order to highlight the relationship between shame and inflation, I will refer briefly to the distinction between "guilt cultures" and "shame cultures," a distinction that goes back to the work of Margaret Mead and Ruth Benedict in particular (Neckel 47–48). The most important distinguishing feature is whether the normative control mechanisms are internal or external to the individual. In "shame cultures," normative control more often occurs in the context of external conventions, whereas in "guilt cultures" this control takes place within the individual's con- science. In a shame culture, the goal is appropriate behavior: one fears the social disapproval of others, and one brings disgrace upon oneself through social misconduct. The objective is to maintain personal dignity under all circumstances. For Ruth Benedict, Japanese society is an example of a "shame culture," while Western cultures tend to be "guilt cultures." Here, the conscience and the fear of pangs of remorse rule human behavior. People aspire to a clear conscience in all their actions (48). Obviously, such a distinction is mainly heuristic, since in reality both Western and Eastern cultures combine aspects of both cultural types.

The distinction between guilt and shame is so important here because of how it takes effect particularly in the experience of inflation. In this experience, another distinction crystallizes: the victim feels shame, while the perpetrator incurs guilt. Shame is combined with an element of helplessness, with defenselessness, or as Canetti indicates in his autobiography, with powerlessness. A middle class that believed itself for many years the master of its financial and economic circumstances was forced to admit, with shame, that it was at the mercy of the dictates of currency depreciation. The guilty party, no matter how heinous the deed, is at least surrounded by an aura of action. Even in the state of contrition, one can become aware of one's autonomy.

Shame is a more fitting term than guilt for the experience of the inflation because the loss of status that many members of the middle class underwent was not accompanied by culpability or moral wrongdoing. The feeling of social shame that arose—for example, at moments of status inconsistency—was all the stronger: the impoverished lawyer who found himself writing advertising slogans for a living, the noblewoman seen standing in line at the pawnshop.

This element of shame recurs frequently in descriptions of the inflation. Walter Benjamin's concludes, "Not without reason is it customary to speak of 'naked' want [nacktes Elend]. What is most damaging in the display of it . . . is not the pity or the equally terrible awareness of his own impunity [eigene Unberührtheit] awakened in the onlooker, but his shame. It is impossible to remain in a large German city, where hunger forces the most wretched to live on the bank notes with which passersby seek to cover an exposure [eine Blösse zu decken suchen] that wounds them" (One-Way Street 56). This fragment draws its dazzling multiplicity of meaning from Benjamin's play on the double meaning of the German word Scham: shame and genitals.[3] The two meanings of the word are united in the "naked want": the humiliation of social decline and sexual shame. The passerby sees the "nakedness" of the victims of inflation, particularly in contrast to his own eigene Unberührtheit, or

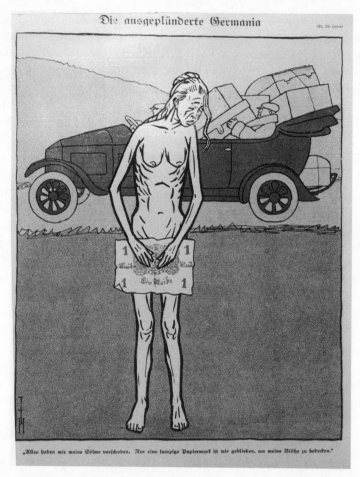

Figure 5. "Looted Germania." Illustration by Thomas Theodore Heine, in *Simplicissimus* 25 (April 21, 1920).

virgin state. Inflationary money, the banknotes *(Scheine),* cannot disguise the fact that they are—and here Benjamin engages in more wordplay—mere appearance *(Schein)* through which shines naked misery. Figure 5, a caricature from the satirical magazine *Simplicissimus,* represents Benjamin's observation in a visually striking way that echoes the relationship between shame, nakedness, and the worthlessness of inflation money. "Looted Germania," says the heading, and the line at bottom explains: "My sons have racketeered everything. A lousy paper mark is all I have left to cover my nakedness *[meine Blöße].*"

Succumbing to the centrality of money, facing an irrational and unpredictable economic phenomenon that often resulted in the loss of social status and therefore inflicted shame—these experiences point to the traumatic nature of inflation on a subjective emotional level. At the same time it is important to conceptualize inflation within a larger sociocultural context.

IV.

In this section I return to the heuristic model inspired by Canetti's writings in *Crowds and Power* that I outlined in chapter 1. This model captures the essential features of inflation both as an economic phenomenon and as a force that links it to a range of fundamental cultural dynamics of modern culture. Simmel's basic insight in *The Philosophy of Money*, that money is far more than solely an economic instrument, that it shapes and informs the way people think, conceptualize, and evaluate their social surroundings, finds its logical extension in Canetti's analysis of inflation.[4] Canetti argues for certain analogies between currency depreciation and sociopsychological developments in the 1920s by stating that people felt the depreciation of money as a degradation of their own personal and social identity. This assumption opens up the possibility of thinking about inflation beyond its monetary and economic significance and viewing it as a grand metaphor that captures the enormous cultural and psychosocial dislocations and displacements in the wake of the currency devaluation. Canetti writes about the dynamics of inflation, "The unit of money suddenly loses its identity. The crowd it is part of starts growing and, the larger it becomes, the smaller becomes the worth of each unit. . . . It is as though the process of sudden increase had deprived the thing which increases of all value" (*Crowds and Power* 186).

By conceptualizing inflation as a process of simultaneous, uncontrolled, and unpredictable massification and depreciation taking place in an ever faster-moving circulation of money, we are able to establish inflation's participation in the overarching cultural dynamics of modern life. Let me point out again that these dynamics of circulation, massification, and devaluation do not constitute new analytic terms for an understanding of modern life. In addition, inflation did not create these phenomena, nor are rapid currency depreciations bound to advanced modern Western capitalist societies. Rather, the basic role of the inflation within the fabric of modern society and culture is one of a giant accelerator that intensified these dynamics.

To illustrate and contextualize the dynamics of circulation, massification, and devaluation within the discourse on modern culture, it is useful to consider Georg Simmel's influential essay "Die Großstädte und das Geistesleben" ("Metropolis and Mental Life") from 1903. He observes, "The deepest problems of modern life derive from the claim of the individual to preserve the autonomy and individuality of his existence in the face of overwhelming social forces, of historical heritage, of external culture, and of the technique of life" (47). For Simmel, modern life is a constant individual struggle of not "being leveled down and worn out by a social technological mechanism" (ibid.). This fight against massification, against losing one's own sense of individuality in modern life, takes many different psychological and social forms, from shielding oneself against the stimuli of modern life to dramatic displays of "metropolitan extravagances of mannerism, caprice, and preciousness" (57). Always present in modern life is a sense of tempo, of rapid circulation: "With each crossing of the street, with the tempo and multiplicity of economic, occupational, and social life, the city sets up a deep contrast with small town and rural life with reference to the sensory foundations of psychic life" (48). Yet the giant maelstrom that lies at the core of this sense of tempo with which modern people circulate through the metropolis, the force that serves as a constant energizer for all this traffic, is the circulation of money. Simmel beautifully captures the essence of the triadic constellation of circulation, massification, and a perceived devaluation in the following description: "By being the equivalent to all the manifold things in one and the same way, money becomes the most frightful leveler. For money expresses all qualitative differences of things in terms of 'how much?' Money, with all its colorlessness and indifference, becomes the common denominator of all values; irreparably it hollows out the core of things, their individuality, their specific value, and their incomparability. All things float with equal specific gravity in the constantly moving stream of money. All things lie on the same level and differ from one another only in the size of the area which they cover" (52). Simmel's notion of devaluation is linked to massification and derives its meaning from the loss of the status of uniqueness, of incomparability. All things begin to float in the constantly moving stream of money and thus affect the status and identity of people connected to these things. Simmel describes the impersonal, calculating, and formal way in which social relations are conducted in modern life. His view on modern life is still rooted in the tradition of nineteenth-century German idealism and certainly expresses the viewpoint of an educated middle class (Habermas 7–17). This explains a certain romantic nostalgia that pervades his analysis of modern culture when he bemoans the loss of the uniqueness und incomparability of things. Yet it would be misleading to characterize Simmel as a cultural pessimist. Modern life for him is defined as a careful and creative process of adaptation, one of accepting these fundamental dynamics and taking advantage of the enormous potential for personal freedom and social mobility, yet at the same time finding modes of resistance against their potentially overwhelming forces.

While observing the fact that inflation brought forth the deeply threatening side of the triadic dynamic of circulation, massification, and change of values (in this context, depreciation or devaluation), it is important not to fall into the trap of adopting cultural pessimism toward modernity. All three dynamics are constitutive for any experience of modernity, yet at the same time they are subject to cultural critique. Without even trying to do justice to their ambivalent and multifaceted appearances in so many representations of modern life, I would like to sketch out some of their general characteristics.

It is evident from Simmel's essay that "circulation" addresses some of the most salient aspects of modern life. It signifies the flow of a currency, of money in general. In general economic terms, the idea of circulation, as Marx observed, captures the essence of the commodity-producing society: "The continual movement in circuits of the two antithetical metamorphoses of commodities, or the never-ceasing alternation of sale and purchase, is reflected in the restless currency of money, or in the function that money performs of a perpetuum mobile of circulation" (Marx, *Capital*, 1:130). In addition, the term *circulation* denotes the number of copies of a distributed newspaper or a periodical. We also think of circulation in connection with traffic in modern urban agglomerations. We can deduct from these examples a number of underlying principles. Circulation presupposes the transmission of a multitude of entities that, while certainly discernible, are related to each other through sameness rather than incompatible uniqueness. Similarly, we associate with circulation a system that tends to be organized more along egalitarian than hierarchical structures. It implies the flow of information, movement, exchange, on a horizontal plane among many different persons. Its opposite would be a strictly hierarchical system of human communication in the form of an order or command that never circulates, but rather is sent out in a one-directional, linear fashion. "Circulation" is a movement that returns to itself and calls into question the existence of an originating source. In addition, it possesses the quality of continuous, seemingly natural, and eternal repetition. This characteristic plays an important role in the oldest use of the word *circulation* describing the flow of blood from the heart to the different vessels of the body.

The term *massification (Vermassung)* has accompanied the development of modern societies as mass societies since the mid–nineteenth century. It carries an inherently negative connotation, partly because it assumes some kind of devaluation of all those entities that are entering a mass. Nietzsche's writings on the masses and the mob as the antithesis to the independent, heroic individual; Le Bon's characterization of the masses as mindless and erratic emotional social entities; and Ortega y Gasset's dire predictions of the downfall of intellectual elites in the "age of the masses" constitute a long tradition that casts the masses as the negative opposite of the rational, bourgeois individual.[5] Even Freud, in his *Group Psychology and the Analysis of the Ego,* follows Le Bon's perspective and cannot imagine masses without the distinct dichotomy of a mass and its superior leader. Elias Canetti stays away from such simplistic and ideological polarizations. Rather, he is interested in the enormous empowerment and liberation individuals may experience by joining a mass—which in Canetti's view by no means depends upon a leader figure. In general, Canetti understands "massification" as a process in which the individual may relinquish some autonomy but experiences an enormous growth of power as a member of the whole.

In contrast, inflation is a mass phenomenon that reverses this process. Instead of empowering individuals by their membership in a growing mass, inflation is characterized by a

> double depreciation originating in a double identification. The *individual* feels depreciated because the unit on which he relied, and with which he had equated himself, starts sliding; and the *crowd* feels depreciated because the *million* is [devalued]. It has been shown that the word million is ambiguous, standing for both a large sum of money and a large number of people, particularly the people inhabiting a modern city. . . . Together people are worth as little as each is worth alone. . . . An inflation cancels out distinctions between men which had seemed eternal and brings together in the same inflation crowd people who before would scarcely have nodded to each other in the street. (*Crowds and Power* 186–87)

Within Canetti's phenomenology of mass formations, the opposite of the bundles of millions of worthless paper marks, the opposite of inflation, is the treasure. Here the single entity, a gold coin or a precious stone, is not diminished in its value, and the treasure becomes worth even more. A treasure is excluded from circulation; it rests underground, in caves, is hidden away. It promises an eternal, untouchable value and invokes a certain nostalgia for a time past.[6]

As with the term *massification,* the notion of depreciation or devaluation *(Entwertung)* has an obviously negative meaning that overshadows the more general and ambivalent dynamic of revaluation or transvaluation *(Umwertung)* that is constitutive for modern life. As Nietzsche argues most persuasively, modernity is characterized by a trend toward relativism of all values, a constant struggle of different value systems with no overarching transcendent moral system. The process may result in emancipatory steps toward greater personal freedoms; at the same time, members of modern societies may be threatened by the absence of one authoritative system of values. The term *devaluation* in our context acquires its negative meaning by being closely related to a process of massification that, as Canetti points out, does not empower people but rather robs them of their material and social status.

Not only is his general understanding of inflation as a phenomenon that transgresses the strictly economical important with regard to its contextualization within the larger cultural dynamics of modern life, but the aspects of circulation, massification, and devaluation will also help us to uncover traumatic and hidden manifestations of the inflationary experience in different cultural and artistic expressions. By being aware of these underlying forces, we will be able to interpret different metaphorical reenactments of the currency depreciation. In addition to this broad description of inflation, Canetti's essay contains several specific insights into the sociocultural impact on inflation that I will address in later parts of this book, most importantly his provocative reflections on inflation and anti-Semitism.

V.

The world of *Crowds and Power,* despite its excess of human conflicts, its scenarios of struggle, violence, and death, remains oddly untouched by any tension or conflict between the sexes. This is all the more striking since Canetti's other central work, the novel *Auto-da-fé (Die Blendung,* 1935), draws its narrative force from the fierce battle of the sexes between its two protagonists, the independent scholar Peter Kien and his housekeeper, Therese Krumbholz (Widdig 178–210). To be sure, Canetti's novel draws its life also from other grotesque figures, such as the brutal building manager, Benedikt Pfaff; the hunchbacked chess player, Fischerle; and Peter Kien's brother, George, a psychiatrist in Paris. But the struggle between Kien and Therese runs through the story like a red thread. It becomes apparent that this grotesque conflict, too, dramatizes inflationary events. Canetti caricatures a cultural tendency closely intertwined with the triangular relationship of money, inflation, and antimodernism: the curious mixture of anticapitalism and misogyny.

"It was necessary to invent extreme individuals with the utmost consistency, like those of whom the world was actually composed, and to place these exaggerated individuals side by side in their separateness" (*Gewissen* 229): this is how Canetti himself describes his construction of the characters who people the world of *Auto-da-fé*. Peter Kien and Therese Krumbholz are extreme in their separateness: they are polar opposites. The sinologist Kien owns the largest private library in Vienna, comprising twenty-five thousand books, mainly Chinese literature and philosophy. This library is his world; it is here that he converses with his books, here that, with a gesture of disdain toward bungling university scholarship, he writes his pathbreaking essays. Kien's library is the realm of letters.

In contrast, the housekeeper, Therese, whose vocabulary, according to Kien, scarcely exceeds fifty words, adores numbers. She lovingly imagines and calculates her future wealth, fantasizing about big money and the grand romance she associates with it. While in Kien's realm the letter consolidates into a text, in Therese's world the figure becomes a sum of money.

Impressed by the solicitous motherly relationship she develops toward his books in her weekly dusting of the library over a period of eight years, Kien makes the fatal decision to marry his housekeeper. After the wedding, however, she suddenly wants regular access to the library, a desire Kien considers incredible. Their relationship becomes truly dramatic when Therese imagines that Kien is going to leave her a large fortune in his will. To her dismay, she discovers that Kien has very little money because he has spent almost his entire fortune on books.

The dialogues between the two, their endless miscommunications, and their already paranoid mutual resentment make the novel a gem of grotesque and often absurd prose. But as diametrically and implacably opposed to each other as these two persons are—he a man of the letter, the word, the intellect; she a woman of the figure, of money and the material—the will, as a form of text that necessarily brings together figures and letters, brings new life to their battle. Therese will gain access to Kien's "code," the alphabet. The weak spot in this "code" is the letter O, which has the same shape as zero. *Auto-da-fé* mentions Therese's deep affection for the letter O several times: "Her favorite letter was O. From her schooldays she had retained some practice in writing Os. (You must close up all your Os as nicely as Therese, the teacher used to say. Therese makes the best Os. . . . All the children had to copy her Os.)" (127). Out of this love for the letter gradually arises a sort of obsession with zeros, which becomes intertwined with fantasies of future wealth. Finally, the day arrives on which she lives out her desire for the big figure. She picks up Kien's will:

> Not only the number itself, 12,650, but the very outline of each figure seemed to be written in her own flesh. She went to fetch a strip of newspaper and wrote down the number exactly as it was written in the will. The figures resembled Kien's to the last hair; not even a graphologist could have told them apart. She made use of the strip of paper lengthwise so that she could put on as many noughts as she liked, and added a round dozen. Her eyes brightened at the colossal result. She caressed the strip two or three times with her rough hand and said: "Isn't it beautiful!"
>
> Then she took Kien's pen, bent over the will and changed the figure 12,650 into 1,265,000.[7]

It takes some time for Kien to recognize that his own will has been forged by Therese and been expanded by two digits. For a short while, before he becomes aware of her doing, the two naively revel in their sudden wealth. Kien fantasizes about expanding his library. One can imagine no more sarcastic fictional portrait of the ignorance with which many intellectuals, independent scholars, and professors like Peter Kien reacted to the rapid multiplication of zeros during the era of inflation.

Therese's assault on the will, whose meaning she transforms with the addition of two zeros, fails of course. This episode is nevertheless of far-reaching significance, for in her obsession with appending as many zeros as possible to sums of money, Therese herself becomes an allegory of the inflation signifying that a wild, female libidinal energy underlies the process of creating enormous value out of nothing by simply adding zeros. The symbolic representation of the inflation as unleashed female desire runs through a number of descriptions of the inflation, and will be the subject of a later chapter in this book. In his memoirs of the inflation era, Thomas Mann, for example, writes of a "witches' dance" in which the witch whirls ever more wildly ("Erinnerungen" 188).

In his representation of the battle in which Kien, the independent scholar and rentier, is finally destroyed by the money-grubbing Therese, Canetti caricaturizes the misogynist discourse of fin de siècle Vienna, as it appears, for example, in Otto Weininger's *Geschlecht und Charakter*.[8]

Therese is hungry for money, has no sense of the intellectual, is blinded and carried away by fleeting impressions. Her thinking consists not of logical strands but solely of associations with particular images strung together paratactically. By naming the housekeeper *Therese*, Canetti plays on *Theresientaler*, for many years the common coin of the Habsburg Empire, to make an ironic commentary on the relationship between money and names.

Just as the library symbolizes the sanctuary and temple of Kien's system of meaning and an allegorical space for an unworldly form of educated middle-class existence, the pawnshop of the city of Vienna, the famous Theresianum, represents the allegorical space for the figure of Therese. Here the housekeeper's principles rule absolutely: everything can be turned into money. Individual objects, particularly "cultural goods" that may once have meant something to their owners, are carried up the Theresianum's long staircase to be transformed into money. Jewelry, works of art, and, as the pinnacle of transformation, on the sixth floor of the state pawnshop, books—everything falls victim to this crude institution of capitalist exchange value. By the second half of the novel, Therese has driven Kien from his library and home. Heavily laden with books she makes the journey to the pawnshop every few days and gradually turns the library into money. Kien, for his part, mustering all his financial resources, desperately tries to buy back his books from the pawnshop. The Theresianum is a place where inflation and culture intersect—in fact as in fiction. It is here where for many intellectuals, the proverbial selling out of culture became reality.

VI.

The period of inflation marked a radical turning point in German cultural history. It meant the final breakdown of the nineteenth-century culture that Kien tried to defend so vigorously against the intrusions of a modernity "out of bounds." At the beginning of the inflation, the Weimar Republic was undergoing a cultural modernization process, and a rapid expansion of mass culture—such as cinema, sporting events, revues, and the mass circulation of various entertainment magazines—under the banner of "Americanization" took place. New forms of entertainment and amusement culture spread. The audience was recruited largely from a new type of middle class, a stratum of white-collar employees. Figure 7 captures this shift. The cartoon presents a classic "before" and "after" situation. Under the heading "The book" we see a

Figure 6. "The impoverished middle class has to sell its cherished possessions." Photo by Sennecke, Berlin, in Ostwald, *Sittengeschichte der Inflation*, 90.

circle of readers carefully studying a book, an idyllic portrayal of intellectual or even spiritual activity. The second picture, "The books," shows German society after the effects of the inflation. The couple dancing in the library would have represented well Kien's worst nightmare and Therese's ultimate fantasy. The two elegant, fox-trotting dancers could be the Bemberg couple from Canetti's Pension Charlotte, profiteers from inflationary speculation who imitate and simultaneously ridicule bourgeois cultural values by amassing books for pure decoration. While the outdated medium of books serves as a background, the new technology of the record player on the floor incorporates the new rhythm of the time. In addition, the cartoon can be read as a graphic representation of the heuristic model of inflation that I introduced in this chapter. Both pictures signify circulation. The first one portrays a circulation "under control," readers around the table exchanging and discussing ideas that emanate from the book. In the second picture, this idyllic, *bildungs-bürgerliche* scene of contemplation and erudition is replaced by the motif of modern dance—a metaphor often used to depict the moral breakdown during inflation. Circulation here signifies erotic and bodily desire and freedom from social constraints associated with the wild and

Figure 7. "The book" and "The books." Illustration by
G. Oelkranz, in *Simplicissimus* 30 (February 22, 1926).

"amoral" new dances that became so popular during the early 1920s.
The process of massification that is accompanied by devaluation is quite
strikingly portrayed by the contrast between the value of the one book
in the first picture attracting the intense attention of the reading circle
and the obvious degradation of the many books constituting a library
that has lost its function. The cartoon builds also on the *Geist* versus
Geld dichotomy assuming that the intellectual exchange of ideas has
been displaced by a superficial "Americanization."

The cartoon invokes a nostalgia for a seemingly idyllic time that has passed, and critically comments on the decline of traditional culture in postinflation Germany. Yet at the same time, the opposing constellation of the two scenes perhaps betrays the existence of the seeds of a resentment that would do more than merely take a critical stand. Soon, National Socialist cultural politics would promise a return to the first scene as the antidote to the confusions that inflation and modern life had brought about. The book would become a piece of "*völkisch* literature" or even Hitler's *Mein Kampf*. The couple in the second scene would suddenly lose their anonymity as typical figures portraying modern life. Instead, they would become Jewish and be made responsible for the destruction of the idyll. The deep-seated memory of the inflation would find its defensive counterimage and its scapegoat.

PART TWO

Money

CHAPTER FOUR

Under the Sign of Zero

Money and Inflation

I.

Next to language, money is the most important medium through which modern societies communicate. As an abstract signifier of our desires, our economic activities, and our intentions and promises, money acts very much like a language. Marshall McLuhan observed, "Like words and language, money is a storehouse of communally achieved work, skill, and experience" (136). The historian Fernand Braudel wrote that money is "an excellent indicator: the way it circulates or stagnates . . . gives us a quite accurate account about people's actions down to the most simple every-day routines" (quoted in Kintzelé 7). And Georg Simmel, in his classic study, *The Philosophy of Money,* links the very essence of modernity to the fact that money has entered all spheres of society. Thus, it is more than simply a tool for economic exchange; its different qualities shape the way modern people think, how they make sense of their reality, how they communicate, and ultimately how they find their place and identity in a modern environment.

The notion of a "culture of inflation" that I invoke in this book evolves from a fundamental insight that all these authors share: money is an essential force in the formation of cultures. Because inflation manifests itself through the medium of money, any serious currency depreciation invariably influences social and cultural practices; money translates and transmits the economic phenomenon of inflation into the lived experience of individuals and groups.

In this chapter, I will look at the medium of money from a range of different perspectives. Considering that money's essential power lies in its different economic functions, in what way exactly did the hyperinflation jeopardize and finally destroy those basic functions? Did it highlight certain characteristics of money? Did it uncover the hidden social contracts that make any monetary function possible in the first place? This chapter will also address the actual physical appearance of money during the inflation. What are the semiotic dimensions of inflation money? Besides these functional and semiotic aspects, I will discuss money's role as an ideological vessel within the antimodernist discourse of the 1920s in which the experience of inflation meant a further step toward an anticapitalist and anti-Semitic sentiment. But first I will put the discussion about money, inflation, and culture into a larger philosophical context.

II.

Throughout Western tradition, the ethical and moral status of money and its proper role in society have been contentious, with a forceful chorus of voices warning us about money's dangerous and immoral powers. Money circulates through society as a medium of exchange, but it can also be used to create more money. The terms "currency" and "capital" express this basic dual quality (Buchan 30). It is especially money's ability to create more money through credit and interest that has been seen throughout much of Western, and not only Western, history as immoral.[1] The debate that was framed in National Socialist ideology as (Jewish) *raffendes Kapital*, or greedy capital, against (German) *schaffendes Kapital*, or productive capital, had already appeared in the canonical teachings of the Catholic Church as the moral condemnation of interest-charging, especially usury, and went all the way back to the writings of Aristotle. The Greek philosopher set the stage when he argued that the "natural" purpose of money is to help people acquire the necessities of life. Aristotle regarded the accumulation of wealth through charging interest as "unnatural":

> There are two sorts of wealth-getting . . . ; one is a part of household management, the other is retail trade: the former is necessary and honourable, while that which consists in exchange is justly censured; for it is unnatural, and a mode by which men gain from one another. The most hated sort, and with the greatest reason, is usury, which makes a gain out of money itself,

and not from the natural object of it. For money was intended to be used in exchange, but not to increase at interest. And this term interest, which means the birth of money from money, is applied to the breeding of money because the offspring resembles the parent. That is why of all modes of getting wealth this is the most unnatural. (15)

Nowhere does the dual nature of money as a medium of exchange and an instrument for speculative enrichment become more apparent than during inflation. As the "natural" function of money as a medium of exchange increasingly withered during the early 1920s in Germany, people became angered by the success of young investors and speculators who created fortunes seemingly out of nothing. To get rich without working, however, one had to take advantage of the peculiar reverse situation between credit and interest during inflation. By betting on the continuing decline of the currency and therefore the increasing devaluation of future interest payments, speculators could borrow huge sums of money, immediately invest it in foreign currency or real estate, and gain an immense profit.

A second voice warning us about the alienating effect of money on all human interactions is that of a man whose own life was constantly overshadowed by financial struggles.[2] Karl Marx's bitter verdict that money is a force that estranges people from themselves and others, that liquefies all identities and objectifies human relationships, remains probably the most vehement critique of money. It was Marx's view, as James Buchan summarizes, "that a social system that evaluated men and women in terms of money and made morality a function of credit was unworthy of the human being" (200). Marx's reflections on money, coupled with his utopian dream of a society that could eventually do without money, are woven like a red thread throughout all of Marxist social and economic theory.[3]

In the third of his *Economic and Philosophical Manuscripts* from 1844, Marx presents us with an apocalyptic description of how money has destroyed any possibility of authentic identity:

That which exists for me through the medium of *money*, that which I can pay for (i.e. which money can buy), that *I am*, the possessor of the money. My own power is as great as the power of money. The properties of money are my own (the possessor's) properties and faculties. What *I am* and *can do* is, therefore, not at all determined by my individuality. I *am* ugly, but I can buy the most beautiful woman for myself. Consequently, I am not *ugly,* for the effect of ugliness, its power to repel, is annulled by money. As an individual, I am *lame,* but money provides me with twenty-four legs. Therefore, I am not lame. I am a detestable, dishonorable, unscrupulous and stupid man, but money is honored and so also is its possessor. (191)

These reflections on money lead to his apodictic statement: "The power to confuse and invert all human and natural qualities, to bring about fraternization of incompatibles, the *divine* power of money, resides in its *character* as the alienated and self-alienating species-life of man. It is the alienated *power* of *humanity*" (192).

Nobody can escape Marx's prison house of money. Money features in his thinking as an independent force that has completely taken hold of humans. The consequences are much more than only the division between rich and poor. Marx assumes that our very identity is a mediated one, mediated not by language in this case but by money. We live in a paradise-lost situation: the emergence of money—which came with private property, the division of labor, and later, capitalism—brought with it an alienation from ourselves. We are what money is: fluid, constantly changing. We serve different kings simultaneously and circulate without a moral compass. He invokes the imagery of the individual's body to argue how radically money can alter even seemingly unchangeable qualities. Money not only fulfills all desires, it also creates a reality according to our desires. With cynical candidness Marx describes the commodity status of women in this endeavor: "I *am* ugly, but I can buy the most beautiful woman for myself. Consequently, I am not *ugly*."

We are all painfully aware of how right Marx's observations are—and how wrong. Indeed, money in many ways constitutes the way we conceptualize the world and ourselves. Yet Marx overlooks, for example, that a capitalist system can only work properly when it is imbedded in a whole range of social structures and relationships that are actually protected from the exchange mechanisms of money. Capitalist systems suffer, and may even collapse, when their legal structure and their business climate are affected by pervasive corruption. Marx also underestimates the modest yet significant achievements that came along with modern society and the emergence of money. For one can argue that a modern money-economy represents an astonishing amount of civil achievement, an intricate network of trusting relationships that serves as a prerequisite for the emancipation of the individual.[4] As Georg Simmel writes, "When one laments the alienating and separating effect of monetary transactions, one should not forget the following. Through the necessity of exchanging it and receiving definite concrete values for it, money creates an extremely strong bond among members of an economic circle.

Precisely because it cannot be consumed directly, it refers people to others, from whom one can obtain what is actually to be consumed" ("Money in Modern Culture" 20).

A massive inflation, however, creates a world that is much better captured by Marx's perception of capitalism than by Simmel's optimistic liberalism. The destruction of a country's currency undermines and damages the social bonds that Simmel describes. People are forced to exchange inflation money, yet they do not receive "definite concrete values" for it. Marx's critique of the capitalist price system as the nonrelation between the "use-value" of an object and its actual "exchange value" on the market can be vividly illustrated by the outrageous price fluctuations during the inflation. His dictum that money has the power to ruthlessly "confuse and invert all human and natural qualities" aptly captures the way in which many contemporaries experienced the inflation. For the German Marxist and Communist movement, therefore, the inflation was yet another proof of the irrational and inhuman qualities of capitalism, another piece of evidence that capitalism was in its death throes.

III.

How exactly did the medium of money translate the economic phenomenon of inflation into the everyday life of Germans and cause such distress and chaos? In other words, considering that money's true essence lies in its different economic functions, how did the inflation actually impair the functional performance of Germany's currency? I will develop this analysis within the context of one of the seminal works of German cultural theory, Georg Simmel's *Philosophy of Money* (1900).[5] Simmel's book continues to be the single most important study on the relationship between money and culture. We may find some of his idealistic arguments questionable nowadays, yet many of his basic observations about the influences of the characteristics of money on modern cultures remain very plausible.

A meaningful discussion of the different monetary functions, however, has to start with a preamble that points out a fundamental condition: in order to function at all, any monetary system relies on trust.[6] As Simmel writes, "The feeling of personal security that the possession of money gives is perhaps the most concentrated and pointed form and manifestation of confidence in the socio-political organization and order"

(179). The seemingly unobtrusive flow of money between people and whole nations works only because all participants put an enormous amount of trust in a piece of paper or an electronic message that in itself is completely worthless. The nexus of trust extends not only between two individuals who engage in a monetary transaction; in each exchange a third party is involved, usually a government or a central bank that we endow with our trust that it will not abuse its power to create money and regulate its circulation. Thus, a government that prints excessive amounts of money and devalues its currency fundamentally betrays the trust of people who believe, at least for some time, that the promised value printed on a banknote corresponds to its future purchasing power.

Trust may be reinforced by past experience, yet its temporal trajectory is future oriented. John Maynard Keynes expressed this fundamental aspect of money in his *General Theory of Employment, Interest, and Money* of 1936: "The importance of money essentially flows from its being a link between the present and the future" (293). The possession of money opens up a window of time that allows us to postpone an exchange and at the same time creates countless opportunities for different exchanges. Money is at the center of the bold, at times hubristic, confidence, with which we take hold of a distant future and integrate it as a matter of course into our daily dealings.

The German hyperinflation undermined all of this. It not only damaged the social fabric of trust and caused Germans, as Thomas Mann wrote, "to look on life as a wild adventure, the outcome of which depended not on their own effort but on sinister, mysterious forces" (63). It also destroyed the strong temporal bond between present and future that a functioning monetary system carries within its core. Those who profited from the inflation, the economist Moritz Julius Bonn (1873–1965) wrote in his book *Das Schicksal des deutschen Kapitalismus* (1930), understood "the secret of inflation"; employing it, they strategized "to always be just one minute ahead with a price increase; to immediately exchange liquid assets into goods or foreign currency; to borrow as much money as possible in order to invest it in tangible assets, and to pay this credit back on a long-term payment schedule when the original sum had lost most of its value" (19). Bonn's brief, but poignant description locates the "secret" of inflation profiteering first of all in the incongruity of people's time horizons: those who had learned to radically disassociate the present from the future outsmarted those who had not changed their time horizons and still had some trust in the German currency. More important, however, Bonn's observations illustrate the distortions in the interplay of the different monetary functions. He argues that inflation profiteers capitalized on the breakdown of a common, all-encompassing time horizon for money's four different yet closely interrelated functions: money serves as a medium of exchange, it functions as a measure of value, we use it for borrowing and lending, and finally, money has an asset function: we can use it to store wealth.

In his *Philosophy of Money,* Georg Simmel regards money's function as a medium of exchange as its most important quality; indeed, he links it to the very emergence of modern society, which is accompanied by an increasing abstraction in the process of exchange. While a barter economy relies largely on the immediate social interaction between producers, a more advanced mode of exchange leads to the emergence of money and a class of merchants. Simmel concludes that "money stands between the objects of exchange as the merchant stands between the exchanging subjects. The equivalence between objects of exchange is no longer effected directly, and its fluctuations are no longer concealed; instead, each object acquires a relationship of equivalence and exchange with money" (176). Another important change marks this development: "When barter is replaced by money transactions a third factor is introduced between the two parties: the community as a whole, which provides a real value corresponding to money" (177). With the widening acceptance of money, its value is increasingly backed by political authorities. In fact, the larger the economic circle of those using a specific form of money, the stronger the value of this money has to be. This is especially the case when "substantive" money, such as gold coins, is replaced by paper money.

Looking at the unfolding of the German inflation, it seems remarkable that even at the height of the currency devaluation people continued to use the German mark as a medium of exchange. They went shopping for scarce, often rationed food and paid with million-mark banknotes. Yet one should not conclude that the inflated German mark had not lost considerable function as a medium of exchange, but as long as the German government insisted on the mark's legitimacy as a currency, as long as employers paid wages in German marks, the average citizen had no choice but to play along. The benevolent state authority that was supposed to watch over the stability of the currency had become a cynical power insisting on the use of a currency that was not worth much anymore. The real deterioration of the exchange function manifested itself mainly through three phenomena that are all part of the culture of inflation: the increasing importance of foreign currencies, the emergence of black markets with a sort of barter economy, and the circulation of emergency money.

As the mark increasingly weakened, the exchange function shifted to other currencies, mainly the American dollar. The possession of *valuta*, of strong foreign currencies, became a powerful weapon against economic misery. Thomas Mann remembers, "My family of eight was able to live tolerably well on the twenty-five dollars I received each month from the American magazine *The Dial* for a letter from Germany. One of my sons was at a boarding school in the country. Every term I gave him five dollars for his fees, which the headmaster received with satisfaction and gratitude" (188). Americans and other foreigners used the situation to their advantage. Border regions, especially the borders with Holland and Switzerland, became hotbeds of smuggling. Newspapers and magazines in the early 1920s expressed strong resentment against Americans who traveled through Germany on buying sprees. It was especially feared that these foreigners would buy up the German heritage, as Figure 8, an illustration from the social-democratic journal *Der Wahre Jakob,* indicates. The representation of the American millionaires is a mixture of two cultural and racial stereotypes. Both men embody a certain casual and nonchalant modern sportsmanship that identifies them as "American" and assumes a disinterest in the actual historical and cultural value of the castles they want to purchase. The caricature of their striking noses suggests that these are Jewish American millionaires, which, in the vocabulary of anti-Semitism, would underscore again the implicit assumption that these two men are primarily interested in real estate profits. While the anti-Semitic resentment certainly prevailed, it is difficult to say how deeply seated anti-Americanism remained after the inflation. As a plan to help Germany reconstruct its economy after the inflation, the Dawes Plan pumped a substantial amount of American money into the German economy. During at least the inflation period, however, the gap between German and foreign currencies served as a painful reminder for Germans that their own nation was impoverished.

Another phenomenon that indicates the collapse of the exchange function of the German mark was the increasing importance of a black market for scarce goods. The *Schieber*, the black marketeer, became a hallmark figure during the inflation. An important aspect of the black market economy was the frequent trips urbanites made to the countryside in hopes that a farmer would exchange butter and eggs for jewelry or rugs.[7] The barter economy existed parallel to the increasingly debilitated official economy. This switch from a money economy to barter re-

Figure 8. "Consequence of the bad exchange rate: American millionaires traveling through Germany to buy castles and villas for a few dollars." Illustration by W. Steine, in *Beilage zum Wahren Jakob* 37 (March 12, 1920).

sulted in many tensions between farmers and urban classes, partly because some farmers ruthlessly exploited the situation by excessively hoarding food, and partly because urbanites often stole food crops from the fields. Farm houses that were imagined to be full of pianos and oriental rugs became popular clichés in Germany's starving cities.

Finally, a third phenomenon that appropriated the exchange function of the German mark was the so-called *Notgeld,* emergency money that local governments and companies printed throughout the early 1920s. *Notgeld* circulated only in local communities, yet it proved to be a valuable alternative to the general currency. I will address this form of money briefly in the next part of this chapter.

When we exchange goods and services, we simultaneously utilize a second essential function of money: it serves as a common yardstick within a price system. In many ways, this measurement function of money can be most directly linked to the economic unfolding of an inflation, which is, after all, defined as a "process of continuously rising prices, and of the currency's persistent loss of external and internal purchasing power" (Holtfrerich 6). The actual destructive effect of inflation, however, is determined by the complicated dynamics of different price-related factors that I have described in chapter 2: price rises were by no means continuous and steady, prices did not increase at the same rate for all products, and salaries and wages were adjusted differently—with different time lags—to the overall increase of the cost of living.

The German mark's impaired ability to serve as a reliable measurement of economic value determined people's lives in countless ways. The constant adjustment to the rising prices caused an enormous frenzy in everyday life. A correspondent for the British newspaper *Daily Mail* reported on July 29, 1923: "In the shops the prices are typewritten and posted hourly. For instance, a gramophone at 10 a.m. was 5,000,000 marks but at 3 p.m. it was 12,000,000 marks. A copy of the *Daily Mail* purchased on the street yesterday cost 35,000 marks but today it cost 60,000 marks" (Angell 336). For those who remembered that a head of cabbage may have cost 25 pfennig not so long before, its 1923 price of 50 million marks became a mind-boggling absurdity. Older Germans can still recount the millions of marks they paid for the most basic groceries. Yet I believe that the actual emotional distress that etched those prices into collective memory has its source less in absolute prices than in the often radically altering price relationship of different goods and services to each other.

Georg Simmel, who touches only briefly upon the phenomenon of inflation in his *Philosophy of Money,* nonetheless establishes a thoughtful context about these changing relationships. He relates any increase in the quantity of money to a "disturbing effect upon the pace of social life" (503). Such changes in money supply increase the tempo of life, yet they also result in price changes. They affect the countless equations that money establishes between objects. We compare these objects

> according to their utility value, their aesthetic, ethical, eudaemonistic and labour value, with reference to hundreds of relationships of quantity and quality. . . . Thus, their money value creates an equation and comparison between them that is in no way a constant function of other values, yet is always the expression of some notions of value that are the origin and combination of others. Every value standpoint that orders and ranks things differently and cuts across the usual mode of ordering things provides, at the same time, a new vitality for their relationship, a suggestion of as-yet unknown combinations and syntheses, of the discovery of their affinities and differences. This is because our minds are constantly endeavouring to counterbalance what is irregular and to force differentiation upon the uniform. In so far as money confers upon things within a given sphere a sameness and differentiation to a greater extent than any other value standpoint, it thereby stimulates innumerable endeavours to combine these with the ranking derived from the other values in the sense of these two tendencies. (Ibid.)

This passage demonstrates how radically Simmel connects price changes to a rearrangement of our sociopsychological reality. He makes us aware that these changes are not simply numerical alterations within an economic universe expressing ever renewed balances between supply and demand. Rather, they reach deep into the fundamental way we make sense of the world by constantly sorting out sameness and differentiation. It is essential to understand that Simmel regards price changes on the whole as necessary and healthy because they force a certain fluidity into the way we think about things and their relations. At the same time, this system seeks balance. And it is precisely here where rapid and radically distorted price increases show their disastrous effect. Simmel writes that "debased paper money" only highlights the effect of price changes "in the same way as some aspects of normal physiology are most clearly illustrated by pathological and abnormal cases" (499). People's endeavors "to counterbalance what is irregular and to force differentiation upon the uniform" become more and more difficult given the "pathological" way in which prices change in an inflationary economy. When people no longer perceive prices as expressions of different types of values, the very fabric of society, the myriad forms of *Wechselbeziehungen,* of interdependencies, begins to unravel.

Whereas the breakdown of money's function as a measure of value became a sort of public spectacle as prices became increasingly outrageous, the collapse of money's function as a standard of deferred payment was much more hidden. The effect of the inflation upon this function is illustrated by a story that repeated itself, with slight variations, countless times:

> Often you were betrayed without malicious intent. During the War, I had invested ten thousand marks in a friend's country house, where I was a frequent guest. In a sense I was part-owner of the house. For all practical purposes, my loan of ten thousand marks was guaranteed by a lien on the house. In the spring of 1923 my friend informed me that circumstances had obliged him to sell his house, so he was returning my money. As a matter of fact, he added with a smile, it was the same ten thousand, the same bank-notes I had given him in 1917; they had been lying untouched in his safe all the while. There I stood, incredulous, baffled and embarrassed holding the clean, almost new, handsomely engraved museum pieces. (Mann, "Inflation," 62–63)

Thomas Mann's ambivalence about the ethical dimension of his friend's action was echoed in a larger legal discussion during the early 1920s.[8] To take advantage of the decreasing values of one's debts was only possible because of the "mark = mark principle." Part of the German currency's definition as a *gesetzliches Zahlungsmittel,* as "legal tender," included the provision that the creditor had to accept the nominal value of the liability in all circumstances (Pfleiderer 71). This meant, simply put, that the mark of yesterday equaled the mark of today. With the increasing depreciation of the mark, the German legal system was increasingly pressured to reconsider this principle. But it was only after the inflation, on November 28, 1923, that a decision by the Fifth Senate of the Reichsgericht paved the way for the readjustment of loans according to their original values, albeit to varying degrees (see chapter 2). In the meantime, some lenders had found different ways to insure the value of their loans, such as basing them on foreign currencies or including specific conditions for inflation adjustments. It is interesting that the Reichsgericht in its reversal of the nominalist law invoked the basic principle of *Treu und Glauben,* of trust, as the overriding principle in all business contracts. The situation is not without irony, because the largest debtor in this game was the German state itself. The inflation has often been described as a kind of indiscriminate taxation that allowed the German state to free itself from all internal war debts. It is impossible to judge exactly what form of residual resentment remained in those who had invested their precious capital in war bonds, and how many friendships, family ties, and business relationships were soured because of this legal form of betrayal.

Finally, money has a fourth important function: it provides us with a way in which to store our wealth and serves as a convenient form in which to hold back income we do not immediately need to use. In that sense, it is a pure expression of *Vermögen* in the literal sense of the word, of ability and potentiality. I will address this asset function only summarily at this point, because its collapse within the inflationary scenario is closely linked to the fate of pensioners and rentiers, whose situation I will discuss in more detail in chapter 7. As the mark depreciated, millions of rentiers, people who lived on pensions and life insurance, lost their livelihood. The father of William Guttmann, coauthor of *The Great Inflation,* was a typical example:

> My father had sold his business during the war together with all the real-estate property he owned, and retired from active business. He was, by middle-class standards, a rich man and intended to live as a rentier on the proceeds of his investments. These were mainly life-insurance policies, fixed-value securities, among them a lot of war loans, and the biggest single item was a mortgage on a large agricultural estate of 300,000 marks, whose yield of 15,000 marks per annum would have provided a very good income. All this depreciated, of course, to zero—my father managed to keep his head above water by resuming some work. The impact on my own life was dramatic. Once upon a time I had dreamed of a glamorous student existence à la old Heidelberg as the birthright of a rich man's son. The reality, as I have described, was very different: even by early 1922 that fabulous income from the big mortgage was not much more than was necessary to maintain me for a couple of terms in very reduced circumstances. (Guttmann and Meehan 130)

One of the actions people undertook to save their assets was the *Flucht in die Sachwerte,* the flight into "real values," into tangible assets, everything from real estate to art collections. Nevertheless, the collapse of money's asset function resulted in a vast redistribution of wealth, especially among the middle class.

The four main functions of money—means of exchange, means of measurement, standard for deferred payment, and liquid asset—are, of course, interrelated. Because money fulfills so many roles, each member of a society encounters money in a different mix of these functions. Thus, during the German inflation their breakdown and the resulting deep sense of chaos was experienced in many differing ways. While the depression in the late 1920s and early 1930s etched itself into collective memory mainly through one phenomenon—namely, large-scale unemployment—inflation's collapse of money's functions created a much wider range of diverse experiences.

IV.

On July 26, 1923, the correspondent for the British *Daily Mail* reported: "The printing presses are working day and night to supply the Reichsbank with 2,000,000,000,000 mark-notes daily but there are still not enough to go around. . . . This morning motor-lorries loaded with paper money kept on arriving at the Reichsbank but messengers with handcarts were also there to take away the bundles of notes passed out by the Bank. Film operators are taking pictures of the scene. The cashier of my bank handed me 4,000,000 marks in 1,000 mark notes, each worth less than one-fourth of a cent" (Angell 335). Eyewitness accounts like this one paint a vivid picture of the hyperinflation "in action"; they highlight the unfolding of the interrelated dynamics of massification, of devaluation, and the rapid circulation of money. To convey the essential narrative of the inflation to his readers, the British journalist relies on inflation's most demonstrable manifestation: the overwhelming presence of huge masses of paper money in its different denominations. Many older Germans still keep *Inflationsgeld* banknotes such as the ones shown in Figures 9a and 9b as memorabilia and striking reminders of those turbulent times. During the hyperinflation, the Reichsdruckerei, the most important agency printing money, had more than seventy-five hundred employees working desperately to fulfill the demand for more money. All in all, 10 billion banknotes were printed during the inflation years (Rittmann 72).

Next to the official banknotes, so-called *Notgeld,* emergency money, was issued by many local communities. Usually, this emergency money served as a local currency, and in some cases it kept its value for longer periods of time than did the official banknotes. *Notgeld* was often issued as a series in which images on the different banknotes retold a local myth or fairy tale, as Figure 10 shows. These often quite decorative banknotes had already become collectors' items during the inflation. With their visually striking designs, they stood in stark contrast to the official paper money. More important, in their imagery they abandoned any national context and relied on a strictly regional and local cultural environment. In that sense, they indicated, on the one hand, the weakness and tenuousness of national political structures in the early 1920s. On the other hand, they resurrected a strong sense of a regional identity that was almost always based on a cultural narrative.

Many photographers attempted to depict the devaluation of money

Figure 9a and 9b. Inflation money: a 100,000-mark banknote and a 10-million mark banknote.

by unveiling that which was left: the sheer materiality of banknotes as paper.[9] Contrary to objects or gold coins, which may offer intrinsic material value to their holders, the *Geldschein,* the banknote, once its valuable signifying power is diminished, reveals to a terrifying degree its lack of any material value. Figure 11, "Banknotes as wastepaper," probably

Figure 10. Emergency money printed in Stadt
Osterfeld depicting "The myth of the castle
of Vondern."

taken in 1923, shows a man selling his inflation money as wastepaper.
The value of banknotes is being decided by weight. The huge stack of paper on the right stresses the overall message that the paper money on the
scale is no different from any other sort of paper being bought by the
shopkeeper. Even though a sense of oddity permeates this scene, the
woman tries to give the impression of "business as usual." The customer,
probably a member of the now-impoverished middle class, stares quite

Figure 11. "Banknotes as wastepaper." Photo by Atlantic, Berlin, in Ostwald, *Sittengeschichte der Inflation*, 47.

perplexedly at the pile of money. One detects a mixture of embarrassment, curiosity, and powerlessness in his demeanor: he wants to display a sort of casualness by keeping his hands in his pockets—as if paper money has always been measured by weight—yet this gesture remains forced and contradicts his more formal suit and hat. One might speculate on how the customer will be paid for his paper money. Will it be newly issued money, perhaps local emergency money, or even some groceries? While Figure 11 drastically disavows that money has privileged status and shows that it is nothing more than paper, Figure 12 displays, perhaps unintentionally, the gap between the obvious madness of the printing excesses and the official attempt to nevertheless give this money an official aura. The money is neatly stacked, and a bank clerk painstakingly counts the bundles. In his left hand he holds what is probably a list into which exact amounts are entered. The photo expresses an atmosphere of order and correctness; it wants to convey the idea that despite these masses of money, the monetary system is still fully under control. There are still loyal, trustworthy civil servants who handle this money as if it were not the product of the inflationary maelstrom. Yet at the

Figure 12. "In the vault of the Reichsbank: mountains of stacked money."
Photo by Scherl, Berlin, in Ostwald, *Sittengeschichte der Inflation,* 95.

same time, these bundles look like bricks, and the idea of a single banknote is barely conceivable anymore. There is something uncanny about
these piles of money, which extend far beyond the man's own height.
How does he count this money? How many zeros will his list contain?

Often children are included in photographic portrayals of the inflation. The photo in chapter 2 of this book showing two children next to
an enormous tower of money presents such an example; in Figure 13
children build a sort of kite with inflation money. The frequent display
of inflation money with children conveys the message that this money
has lost all seriousness. In the hands of children money becomes *Spielgeld,* that is, to be used for play. On a semantic level, one is reminded of
the double meaning of *spielen* and *Spielgeld,* of play and gamble, of children's play money and gambling chips. The notion of gambling, as I will
address in chapter 5, combines the moment of play with monetary speculation; the children's play with money seems to indicate that inflation
money has become part of a decidedly noncapitalist, noneconomic
world of children. These three children seem to be unconcerned that they

Figure 13. "Playing with money." Photo by Atlantic, Berlin, in Ostwald, *Sittengeschichte der Inflation,* 214.

are playing with money. As much as one might lament the situation, there is also a kind of Rousseauian atmosphere in this photo, a moment of creative playfulness and innocence.

All these photos express the different characteristics of the inflation by situating its most important visual signature, namely, paper money, in concrete social situations. Inflation money inundated Germans' (and Austrians') daily lives. Printed on these banknotes, visible in every shop window, following people into their dreams was the sign that I regard as the most essential and most telling semiotic symbol of the inflation: the number zero.

V.

Bank clerks complained about how much the counting of endless tails of zeros frustrated them and caused them to lose any relationship to the money they were handling (Guttmann and Meehan 46–47). In an article in *Berliner Tageblatt* on February 9, 1921, Walter Rathenau had warned that those producing rows of zeros were in danger of losing a sense of reality: "They write down zeros, and nine zeros mean a billion. A billion comes easily and trippingly to the tongue, but no one can imagine a billion. What is a billion? Does a forest contain a billion leaves?" (quoted in Fergusson 48; translation slightly altered). Rathenau's warning links the zero to the power of a sudden multiplication that evades the imagination. Like the magic spell in Goethe's *Zauberlehrling,* the zero, to Rathenau's mind, can unleash uncontrollable powers beyond reason. The zero is not only an abundantly frequent sign during an inflation, but its unique qualities as a mathematical number and a cultural sign also harbor and exemplify essential aspects of an inflation.

The number zero possesses certain mathematical qualities that are different from those of other numbers. Brian Rotman writes that the zero affects "values of numerals wherever it occur[s] but ha[s] no value itself" (12). It indicates the absence of other numerals, and in that sense it is a "sign-about-signs," or what Rotman calls a "meta-sign" (13). Additionally, the zero indicates the starting process of counting. As "a number declaring itself to be the origin of counting, the trace of the one-who-counts and produces the number sequence, zero is a meta-number, a sign indicating a whole potentially infinite progression of integers" (14).

For Rotman, the introduction of the zero during the Renaissance, together with the vanishing point in perspective art and the introduction of "imaginary money," mainly paper money, created a crucial change in conceptualization. All three codes are signs about signs indicating the absence of certain other signs.[10] The mathematical sign of zero came to Western Europe during the fourteenth century with the introduction of the Hindu system of numerals already widely used by Arab merchants. The emergence of mercantile capitalism during the Renaissance necessitated new ways of calculating and processing monetary transactions, most importantly the need for double-entry bookkeeping. The Roman numerical system did not have a sign with the properties of the zero. Yet the introduction of the mathematically superior Hindu system, with the zero as an integral part of its numerical system, was long resisted because of hostility toward the concept of "nothing" in Christian orthodoxy (Rotman 8). The idea of "nothing" touches indeed at the very center of any theory of origin and creation. Already Greek philosophers, especially Plato and Aristotle, reacted to the idea of "nothing" with unease and fear. Rotman observes, "Within the full indivisible universe of Being there could be no fissure, absence, hole, or vacuum; the void did not exist, it could have no being, it was not" (63). This *horror vacui* continued in Christianity. For Saint Augustine, "nothing" presented "a kind of ultimate privation, the final and limiting term of that which was absent, lacking, lost, which had been subtracted and taken away from the original presence and fullness of God" (ibid.). "Nothing" marked the sphere of the ultimate evil, the reign of the devil, the complete absence of God. The deep-seated unease about the zero in Western philosophical tradition is linked to its state of nonidentity, to the deeply paradoxical structure of a signifier that signifies the absence of something.[11] This nothingness establishes itself through the opposites of both void and infinity. The number zero both indicates an empty plurality and stands at the beginning of a potentially infinite numerical progress.

The enormous significance of the zero for the dynamic of an inflation should be apparent now. An inflation marks a catastrophic meltdown in which the opposites of infinite growth and void collapse into each other. As long as these opposites are separated, the zero enables us to, on the one hand, perform powerful multiplications. By simply adding a zero to a number, the power of the counting process—and indirectly the subject that counts—reveals itself in its purest, most abstract form. As long as these opposites are separated, the zero allows us, on the other hand, to indicate moments of absolute silence and emptiness. This is the strange beauty of double-entry bookkeeping: the zero on the balance sheets, indicating that countless income and expenditure transactions balance each other in perfect harmony, has filled generations of accountants with joy and deep satisfaction.

During an inflation, however, zero's power to signify growth and multiplication is fused with zero's signification of a void. As Elias Canetti writes in *Crowds and Power*, "The growth negates itself. . . . What used to be one Mark is first called 10,000, then 100,000, then a million. The identification of the individual with his mark is thus broken, for the latter is no longer fixed and stable, but changes from one moment to the next. . . . Whatever he is or was, like the million he always wanted he becomes nothing. Everyone has a million and everyone is nothing" (186). Void manifests itself through rapid growth and results in a *horror vacui*, a moment of radical nonidentity, in which all balances are broken, the moment in which Saint Augustine locates all evil.

An additional link between the number zero and an inflation is paper money, which serves as the visual carrier for the zero. Brian Rotman argues that paper money and the zero are not only signs about signs, and signify absence, but they also "articulate a central, and previously implicit, feature of the meta-signs which gave rise to them: namely that the opposition between anterior 'things' and posterior 'signs' (for things) is an illusion, a fiction of representation unsustainable when faced with the inherently non-referential status of a sign for the absence of signs" (57). Rotman points out the development of monetary systems, from gold coins to paper money backed by a gold-standard system to the emergence of money that promises its holder nothing else but its identical replacement. He argues that a radical break takes place when money is "recognized as an instrument for *creating* money" (49), and concludes, "The scandal is the loss of anteriority: paper money, instead of being a representation of some prior wealth, of some anterior pre-existing quantity of real gold or silver specie becomes the creator, guarantor and sole evidence for this wealth" (50). This is, as noted at the beginning of this chapter, Aristotle's worst nightmare becoming reality.

The creation of money ex nihilo becomes, of course, most apparent with the abolition of the gold standard. Germany had stopped backing the German mark with gold reserves at the beginning of World War 1, in 1914.[12] All the paper money of the inflation was, in Rotman's sense, strictly self-referential: its creation did not point to any specific anterior object such as gold reserves. Marc Shell, who has traced the debates on the introduction of paper money in the United States, observes that while proponents of a gold currency could always insist that this money is ultimately a "thing," and not just a sign, paper money is based on pure appearance, on *Schein,* and refers to nothing other than itself. With their common trait of self-referentiality, with their lack of origin outside or before themselves, the duo of paper money and the zero provided the framework for a specific mental and psychological experience. While many may have subconsciously been aware of the fact that their money was created out of nothing, money's ultimate collapse into nothing nevertheless proved to be traumatic.[13] All the hidden fears about the "artificial" creation of money ex nihilo that Aristotle had already condemned as blasphemous, all the deep-seated fears about the zero, proved to be true.[14]

VI.

The devastating German inflation was an ideal breeding ground for all kinds of "money reformers." Although the specter of a society without a monetary system may seem improbable to us, we should not overlook the powerful utopian dream of drastically curtailing certain functions of money or even abolishing it altogether. Different pamphlets, manifestos, and theoretical treatises bear witness to those long-forgotten and seldom-researched economic crusaders of the 1920s who wanted to free humankind from the scourge of money. On the whole, these visionaries remained on the margins, except those whose radicalism would eventually merge into a political norm, as in the case of Gottfried Feder, one of National Socialism's most important economists. I will explore his ideas on money, anti-Semitism, and the creation of a National Socialist economy in the last chapter of this book.

The economist Franz Haber undertook the task of collecting and criticizing some of these theories in his book *Untersuchungen über Irrtümer moderner Geldverbesserer (On the Errors of Modern Money-Reformers,* 1926). Feder, with his National Socialist critique of "interest-capitalism," is just one of the money reformers Haber investigates. Yet right-wing authors were not the only ones to inveigh against the uncontrolled forces of money. On the other end of the ideological spectrum stands Silvio Gesell (1862–1930), for example, a monetary and social visionary whose influence had already begun before World War 1, and increased in the wake of the inflation. Gesell was born in Germany, had lived in Argentina, where he became a successful businessman, and had moved back to Germany in 1900. In 1919, he became minister of finance in the short-lived socialist Bayrische Räterepublik. Gesell spent the last years of his life on a reform-oriented farm project in Eden-Oranienburg, near Berlin.[15]

Gesell's economic and social programs have become known under the name Freiwirtschaftslehre, which was propagated during the 1920s by the Freiwirtschaftsbund and several other smaller factions. Like Marx, Silvio Gesell sought to overcome capitalism. Yet whereas Marx located the source of capitalist exploitation in the private ownership of the means of production, Gesell believed that exploitation and economic misery were the results of a faulty monetary system (358). His basic assumption was that money and products are not really in a relationship of equivalence as Marx assumed. Gesell argues that goods and services have a distinctive disadvantage against money because they are to be brought to the market quickly. Any delay results in costs and the risk of spoilage by breakage, rust, natural disasters, diseases, and so on. Money, on the other side, can potentially be exchanged for goods or services—or not. One always has the option of lending money and earning interest with it. Gesell's chief aim was, therefore, to put money and products on an equal footing. He believed this could be achieved by abolishing all interest and replacing it with a negative form of interest: the longer one kept a banknote from circulation, the more it would lose in value. As a consequence, Gesell argues, nobody could gain wealth anymore through *arbeitsloses Einkommen* (workless income), and the economy would flourish because everybody would be more than willing to invest. Gesell believed that this, together with radical land reform that would nationalize all privately owned land, constituted the solution to economic misery. The feasibility of an economic system that basically abolishes the possibility for any savings is only one of the many questions that Fritz Haber discusses in his in-depth critique of Freiwirtschaftslehre. Gesell's theoretical terrain is more wide-ranging and complex than I can describe here.[16] In general, his work combines anarchism, especially the work of the anarcho-socialist Pierre-Joseph Proudhon (1809–65), with ideas from the German youth movement, the ecological nature-reform movement *(Natur-Reform Bewegung)*, and basic aspects of socialism.

While Gesell's critique of the capitalist monetary system is part of a larger socialist and romantic tradition, another money reformer can be linked much more closely to the cultural context of the German inflation: Berthold Otto, author of the 1924 booklet *Abschaffung des Geldes: Arbeitswährung, Rechenwirtschaft (The Abolition of Money: Work Currency, Accounting-Based Economy)*. Otto (1859–1933) was by no means an economist. As a teacher and educator he became an important force in the German pedagogic reform movement around the turn of the century; in 1906 he founded his own school in Berlin. In the foreword to *Abschaffung des Geldes* he informs his readers that in early 1924 he had sent a draft of his book to all representatives of the German Reichstag in order to advise them on future financial politics—"of course in vain," he adds indignantly (4).

Viewing Otto's treatise from the standpoint of a sober economist, Franz Haber was right to call Otto's ideas "unbelievably half-baked" and "without any sense of reality" (38). Yet as bizarre and nonsensical as Otto's crusade for the abolition of money may be, it offers us an interesting insight into what one could call the "socioeconomic unconscious" of a layman who reacted to the trauma of the money depreciation. And as we will see, Otto's positions do intersect with many popular reactions to the effects of inflation. He laments that, once and for all, the inflation had shown to the world the destructive powers of monetary speculation and the overall spreading of *Mammonismus*, the total commodification, and ultimately *Käuflichkeit*, the venality, of everything. He locates the source of such speculation abroad. In his opinion, foreign interests in the German economy dictated the price of domestic goods and

services: "Why should the [German] miller buying rye, the baker buying flour, the consumer buying bread care at which exchange rate speculators in New York purchase German marks with which we buy our rye,
flour and bread?" (6–7). He admits, however, that many Germans had
succumbed to the seduction of speculation as well. In addition, he notes
that money in itself has a tendency to move everything into the circle of
Käuflichkeit. Berthold Otto's cure for the contagious disease of *Mammonismus:* quit cold turkey, abolish money, and turn society into a
work-based community, a *Werkgemeinschaft*.

His vision of a moneyless society is squarely grounded in an organic
model of a *völkisch* community with rigid borders and a strong sense of
autarky. He appeals to his readers: "In the future, no German who wants
to be worth that name, should possess any capital abroad" (15). The
Volksgemeinschaft would own all means of production and all products.
Monetary exchange would be replaced by a statewide accounting system.
Through work, individuals—primarily men between 18 and 65 years of
age—would earn a certain amount of "demand units" for themselves
and their families. Aware of the rather patriarchal aspect of this system,
the "economist" Otto assumes a role as a prominent educator and de-
fends women's part as mothers, who should be limited mainly to raising
children (28–29). The relation between accomplished work and the
price of goods and services would be set once and for all by a group of
experts. When people bought something, the exchange would be entered into both an individual account and the nationwide accounting
system. Instead of money values, the system would compile the exact
number of the different products being purchased. According to Otto,
this method would allow for an instantaneous and complete transparency of the national economy. Every day, consumer statistics would
be published. They would instill a "joy of statistics" in everyone (83),
says Otto, because the clarity and directness of these statistics would
give people a sense that they were an intimate part of the overall economy: "I am convinced that very few readers will want to miss the evening local newspaper that not only reports how much cheese but also
how much [of the] different cold cuts, meat . . . and other kinds of groceries were sold in one's own hometown. . . . There are other joys of statistics the reader will experience. For example, a compilation of the average consumption of bread and meat, comparisons with other towns,
information about rising or sinking consumption of certain goods. . . .
Over time, not only smart businessmen . . . but even the simplest work-

man will be able to judge the future sales prospects of his company"
(83–84). Berthold Otto assures us that the complete transparency of
this demand-driven economy would not only make production adjustments easy but would also streamline the complex task of allocating resources for future investments. These decisions would be made by a
council with the overall premise that they would insure the "organic
health of the economy" (28). Not greed for more money, but rather a
basic "joy of work" and respect from their community would motivate
people to give their best in this system (89).

In many ways, Berthold Otto's economic utopia is a planned economy
in which a central agency replaces a market mechanism and regulates
the allocation of resources in order to reconcile supply and demand.
Franz Haber addresses the many economic faults and shortcomings in
Otto's system, offering, among other things, a major critique of any
planned economy, observing that rigid price fixing distorts the necessary
interaction between supply and demand structures (82–86). However,
more relevant to my topic are the specific cultural messages contained in
Otto's *Abschaffung des Geldes.* Central to his concept is the notion of
work and an unmediated relationship between production and consumption, which I will explore in detail in chapter 6. Along with "transparency," the notions of order and orderliness appear repeatedly. He describes the move from capitalism to a moneyless society as the change
from "economic anarchy to economic order" (42).

What I find most interesting, however, is Berthold Otto's passion or,
might I say, obsession, with statistics, lists, and compilations that replace
money as a medium of economic information. In loving detail he designs
possible templates and chart arrangements for all kinds of economic exchanges. Yet his desire for documentation does not stop here. He envisions registers that give precise and immediate access to people's personal lives: an *Ortsbuch* that compiles current and past home addresses,
a *Stammbuch* that stores all significant data about their families, and
even a *Besitzverzeichnis* that painstakingly reports individuals' possessions, such as one's neighbor's type of furniture or bicycle (93–103).
Here, the anonymity of a market economy with a monetary system finds
its opposite in the seemingly benevolent attempt to register everything in
order to alleviate all economic and social distress. Otto's obsessive demand for listings and compilations is a telling reaction to the inflationary chaos with all its opacity and disorder.[17] With regard to a larger historical picture, it should be noted that both National Socialism and
Stalinism responded in a sense to Otto's vision with the promise that a

master plan as the result of centrally accumulated data would guarantee the orderly and efficient development of the economy.[18]

VII.

Germany's loss of the world war, the abdication of the Kaiser, the tumultuous beginnings of the young republic, and the unfolding of the inflation—all these experiences left many Germans with a deep sense of chaos and a search for a framework that would give meaning to history's rather unpredictable twists and turns. Large parts of the middle class found answers in arguably the most powerful catalyst for all forms of cultural pessimism throughout the 1920s: Oswald Spengler's *Der Untergang des Abendlandes (Decline of the West)*. The philosopher Ernst Cassirer once remarked about this book, "Maybe never before has a philosophical work had such a sensational success. The book was translated into almost all languages and was read by all kinds of readers—philosophers and scholars, historians and politicians, students and researchers, businessmen and the person on the street" (378). The first volume of *The Decline of the West* was published in 1918 and sold out in no time. In the summer of 1922 the eagerly awaited second volume appeared with the subtitle *Perspectives of World History*. While the critical reception of this second part was more subdued, *The Decline of the West* continued to be a commercial success. By the end of 1926 more than a hundred thousand copies had been sold. One wonders how many readers actually made it through the twelve hundred pages of Spengler's tour de force, which spanned eight different world cultures. Yet the title of this book became a household phrase during the 1920s; and such familiar and popular dichotomies as culture/civilization, community/society, province/metropolis, instinct/intellect, and so on that give structure to Spengler's arguments resonated strongly within the ranks of an insecure and beaten German middle class.

Oswald Spengler (1880–1936) was a typical representative of the "Conservative Revolution": he was elitist and misogynist, disdained modern mass society, and rejected the parliamentarian system of the Weimar Republic.[19] His initial support for the emerging National Socialist Party in Munich, however, soon waned. Like many other intellectuals of the "Conservative Revolution," Spengler became disillusioned with the development of National Socialism, accusing the party of having a "low intellectual level." The National Socialists in return started a press campaign against him. Spengler and Hitler met once during the Wagner Festival in Bayreuth in 1933, only to confirm their mutual dislike for one another (Felken 194). Spengler retreated from public life and died in Munich in 1936.

Why read *The Decline of the West* within the context of money and inflation? Although the book's merits as a scholarly contribution to an understanding of cultural history are questionable, *The Decline of the West* served as a kind of cultural compass for many Germans throughout the 1920s and 1930s, mainly affirming their disillusionment with modernity, yet also encouraging them to fatalistically accept the status quo. Central to Spengler's cultural theory was the role money plays in the eventual decline of cultures. I am not arguing that *The Decline of the West* was written as a direct reaction to the inflation. Spengler's ideas for this work originated in the beginning of World War 1, and his book was enthusiastically read throughout the 1920s. Even though money plays a crucial role in his understanding of cultural dynamics, the German inflation does not appear in his wide-ranging cultural analysis that spans more than three thousand years of human activity. Yet the inflation presented itself as "living proof" of Spengler's theorems. *The Decline of the West* gave its readers an ideological framework to integrate the destructive power of money into the larger scope of things. As I will show, money stands at the center of Spengler's work, which, despite its myriad of historical details, is above all a cultural ideology. Spengler uses the term *money* as part of a powerful binary construction whose other pole is *blood*. Both terms serve as cultural metaphors and are overloaded with the cultural imagery of an organic, antimodern discourse. I have chosen Spengler's work not because it provides us with a unique perspective, but rather because it is so typical, so "replete with the familiar catalogue of antimodernism" (Herf 49).

While Simmel in his analysis of money and culture carefully balances his own melancholia about a perceived loss of immediacy with his embrace of a modern society, Spengler indulges in a heroic pessimism and transforms money into a largely ideological force. Spengler's main argument in *The Decline of the West* is that human cultures follow the same cycle of birth, youth, prime, decline, and death as all natural organisms: "That which Goethe called *Living Nature* is exactly that which we are calling here world-history, *world-as-history*. Goethe, who as artist portrayed the life and development, the thing-becoming and not the thing-become . . . hated Mathematics. For him, the world-as-mechanism stood opposed to the world-as-organism, dead nature to living nature, law to form. . . . And just as he followed out the development of the plant-form from the leaf . . . —*the Destiny in nature and not the Causality*— so here we shall develop the form-language of human history, its periodic structure, its *organic logic* out of the profusion of all the challenging details" (1:25–26). In other words, just as a botanist knows the developmental stage of a flower, Spengler argues that with the help of his cultural morphology it is possible to trace the development of different cultures. Consequently, Spengler believes that he not only can assess the current life-moment of a specific culture, including his own, but also can predict its inevitable decline and death.

For our purposes it is not essential to go in detail through the various stages of the different Egyptian, Indian, Arab, and European cultures that he investigates. Basically, Spengler understands cultural development to mean the increasing abstraction in thinking, accompanied by the rising importance of mathematics and of money. It means a development from the intuitive and mythical to the rational and calculable. The increasing spread of these developing cultures is accompanied by a widening separation between city and country. While Spengler locates this stage in Arab culture as having developed between the fourth and fifth centuries, in Western European culture this period begins in the fourteenth and fifteenth centuries. The final stage in the decline of a culture—which Spengler calls "civilization"—takes place in the modern metropolis with its urban, modern lifestyle: "In place of a type-true people, born of and grown on the soil, there is a new sort of nomad, cohering unstably in fluid masses, the parasitical city dweller, traditionless, utterly matter-of-fact, religionless, clever, unfruitful" (1:32).

Modern civilizations for Spengler are dominated by cold calculation, by the spirit of money. Influenced by Simmel's *Philosophy of Money,* Spengler observes how money influences modern thinking: "Abstract money corresponds exactly to abstract number. Both are entirely inorganic. The economic picture is reduced exclusively to quantities, whereas the important point about 'goods' had been their quality" (2:481–82). Accordingly, the trader begins to dominate the economic life.[20] "He forces the producer to offer, and the consumer to inquire of him. He elevates mediation to a monopoly and thereafter to economic primacy, and forces the other two to be 'in form' in *his* interest, to prepare the wares according to *his* reckonings, and to cheapen them under the pressure of *his* offers" (2:483–84). We already noticed this distinctly negative reaction to any mediating agent in Gesell's Freiwirtschaftslehre, present even more strikingly in Otto's *Abschaffung des Geldes.* One can argue that Spengler's rhetoric of dichotomy does not allow for any third element. Consequently, the merchant or trader is positioned as the oppressor of both the consumer and the producer. Equally important here is the influence of Lebensphilosophie in the tradition of Nietzsche, Bergson, Klages, Simmel, and others. Paramount to Lebensphilosophie is the notion of immediacy, of experience that is not mediated by any institutional or legalistic social construct. For Spengler, money and its main agent, the modern trader, foreclose such immediate experience. While Simmel is able to see the price for such "natural" immediacy—namely, the imprisonment in a static "organic" community that does not allow for personal freedom and autonomy—for Spengler money represents the main force behind the spreading decay of the cultural organism.

In the final analysis, Spengler's book is a grandiose attempt to come to terms with a deeply rooted cultural anxiety that found renewed affirmation during the inflation. His organic model of culture allows him to develop a whole set of metaphors and scenarios that all circle around the dynamics of circulation. He develops two models of circulation with two opposite "fluids"—blood and money: "Through the economic history of every Culture there runs a desperate conflict waged by the soil-rooted tradition of a race, by its soul, against the spirit of money" (2: 485).

He constructs a sequence of circulation models. In prehistoric time, humans were nomads, "roaming animals," pure objects within the natural cycle of nature. This Urzirkulation is important because it serves Spengler in his effort to establish a ring structure, claiming that in the last stages of cultural decline the modern human becomes an "intellectual nomad." The decisive break in the history of humankind begins with the start of agriculture. People begin to put down roots. The hidden anxiety that stands behind Spengler's model of history—humans as circulating, homeless, and rootless entities—seems to be contained. Spengler's ultimate hero arrives on the scene: the peasant who puts down roots and lives in an intuitive symbiosis with nature. Instead of this peasant being the object of circulation, a circular inversion happens: the person becomes static, and a new circulation emerges: the circulation of blood: "Let the reader try to merge himself in the soul of the peasant. He has sat on his glebe from primeval times, or has fastened his clutch in it, to adhere to with his blood" (2:104). While "money" becomes the sole signifier for the historical trajectory of the Enlightenment, for rationality and modern capitalism, "blood" is the "symbol of the living. Its course proceeds without pause, from generation to death, from the mother's body in and out of the body of the child. . . . The blood of the ancestors flows through the chain of the generations and binds them in a great linkage of destiny, beat, and time."[21] It is a scenario in which human existence remains in a sort of infinite prenatal regression. The absence of progress and historical development is outweighed by the promise of nonalienated, "natural" existence.

The circulation of blood is eventually attacked and pushed back by a new mode of circulation: the circulation of money, which removes cultures from their contact with the soil and then causes the ultimate sacrilege: it drags the soil itself into the circulation of money. The *Immobilie* (real estate) becomes mobile: "Stein's warning that 'he who mobilizes the soil dissolves it into dust' points to a danger common to *all* Cultures; if money is unable to attack possession, it insinuates itself into the thoughts of the noble and peasant possessors, until the inherited possession that has grown with the family's growth begins to seem like resources merely 'put into' land and soil and, so far as their essence is concerned, mobile. Money aims at mobilizing *all* things" (2:485). While blood circulates between nature and the *Volkskörper* in an eternal, never-changing mode of repetition, money carries in itself an expansionary, inflationary dynamic: "*Thinking in money generates money*— that is the secret of the world-economy. When an organizing magnate writes down a million on paper, that million exists, for the personality as an economic centre vouches for a corresponding heightening of the economic energy of his field" (2:492). Finally, financial power dominates industrial production and modern technology. Spengler finishes his book with a somber prediction:

> The dictature of money marches on, tending to its material peak. . . . The machine with its human retinue, the real queen of this century, is in danger of succumbing to a stronger power. But with this, money too, is at the end of its success, and the last conflict is at hand in which the Civilization receives its conclusive form—the conflict *between* money and blood.
>
> The coming of Caesarism breaks the dictature of money and its political weapon democracy. After a long triumph of world-city economy and its interests over political creative force, the political side of life manifests itself after all as the stronger of the two. The sword is victorious over the money, the master-will subdues again the plunderer-will. If we call these money powers "Capitalism," then we may designate Socialism the will to call into life a mighty politico-economic order that transcends all class interests. (2:506)

Many National Socialists later admired Spengler for basically predicting in 1922 the rise of the "ceasarian" Hitler and the regime of National Socialism, with its overcoming of the "plunderer-will" and the victory of "blood" over "money." These enthusiasts forgot that Spengler locates this battle in the last, declining days of Western culture: for Spengler this scenario represents the last hurrah of Western culture rather than a new beginning.

The Decline of the West harbors a well-established and well-known organic and irrational discourse on society and the self whose roots reach back to German romanticism. What makes this book important for the attempt to come to terms with the experience of inflation is not only the central position that money occupies in Spengler's notion of civilization but also the fact that Spengler links the phantasm of a society beyond the perils of monetary circulation to the highly ideologically loaded, irrational term *blood*. Spengler does not directly relate his concept of an organic community to the anti-Semitic discourse of his day. Yet it is obvious to see how easy such a discourse flows within the broad and often diffuse stream of an irrational Lebensphilosophie. The ideologically powerful dichotomy between Jewish money versus German blood was not one that had to be fabricated by National Socialists. They needed only to tie the knots Spengler and others had intentionally or unintentionally prepared for them.

PART THREE

Figures

CHAPTER FIVE

Uncanny Encounters

Dr. Mabuse, the Gambler

I.

On April 30, 1922, the *Berliner Illustrirte Zeitung* reported: "The film *Dr. Mabuse, der Spieler* . . . is the attempt to create an image of our chaotic times. It is a kind of cultural-historical document, a characteristic portrayal of the years immediately after World War I with all their peculiar features. . . . *Dr. Mabuse, der Spieler* will give people fifty or one hundred years from now an idea of an age that they could hardly comprehend without such a document" (quoted in Scholdt 181). Two days earlier the first part of Fritz Lang's *Dr. Mabuse, the Gambler: An Image of Our Time* had premiered at the Ufa Palast, Berlin's most famous film theater. A month later, on May 22, 1922, the second part, with the subtitle *Inferno—a Play about People of Our Time*, followed. The film was an immediate success. Its director and leading actor were showered with ovations. "Rolf Klein-Rogge [as Dr. Mabuse] gave a brilliant performance," attested the *Film Kurier*, and Fritz Lang's "sensitive, yet experienced" directorship received equally high praise (quoted in ibid. 179).

The method of promotion and selling of *Dr. Mabuse, the Gambler* was in many respects an early forerunner of today's carefully orchestrated marketing strategies in which the film itself is only one component. With a lot of fanfare, the *Berliner Illustrirte Zeitung* had begun to publish the serial novel *Dr. Mabuse, der Spieler* by Norbert Jacques on September 25, 1921. The title page of the *Berliner Illustrirte* that day portrayed the bearded author with his wife, both sporty types, on their yacht, a dream-like scene that stood in stark contrast to the general misery of the time.

Installments of the novel were published through January 1922. Readers devoured Jacques's novel, and the newspaper registered a big sales increase. In February 1922, Ullstein put the book on the market. One hundred thousand copies were sold in its first year of publication, and its publishers ultimately printed a record half-million copies. All these readers were now anxiously awaiting the film adaptation. Thanks to the successful and amicable cooperation between Jacques, Lang, and Thea von Harbou, who wrote the screenplay, the production of the film was swift and without major problems.

The critical response to the film was dominated by the film's attempt to capture the peculiarities of the early 1920s. The reviewer in the social-democratic newspaper *Vorwärts,* for example, wrote, "All the racketeering and prostitution going on today, the police raids and exploitation in the gambling parlors, the whole current obsession with gambling, the craziness of the stock market, the fraud surrounding the occult, the nightly pimping, the phoniness of a degenerate society—all of this is very skillfully captured and finds its fictional yet timely expression in the figure of Dr. Mabuse" (quoted in Scholdt 182). The official film program published by the film's production company, Uco/Decla-Bioscop, informed the audience how essential the chaotic atmosphere of the year 1922 was to the making of *Dr. Mabuse, the Gambler:* "Just as the intent of the novel was to paint a portrayal of our times, so the year of the film's production is as important and significant as the work of its main actors, its stage designers or cameramen" (quoted in ibid. 173).

What did this year 1922 look like? Although the Versailles treaty had been in effect since January 1920, the question of German reparation payments was still an embattled issue and it continued to cause ongoing political insecurity. In April 1922, the exchange rate for 1 dollar rose to 290 marks. In a city like Munich one liter of milk cost 4.5 marks in December of 1921; by March this price had risen to 6 marks, and by April to 7 marks. For most Germans, increases in salaries did not keep abreast of such prices. Crime rates, especially thefts and burglary, increased dramatically. Police statistics and reports indicate that, while in 1913 115,000 persons in Germany had been convicted of such crimes, the number rose to 365,000 in 1923. A study of schoolchildren in Frankfurt in 1922 reported widespread hunger and malnutrition, concluding that these children were significantly backward in their physical and mental development. According to Adam Fergusson, "It was a not uncommon sight to see anxious mothers searching in the dustbins of private residences in the richer neighborhoods in the hope of retrieving scraps of food from the garbage" (78). Only two months after the premier of *Dr. Mabuse,* on that fateful morning of June 24, 1922, members of the Freikorps murdered the German foreign minister Walter Rathenau on his way from home to work at the Foreign Ministry. After his assassination, even the most risk-taking investors lost their last ounce of trust in the German economy and society. Beginning in the late summer of that year, the inflation would turn into a runaway hyperinflation beyond anybody's imagination. By the end of 1922, the value of the dollar would stand at 7,589 marks.

With its vivid images that capture the frantic stock market, the feverish atmosphere in the secret gambling parlors, and the shabby living conditions of the poor, *Dr. Mabuse, the Gambler* is indeed, as the many contemporary voices insisted, a cultural-historical document of the inflation. Lang includes, for example, a short sequence of scenes that portrays the biography of Emil Schrammt, the owner of a small entertainment empire. In an almost Brechtian fashion, Lang interrupts the fictional flow of events, and we first see Schrammt in a brief shot as a poor street vendor in 1912. The next shot, under the heading "1913 to 1918," shows him behind piles of paper, indicating that he spent the war years not on the battlefield but safely in some administrative position. In a third segment, with the heading "Vice Pays Well," his success as the owner of an illegal gambling parlor is depicted. Having grown considerably around his waist, Schrammt is counting money while drinking champagne.

At the same time, the film's larger-than-life protagonist, Dr. Mabuse, defies all the conventions of a realistic character. He is a truly fantastic figure, not bound by any logic or social constraints, and his magic abilities lead us to expect the seemingly impossible. This phantasmagoric quality of the protagonist prompts Siegfried Kracauer to conclude that *Dr. Mabuse, the Gambler* "is by no means a documentary film, but it is a document of its time" (*From Caligari to Hitler* 82). Kracauer sees this film primarily as another example of German Expressionist filmmaking and, therefore, concerned with an inner reality, an "emotional vision" that "belongs in the *Caligari* sphere" (ibid.). I believe that neither interpreting Fritz Lang's film solely as a "documentary" nor reading it simply as a more or less abstract parable that depicts the power of evil or a distorted inner psyche, does justice to this film. The multitude of anxieties, the volatility and imbalance of social positions, as well as the visions of grandeur in the face of actual shameful defeat, all these sociopsychological aspects of a deeply wounded German postwar society are brought to life through the character of Dr. Mabuse. They are matters of the social unconscious, yet they emerge from a very specific historical context and are not the result of an ahistorical expressionist drama about the evil in the human soul.

This chapter argues that the true mastery of Fritz Lang's cinemato-graphic art lies in the fact that his film swings between the social and in-dividual unconscious of its viewers, the fantastic nature of the protago-nist, and realist depictions of the contemporary postwar society. I have chosen three thematic aspects to show this triangular dialogue. The sec-ond part of the chapter will emphasize the complex and ambiguous rela-tionship that the film establishes between the audience and Dr. Mabuse. The third part will link Mabuse to an important characteristic of the postwar German society, its pervasive sense of cynicism. Finally, the last part of the chapter will pay tribute to Mabuse's favorite activity: gam-bling in the secret casinos that were one of the hallmarks of the culture of inflation.

II.

On a narrative level, the film depicts a classical structure: the fight be-tween Dr. Mabuse, the lawless, anarchic, and charismatic individual, and the state forces of order and justice represented by the district attorney von Wenk. Yet we have a hard time identifying with von Wenk in his at-tempts to arrest Mabuse. Instead, the film celebrates Mabuse's ingenu-ity. Often the different scenes are arranged to display Mabuse's might rather than provide the film with a progressing plot. The inefficient, bu-reaucratic state apparatus of von Wenk seems to be no match for the in-dividual genius of Mabuse. There are countless moments in the movie when von Wenk comes either too late or is duped by his powerful en-emy. Leslie Pahl describes this pattern quite aptly as an "asymmetry of pursuit" (114).

On a visual level, the brilliant first scene of *Dr. Mabuse* underscores the peculiar relationship we as viewers have with the mad psychoana-lyst.[1] We first gaze at three portrait photographs stacked in one hand like playing cards (see Figure 14). Then the other hand takes five addi-tional cards from a stack. One card remains on the table, the image of a Jewish peddler. At this point, we do not know whose hands these are. Yet it is our gaze that looks through the camera's eye at the cards, and these hands could be our hands holding the cards. We are taking the

Figure 14. Opening shot of *Dr. Mabuse, the Gambler.*

place of someone else, who remains anonymous but stays in definite kin-
ship with us. For a moment, our gaze merges with that of this unknown
person. As the next shot reveals, this gaze belongs to Dr. Mabuse. Several times throughout the film we see through Dr. Mabuse's eyes. Yet we
also become his victim, when he directs his powerful gaze at us (see Figure 15). The most impressive scene that reflects on the position of the
viewer with regard to the fictional space and the protagonist of the film
takes place toward the end of the movie. Mabuse, disguised as the hypnotist Sandor Weltmann, presents his audience with an example of mass
suggestion. He concentrates, and suddenly we see a desert landscape
with palm trees on the stage. An Arabian caravan moves from the background toward the center of the stage, reminiscent of a mirage. The rupture of the filmic-fictional code begins when the caravan leaves the stage,
which is the space of fiction, and steps down the stairs into the auditorium. Audience members turn their heads in order to see the caravan
move toward the exit. What kind of fictional status does this moment in
the film have? Do we become one with the audience and see the caravan
as real? In the next moment we are unmistakably told who directs this
scene. Mabuse makes a gesture that resembles a director's instruction to

Figure 15. Dr. Mabuse hypnotizing one of his victims.

cut—and suddenly the caravan disappears. By seeing the caravan, we ourselves succumb for a moment to Mabuse's suggestive powers. Mabuse presents us with his own movie. He not only decides on the content but also directs its beginning and end. Mabuse's thirty-second spot constitutes, with regard to Lang's film, an astonishing moment of reflexivity. We are challenged to think not only about the status of Mabuse's spectators in the auditorium but also about our own status as spectators of Lang's film.

How can we conceptualize these simultaneous forces of identification and repulsion that the protagonist seems to radiate throughout the film? Dr. Mabuse is a genuinely uncanny character, and Freud's essay on the uncanny can help us to situate Lang's protagonist within the sociopsychological dynamics of the film. In "The Uncanny" (1919) Freud makes the intriguing observation that "the 'uncanny' is that class of the terrifying which leads back to something long known to us, once very familiar" (123–24). These repressed materials can be either original fears or unmitigated archaic desires. "An uncanny experience occurs either when repressed infantile complexes have been revived by some impression or when the primitive beliefs we have surmounted seem once more to be confirmed" (157). Freud undertakes an elaborate interpretation of

E. T. A. Hoffmann's truly uncanny story *The Sand-Man*, in which he relates one terrifying theme of the story, the Sand-man tearing out the eyes
of children, to boys' childhood fear of castration. Freud then names several other themes of the uncanny, among them the idea of a "double":
"Hoffmann accentuates this relation [of the double] by transferring
mental processes from the one person to the other—what we should call
telepathy—so that the one possesses knowledge, feeling and experience
in common with the other, identifies himself with another person, so
that his self becomes confounded, or the foreign self is substituted for
his own—in other words, by doubling, dividing, and interchanging the
self. And finally there is the constant recurrence of similar situations, a
same face, or character trait, or twist of fortune, or a same crime" (140–
41). Freud concludes that these uncanny powers of telepathy can be
traced back to "the old animistic conception of the universe, which was
characterized by the idea that the world was peopled with the spirits of
human beings, and by the narcissistic overestimation of subjective mental processes (such as the belief in the omnipotence of thoughts . . .), as
well as by all those other figments of the imagination with which man,
in the unrestricted narcissism of that stage of development, strove to
withstand the inexorable laws of reality" (147–48).[2]

Freud's ideas on the uncanny accurately describe the two different yet
related uncanny powers of Mabuse. First, he can take on any number of
identities. During the film the audience quickly learns that Mabuse appears in all kinds of roles: sometimes as an elegant gambler, sometimes as
a revolutionary, sometimes as a banker who manipulates the stock market. And second, Mabuse possesses "hypnotic" powers that enable him
to control other people's thinking.[3] Indeed, the fascination with Dr. Mabuse certainly stems from the age-old dream of possessing an "omnipotence of thought" (147).

In addition, Freud observes that within a fictional story two conditions have to be met in order to ensure that the audience perceives it as
truly uncanny. First, the uncanny should be imbedded into an otherwise
seemingly realistic world, a recipe Lang faithfully followed. And second,
we have to identify to some degree with the person who experiences the
uncanny event or, in the case of the uncanny powers of omnipotence,
with the character who exerts these powers. Thus, the shifting positions
of identification and victimization we feel in relation to Mabuse result
from the different aspects of the uncanny that are related to our own repressed fears and longings.

Through Freud's concept of the uncanny, I have so far established a

general sociopsychological connection between the audience and the protagonist of Lang's film. Although the archaic fears and desires of the audience form a psychoanalytic link to the uncanny character of Mabuse,
it is an actual historical experience that both mediates and triggers this
link. As Freud argues, it is the infusion of "common world reality" into
the fictional sphere that "multiplies" the experience of the uncanny
(159). How then does the historical reality come into play in shaping the
uncanny figure of Mabuse? To what experience do Mabuse's uncanny
changes of personality or the omnipotence of his thoughts respond?

Looking at Mabuse's interaction with his social surroundings we can
observe that his two uncanny powers correspond to distinctly different
ways in which he executes these powers. The first way comes to the fore
in his relationships to Cara Carozza, to the Countess Toldt, and to his
criminal gang. Here he displays the power of a type of leader that Freud
describes extensively in his essay "Mass Psychology and Ego Analysis":
unrestrictedly narcissistic, loved and feared by his subjects, charismatic,
independent, and controlling. In this aspect the film acts out a fantasy
of total control that obviously stands in stark contrast to the traumatic
experience of being controlled by the unpredictable frenzy of inflation
during the early 1920s. By secretly identifying with this vital yet amoral
figure, one could find a few hours of refuge from the harsh realities of
1922. One might also add that Mabuse's radical individualism and resentment of government forces offer an attractive way to compensate for
the fact that many Germans experienced the inflation as a betrayal by
their own government. "I don't recognize your justice," responds Mabuse when asked by von Wenk to surrender to the police. The film ex-
cuses such subversive projections by the final outcome, which results not
in the death of Mabuse, not in total victory for von Wenk, but rather in
Mabuse's escape into insanity.

While this way of executing a leadership-power invites an identifi-
catory participation in the archaic dream of omnipotence, the second
form of Mabuse's power is much more complex and variant. Once
Mabuse moves outside his compounds and enters society, he is everywhere and nowhere and invokes the uncanny powers of the double. Kracauer notes that "the film succeeds in making of Mabuse an omnipresent
threat which cannot be localized" (From Caligari to Hitler 83). His uncanny ability to take on different personae points to a depersonalized,
decentralized, Foucaultian scenario of power beyond the borders of a
subject-oriented tradition. Like water, such power seeps into all cracks
in society. It divides itself as easily as it flows together again. This is pre-

cisely the way Mabuse moves through the society of the early 1920s: sometimes as a beggar, sometimes as a rich bon vivant, then as a charismatic revolutionary in a workers' pub. With this uncanny ability, Mabuse is in many respects an allegorical figure of the inflationary dynamic itself. "Mabuse is like money: thanks to his many faces he is an universal equivalent," writes Georges Sturm (350). He is indeed a circulating medium penetrating all social classes. Yet like inflationary money, he cannot be trusted; his circulation is unpredictable and causes destruction, wherever he appears. He embodies a threatening force that cannot be pinned down, because it constantly multiplies itself.

While the film captures the uncontrollable, decentralized aspects of inflation, it offers at the same time some psychological relief for audiences of the time. For behind the seeming disorder, behind the crazy ups and downs of the currency exchange that transformed the once trustworthy *Reichsmark* into a kind of Monopoly money, ultimately stands Dr. Mabuse. Nowhere does this become clearer in the film than in the final shot of the stock market episode. The face of Mabuse is superimposed on the trading room littered with paper and trash after a day of frenzied activity. Thus Dr. Mabuse both captures the peculiarities of inflation as an anonymous, threatening force and offers a pathway out of the unbearable thought that there may be no one in control of such forces.

For one who reads Dr. Mabuse as an allegorical figure of the inflation, the last scene of the film acquires a special vividness. Mabuse flees the police through a system of underground tunnels, and ends up in his counterfeiting workshop, from which no further escape is possible. Having gone mad, Dr. Mabuse is, in the end, engulfed in a pile of counterfeited money. These final images stick with the viewer because they offer a striking visual merging of the protagonist into the contemporary context of the inflation. Mabuse, the genius who once controlled and directed inflation, is now swallowed up himself by the sea of paper money. His insanity and that of the inflationary process have become one (see Figure 16). Dr. Mabuse stands out as a strange figure who nevertheless allows projections of the audience's fears and fantasies; he has secret control, yet also serves as a scapegoat. Thus, the question arises: to what extent did Fritz Lang's film participate in an anti-Semitic discourse that built on the mechanisms of imagined Jewish control resulting in scapegoating? While *Dr. Mabuse, the Gambler* is certainly not an anti-Semitic film, the film nevertheless appeals to an anti-Semitic unconscious. On the surface, most of Mabuse's different masks are connected to an iden-

Figure 16. Dr. Mabuse in a pile of money, having gone insane.

tity that the contemporary audience could very well consciously or subconsciously have deciphered as "Jewish": his roles as the psychoanalyst,
as the banker in the stock market, as a revolutionary in the workers'
pub, and, most obviously, as the Jewish peddler.

Eric Rentschler, in his interpretation of Veit Harlan's anti-Semitic film
Jud Süss, reminds us that many of the anti-Semitic stereotypes that Harlan's film openly embraces are also contained in the figure of Dr. Mabuse.
Both Oppenheimer, the protagonist in *Jud Süss,* and Mabuse are apparently without social or geographical roots. Both change appearance, observes Rentschler, both disguise themselves, both control a state's economy, abduct women, and threaten to bring destruction to a community
(156). A National Socialist critic wrote in the *Völkische Kurier* on September 1, 1925, that Mabuse is a "quintessential Jewish figure" and continued: "This is the image of the Eternal Jew . . . marching through the
centuries, always with one great goal in mind: mastery of the world,
even if entire nations must perish" (quoted in Scholdt 149). The Nazi
critic then describes Mabuse's escape into insanity and remarks that "his
crimes remain unpunished. In that sense the film is very valuable: the
typical case of the Jewish criminal" (150). The last part of this critique
barely disguises the coming threat to the Jews. In National Socialist ide-

ology, the Jews were responsible for the inflation and any other economic disaster. My final chapter will discuss in more detail the linking of monetary circulation, inflation, and Jews in the National Socialist ideology.

For all those who, in the tradition of Siegfried Kracauer, have seen in Mabuse the coming of the tyrant Hitler, this National Socialist interpretation may come as a surprise. And yet one could argue that this indicates how deeply intertwined National Socialism was with its own enemy-phantoms; the "quintessential Jew Mabuse" could easily reappear in Hitler's megalomaniac psyche: "Now the whole world will learn who I am. I—Mabuse. I will be a giant, a titan, who will whirl up the gods and laws like fallen leafs."

III.

The same ambivalent combination of attraction and repulsion that structures our relationship to Dr. Mabuse reappears in other thematic configurations in Lang's film. Cultural history of the twentieth century is not lacking in cynical figures, yet Dr. Mabuse certainly earns a prominent place among them. He is the embodiment of the cynical character; his unlimited selfishness motivates him and demonstrates an outspoken contempt for any moral standards. As a cynic, he calculates that unscrupulously betraying or exploiting others is a good safeguard against being betrayed or exploited by others. Mabuse's cynicism is intimately linked to the overall cultural atmosphere of the early 1920s.

In his much-discussed book *Critique of Cynical Reason*, Peter Sloterdijk introduces an important framework for the discussion of a cynical tendency that characterizes much of the culture of the Weimar Republic: "For reasons that can be enumerated, Weimar culture was cynically disposed like scarcely any previous culture; it gave birth to an abundance of brilliantly articulated cynicisms, which read like textbook examples. It experienced the pain of modernization more violently and expressed its disillusionment more coldly and more sharply than the present could ever do" (7–8).

Sloterdijk develops his critique of cynical reason from the basic assumption that "cynicism is *enlightened false consciousness*. It is that modernized, unhappy consciousness, on which enlightenment has labored both successfully and in vain. It has learned its lessons in enlightenment, but it has not, and probably was not able to, put them into practice" (5). Dr. Mabuse represents an extreme case of such "enlightened false consciousness." He acts against his better knowledge and thus ridicules the basic hopes of the enlightenment's social and political project: the hope that people, once they have gained better insight and knowledge of the world, will turn that knowledge into action and thus advance humanity. In a culture of inflation, in which betrayal becomes an everyday experience, Mabuse represents an extreme form of cynical adjustment, someone who no longer bothers with the notion of honesty.

On the inflation, Sloterdijk argues: "In 1923, inflation in Germany reached its peak. The state, which let its printing presses run hot without having any backing, was thereby itself caught in the role of the grand deceiver, even if it was not drawn to account, since nobody could take legal action against loss through inflation" (485). He observes the "expectation of being deceived" in German culture, yet at the same time also sees a real increase in impostors and "cases of fraud, deception, and misleading" (484).

Ostwald's *Sittengeschichte der Inflation* cites many cases of widespread fraud, among them the famous betting scandal that revolved around the photographer Max Klante in 1921–22. Klante managed to persuade hundreds of Germans that he had special inside knowledge about horse racing and encouraged people to invest in advance in a fund. He then would use the money to bet on horses. Klante promised an investment return of 600 percent per year. In the beginning, Klante was quite lucky with his bets, and each profit distribution was widely publicized. His business boomed for a short while, but, needless to say, it collapsed as quickly. The System Klante, as he called his betting strategy, did not work. By then, he had amassed 90 million marks in debt. His many victims, who lost all their investments, were, as Ostwald remarks, members from all social classes (38–40).

The figure of the impostor became a frequent figure in literature—for example, in Thomas Mann's *Die Bekenntnisse des Hochstaplers Felix Krull* (the first part was published in 1922) and the popular figure of the Captain of Köpenick. Sloterdijk summarizes the attraction of these figures: "Swindle, like poetry and dramaturgy, is dominated by the pleasure principle. It obeys the magical spell of great roles, the pleasure in playing games, the need for self-aggrandizement, the sense of improvisation" (486). With Dr. Mabuse, a rather dark exemplar joins the ranks of these otherwise endearing characters. Felix Krull and the Captain of Köpenick play with social hierarchies whose existence is the prerequisite for their roles. At the center stands the vision of a playful, easy upward mobility. Mabuse shares with Felix Krull the desire to play, yet instead of playful improvisation he personifies an almost terroristic calculation in his games. In Mabuse's world, nothing is left to chance. Furthermore, his frequent masquerades cannot be explained by the desire for upward mobility. He despises the ruling classes; his plan is to control all milieus of society, down to the blind beggars who print the counterfeit money for him.

Dr. Mabuse as the incarnation of a cynic corresponds to the then-contemporary assessment of inflation as a cynical force. In his 1924 introduction to *Könige der Inflation (Kings of Inflation)*, a collection of biographies of ten well-known profiteers, Paul Ufermann notes, "Even more than war, its daughter 'inflation' upset all notions of loyalty and trust, of ethics and morals, of love and patriotism. They were superseded by brutal violence, naked arbitrariness, and cold calculation—a madness of numbers and zeros, that drowned everything that could have been seen as a sign of human civilization into a sea of deceit and brutality." [4] His description of inflation not only coincides with the patterns of violence, arbitrariness, and cold calculation in Mabuse's character, it also indicates a cynical disregard for established normative codes. [5]

Inflation's cynical nature appears beyond the social and economic context as well. Looking back, it is clear that the political elite in Germany in the early 1920s was hesitant to stop the inflation because, as I pointed out earlier, it served several political purposes. For example, the payment of reparation costs could be postponed again and again. For millions of Germans, *Vater Staat* (Father State) itself proved to be a rather cynical character: during World War I, they had turned their savings into war bonds, yet the state's assurances that they would be paid back with good interest became a hollow promise after the war.

Finally, as much as the figure of Dr. Mabuse signifies the cynical dimension of Weimar politics in the early 1920s, there is an added side to this character that is related to, yet also moves beyond, this nexus of cynicism. Sloterdijk introduces in his book a genealogy of cynicism and observes that over time a splitting of the term occurred:

> A tension becomes apparent that, in the ancient critique of civilization, had first found expression under the name of kynicism: the urge of individuals to maintain themselves as fully rational living beings against the distortions and semirationalities of their societies. Existence in resistance, in laughter, in refusal, in the appeal to the whole of nature and a full life. . . . We reserved the concept of cynicism for the reply of the rulers and the ruling culture to the kynical provocation. . . . The concept here undergoes a split into the dichotomy: kynicism—cynicism that, in substance, corresponds to resistance and repression, or more precisely, self-embodiment in resistance and self-

splitting in repression. . . . Kynicism and cynicism are . . . constants in our
history, typical forms of a polemical consciousness "from below" and "from
above." In them, the opposition of high culture and people's culture is lived
out as the exposure of paradoxes within high-cultural ethics. (217–18)

It seems to me that in Lang's Mabuse the split between cynicism and kynicism is retained. While he is certainly a cynical ruler, there is also a hidden kynical element in this figure that attracts and fascinates us. He reacts with laughter to a society that, in the face of a lost war and inflation,
can only barely maintain values such as order, honesty, and justice.
"These days, everything is a gamble" is one of his mottoes—and who
could seriously contradict him in the face of the inflationary spectacle?
He has only contempt for the ruling classes he meets in the gambling
clubs. Mabuse draws his own consequences: a radically individualized
life that radiates with vitality and forceful action. For everyone who seeks
to find a figure of radical opposition not tied to any ideological perspective, Mabuse offers ample space for projection. Among other differences, it is this kynical element that separates him from his opponent
von Wenk and that explains part of the fascination generations of viewers have felt for this character.

IV.

With its focus on gambling, Lang's film takes up one of the most important attributes of the cultural atmosphere during inflation: life as a
mere game of chance, an existence that is completely unpredictable and
random, in which traditional values are turned upside down. The notion
of gambling was more than just a cultural metaphor. A widespread gambling mania had beset all big German cities during inflation. In prewar
Germany of 1913, according to the *Reichskriminalstatistik,* 4,400 persons were pronounced guilty of illegal gambling. In 1923 this number
had skyrocketed to 26,667, while after the end of inflation and with the
currency reform in place, the numbers decreased sharply down to 6,466
in 1924 and 3,736 in 1925.[6] A report in the *Berliner Tageblatt* in February 1923 indicated that according to police estimates about 200,000
persons frequented secret gambling clubs each day (Kreudener 273). As
early as 1919 Max Epstein had warned in *Die Weltbühne:* "Gambling
clubs mushroom in the moral swamps of Berlin. Their morbid dampness
infects the best social elements. People of rank and reputation not only
gamble in these clubs, they even rent out their apartments, they sell their
houses to these dubious gambling associations" (654).

In addition to this gambling mania, thousands of people participated in speculative activities on the stock market and currency exchange, especially during 1922 and 1923. The borders between gambling and the stock market blurred more and more. The rapid changes of stock prices and currency value became for many a gamble that, with the right instincts, promised fast money. Hans Ostwald remembers:

> At that time the tip was the dictator. Everybody worshipped it. At night in the bar, mornings at the barber, in the bus and in the trolley, everywhere there was an expert on the stock market who would give you a tip. . . . Even lovers communicated in the language of the stock market, between two kisses they exchanged the hottest tip: *IG Farben, Zellstoff* or *Sarotti*. Everybody knew then what kind of stock they had to buy.
>
> But these speculations were by no means a smooth enterprise. Between boom markets you had periods of bust and stagnation. During boom periods things became that much crazier, for example during the fall of 1922. During that time a mid-size bank received up to 50,000 commissions per day. . . . Everybody speculated, whether they were a chauffeur, a hungry landlord, an artist or a female accountant. (*Sittengeschichte der Inflation* 57)

Thus, Lang's long excursions into the world of gambling are a barely disguised allusion to German society in general during inflation. The different gambling clubs in *Dr. Mabuse, the Gambler* serve as a social space representing and symbolizing the moral decline of German society as a whole. By depicting the demise of such figures as Count Toldt or the millionaire Hull, the film emphasizes a message that is also at the heart of Norbert Jacques's novel: Inflation destroys the moral and social fabric of the ruling elites.

It is no wonder that Dr. Mabuse commutes between a gambling hall and the stock market. Lang gives us a detailed picture of the hectic atmosphere at the stock market. Mabuse's financial manipulations are an elaborate documentation of what one would call nowadays "insider trading." Over a period of several minutes, the film shows in painstaking detail how Mabuse makes his money. His gang has gotten possession of a secret trade deal. He then manipulates the stock market by launching a press announcement about the disappearance of the important trade treatise between Switzerland and the Netherlands. Stocks fall drastically to an almost worthless value. Now Mabuse buys massively. Shortly thereafter, Mabuse launches another press announcement: The secret deal has been safely delivered to the Swiss consulate. Stock prices rise frantically. Just before the stock market closes, Mabuse completes his coup by selling everything at a huge profit.

The view of the stock market as a form of gambling was by no means a new notion and had always been part of a disapproving view of the capitalist monetary system. This doubtful and unpredictable side of capitalism was forcefully expressed by the French socialist Paul Lafargue, the son-in-law of Karl Marx and the cofounder of the French Workers' Party, in 1906:

> It is impossible to expect that a bourgeois person will ever manage to understand the phenomena of distribution of wealth. As mechanical production evolves, property becomes depersonalized and transformed into the collective, impersonal form of the stock corporation, whose shares finally whirl around in the maelstrom of the stock market. . . . They are . . . lost by some and won by others in a manner so closely resembling a game of chance that indeed all stock market activity can be called gambling. The entire development of the modern economy tends to transform capitalist society increasingly into a huge international gambling saloon where the bourgeoisie wins or loses due to circumstances that remain unknown to them. . . . The "unfathomable" reigns in the bourgeois society like in a gambling hole.[7]

During the inflation year of 1922, speculation on the stock market had reached a dimension in Germany that even Lafargue had not foreseen. Commerce increasingly resembled a game of chance rather than a long-term, rational system of planning based on supply and demand. I would like to step back from the obvious economic nexus between inflation, stock market speculation, and gambling and inquire into some of the specific features of gambling.

The following reflection on the nature of gambling is guided by the premise that the essence of gambling is synonymous with the core of the inflation experience. Gambling resembles and intensifies the up and down of inflation to an extreme. It is important to remember that gambling revolves around money, not material goods. Only money enables the incredible circulation that is both the hallmark of inflation and the essence of gambling. In gambling, money circulates as it changes ownership several times within a single night; in inflation, the rapid devaluation prohibits saving and forces people to immediately exchange it.

Gambling is unpredictable and is usually set up in such a way that losing and winning are felt as an emotional spur of either pain or joy. Like inflation, gambling condenses the present moment. Luck rules over people regardless of social standing, background, gender, or class. Once the barrier of the secret entry to a gambling club is passed, class barriers disappear. A new order results, one of winners and losers. Fate affects only the individual player, and the autonomy of the individual becomes both magnificent and horrifying. The player is stripped of all social ties; neither family nor friends can help the player with decisions at the gambling table. Thus the game of chance becomes the site where the egalitarian utopia of radical individualism is, in a grim way, fulfilled.

Gambling mirrors the heightened circulation of money that is so typical of the inflation. The piles of money in front of the gamblers are not created for the duration; they do not represent their savings accounts, but rather they change with the flow, with the exchange brought about with each new game. What is the relationship between money and the gambler? In a legal sense, the gambler may own the money for a moment, but their relationship is very loose. Gambling enables the player, in a literal sense, to remain liquid. It is not *das Bildende,* the savings aspect, that interests the player about the money, but rather its agility.

This peculiar relationship between the fateful moment and rigid repetition in gambling is well described within the framework of a concept that Walter Benjamin mentions as constitutive for gambling: the *Schwellenerfahrung,* the moment of a threshold experience:

> "Rites de passage"—in folklore this is the name for the ceremonies that accompany death, birth, marriage, manhood, etc. In modern life these thresholds *[Schwellenerfahrungen]* became more and more absent or invisible. Our modern life is deprived of such threshold experiences. Falling asleep is the only one that has remained with us. (And with that, waking up). . . . The threshold has to be distinguished sharply from the border. The threshold is a zone. Change, transition, floods are associated with the word swell *[schwellen],* and this etymological meaning cannot be overlooked. At the same time it is necessary to state the immediate tectonic and ceremonial character that gave the word its meaning.[8]

The game of chance, according to Benjamin, is such a modern rite de passage, a threshold experience in which the up and down of life is condensed to the utmost degree. He stresses the ceremonial and tectonic character of the threshold experience. While luck remains unpredictable, the formal course of the game is rigidly determined by its rules. One game obeys the rules as much as the next. The beginning and end of each game are clearly marked. Through the constant repetition of the game, a night in a casino acquires an almost ceremonial character.

With its rigid rules, the rites de passage provide the cultural and social setting that can hold, contain, and help to express personal emotions of the most extreme kind. The very intimate and the communal are bound together in a dialectical relationship. The ceremony offers the public space in which deep moments of mourning and happiness, of achievement and loss, of entering and departing certain phases of one's life become bearable and livable. The game of chance constitutes such a ceremony in the sense that it enacts and channels extreme moments.

It is precisely the thrill of these moments that prompts Gräfin Toldt in *Dr. Mabuse, the Gambler* to frequent the secret gambling clubs. She sits with von Wenk at a nearby table when a Russian countess who loses a game becomes hysterical. "When she loses, she is so beautiful," comments Countess Toldt. Gambling allows for ever-new constellations of fate—yet the shuffling and dealing of the cards, the turning of the roulette wheel, the *rien ne va plus* always remain the same.

The lust for gambling has many causes—and this desire may also help to explain why for some the hyperinflation was remembered as such an exhilarating experience. Like the dynamic of inflation, gambling arouses people through the waves of circulation that confront them with each new game. Like a surfer, the gambler must decide instantly whether to ride the wave that can take him or her up to a moment of intense pleasure, but that can also come crashing down. Walter Benjamin writes, "The greater the risk, the more hazardous the game, the more entertaining it is. . . . In other words, the greater the role of chance, the more quickly the game transpires. It is the nature of gambling to demand a total presence of mind *[Geistesgegenwart]*. It does so by calling forth a series of constellations in rapid succession, each one quite independent of the other, and each requiring a new, original reaction on the part of the player" (5.1:638–39).

"Presence of mind" signifies the focus of all human faculties on the single moment. The hand that draws a new card, that throws a chip on the roulette table, or for that matter, invests in the rapidly changing stock market during inflation immediately carries out a decision that was reached within a fraction of a second. *Geistesgegenwart* can also be translated as "presence of the spirit." The term thus opens up spiritual or religious connotations. The presence of the Holy Spirit may signify a conversion experience or a moment of redemption. In any case, it signifies an encounter with fate. "Presence of mind or spirit" replaces the belief in one's ability to plan life with the notion of the fateful moment. Fate expresses itself in the contingency of the moment that is not compatible with the notion of a logically ordered life. Benjamin draws an interesting conclusion from this transcendental aspect of *Geistesgegenwart* that is present in gambling: "The contempt for gambling may have its most profound explanation in the essence of presence of mind. Such presence of mind is a natural gift that humans apply to the highest things,

which lets them rise beyond themselves. In gambling, however, it is applied to one of the lowest things, to money, which draws them down"
(5.1:639).

"Presence of mind" also means the opposite of physical labor. While
bodily labor can be measured relatively easily by an individual's physical abilities and limitations, the notion of *Geistesgegenwart* condenses
the enormous, often uncanny powers of the intellect. We can certainly
labor intellectually, yet in contrast to physical labor, as we do so we can
encounter sudden moments of insight, a revelation, a thought that can
bring to a successful end months' worth of endeavor and deliberation.
We may experience the same in the game of chance: the possibility that
enormous gain may result from a mental revelation that can come about
with every new game. As the gambler participates with his or her presence of mind, the game responds with the shocklike experience of win or
lose. Each game, even though similar in its structural unfolding, is strictly
separated from the next, establishing a discontinuum between the different games. In that sense, the game of chance knows no history, it unfolds in a series of moments of presence that are separated by the borders of each new game. Again, it is precisely this time structure that also
characterized life during the hyperinflation.

Presence of mind promises the gambler a moment of empowerment
and, for a brief second, the belief, the thrill, that the game will follow his
or her instructions and thoughts. In this sense, Mabuse incorporates the
ultimate fantasy of every gambler. He is indeed able to rule the game
through the presence of his mind. To be precise: he cannot control the
game itself by manipulating the exact sequence of the cards, yet the presence of his mind is so strong that he completely overrides and replaces
the minds of other people. He possesses, in Freud's words, an "omnipotence of thought." With the invisible beam of his willpower he controls
his victims and forces them to play in such a way that the game ends to
his advantage. Only von Wenk, in a heroic battle that requires all his
concentration and mental energy, is able to resist his enemy's willpower.

In his 1919 essay "Spielclubs" ("On Gambling Clubs"), Max Epstein
warns his readers about the devastating moral effects of gambling: "The
lowest instincts come to the fore. A regular workday seems worthless.
Persevering labor is seen as crotchety" (651). "Gambling" stands for
one of the great destructive forces of traditional values. The link between
hard work and honest money fails in this cinematic world—as it was
failing outside the theater with the increasing depreciation of the currency and the feverish speculation on the stock market. The intricate so-

cial fabric that underlies work and production is replaced by a fragmented group of individuals around the roulette table trying to change
their fate in the next moment.

V.

Those familiar with Lang's films will notice how much the end of *Dr. Mabuse, the Gambler* anticipates the final scenes in *M* (1930–31). Both films
portray the fates of social outcasts who ultimately fail because of their
inner obsessions. In both cases the mise-en-scène of the final scenes is
remarkably similar: caught in a prisonlike cellar, the protagonist ham-
mers desperately against a locked door blocking his escape to the outside.
Imprisoned in their insanity, they both cast themselves onto the ground.
In *M* the child-murderer writhes on the floor and screams to the mob, "I
must, I must kill, I can't help it!" This confession sums up the entire di-
lemma of the character. *Dr. Mabuse, the Gambler* ends with an equally
poignant scene. Symbolizing once again his status as a figurative expression of the inflation, the protagonist wallows in a pile of forged
money, having gone mad. Once in control of such masses of money, he
is now himself swallowed up by it. The madness of the inflation he once
controlled and his own insanity merge. And just as in *M,* the protectors
of law and order arrive from upstairs through the door to take away the
criminal outcast.

There is another interesting parallel: in both films, blind beggars are
involved in the demise of the protagonist. In *M,* Lang uses the new technical possibilities of sound: the blind beggar recognizes the leitmotif of
the murderer's whistling. The roles of the blind beggars in *Dr. Mabuse*
are more complex. One can only speculate why none but blind beggars
work in his counterfeit shop. Possibly their blindness protects them from
the temptation to steal the money they have to count and bundle. Yet if
this is Mabuse's calculation, it turns against him in an unexpected way.
After Mabuse has mistakenly locked himself in, the blind beggars invite
him to a last game of cards. In stark contrast to the first scene of the
movie, Mabuse does not control the cards anymore. After just a few moments, one of the beggars reaches over to Mabuse, touches his hands
with the stack cards, and yells: "You cheat!" The power of this statement causes Mabuse's final mental collapse. The truth value of the beggar's exclamation derives precisely from his blindness. It is not only the
long, emblematic tradition of the blind as the bearers of truth that Lang
invokes here. The blind can "see through" Mabuse because they are im-

mune to his powerful gaze. They do not register his frequent change of appearance, and Mabuse's gaze cannot penetrate into their minds. He, who once played the game of life with the certainty that he could manipulate it to his favor at any time, is now stripped of all control and told the quite humiliating truth that he is a cheater.

Dr. Mabuse as the figuration of inflation, as the cynical force that nevertheless generates meaning, as a frightening spectacle of a power that is everywhere and nowhere, and gambling as an expression of the social and cultural turmoil during inflation link this film closely to the inflationary period. *Dr. Mabuse, the Gambler* is not only a remarkable historical documentation of this time, but it also responds to its contemporary audience's anxieties and fantasies of omnipotence that were triggered by a widely felt loss of control over their lives.

It is highly significant that the film does not end with Mabuse's death. A shoot-out could have been Lang's alternative. Instead, in the last scene, we see Mabuse taken by von Wenk. Mabuse will be brought to a mental asylum, but he is by no means finished. He will reappear in Lang's sequel film, *Das Testament des Dr. Mabuse* (*The Testament of Dr. Mabuse,* 1932), and in his final film, *Die tausend Augen des Dr. Mabuse* (*The Thousand Eyes of Dr. Mabuse,* 1960). For the contemporary audience of 1922, the stairways leading out of the dark auditorium and Mabuse's fictional world did not promise the escape into an orderly, predictable reality. All too quickly they would remember Mabuse's analysis of the time: "These days, everything is just a gamble."

CHAPTER SIX

Visions of Work

Hugo Stinnes and His Doubles

I.

Wheelbarrows with bundles of money, severely undernourished children, once-prosperous members of the middle class queuing in front of pawnshops—the collective memory of the German inflation is full of moments that highlight and condense the humiliating effects of an economic and social devaluation. Yet at the other end of the social spectrum, inflation produced scenery that contrasted garishly with the experience of millions of Germans. For a small number of people, inflation meant the opportunity to amass enormous wealth and economic power in just a few years.

These were the "kings of inflation," as Paul Ufermann called them in his 1924 collection of biographical portraits. Ufermann's list contains famous industrialists such as the steel magnates Otto Wolff and Alfred Ganz, the department store owner Rudolf Karstadt, and a number of young profiteers such as Richard Kahn and Hugo Herzfeld, whose fortunes were almost exclusively linked to speculations on the stock market.

Yet towering above them all, the giant among the "kings of inflation," was the industrialist Hugo Stinnes (see Figure 17). He personifies like no other the nexus between inflation, industrial concentration, and wealth. It is barely imaginable today what a wave of emotions, what deep hatred and boundless admiration, the mere mention of his name aroused. "Stinnes"—these two syllables, hard, precise, with undertones of aggression and a certain boorishness, provoked as many associations in the minds

Figure 17. Hugo Stinnes (1870–1924).

of Germans as were conjured up by legendary names such as Rockefeller and Vanderbilt in the imagination of the American public.

When Hugo Stinnes died on April 10, 1924, he was considered "the richest man Germany has ever known" (Neckarsulmer 61). Yet his legendary status was not based on his vast assets alone. His contemporaries were equally awed by the unbelievable pace at which Stinnes was able to amass his wealth within a few years. Neckarsulmer notes, "It is commonly assumed that the fortune he left behind far exceeded a billion in gold, indicating that his assets increased by a factor of more than thirty in the decade following 1914. Not even in the 'land of unlimited possibilities,' America, had a fortune ever grown so rapidly" (ibid.).

Stinnes was born in 1870, the second son of the industrialist Hermann Stinnes in Mühlheim/Ruhr in the heart of the Rhine and Ruhr district. Hermann Stinnes headed a successful family-owned mining and transportation business whose considerable armada of barges was a familiar sight in the Ruhr district and up and down the Rhine. The Stinnes family was one of a small group of German families—such as the Thyssens, Klöckners, Krupps, and Siemens—who dominated the industrial development of the Ruhr region.

Hugo Stinnes was, therefore, an insider in Germany's big business. He began his career by learning both business and mining in his father's company. In 1892, at the age of twenty-three, Hugo Stinnes founded his own company in Mühlheim. Soon his widely acclaimed business acumen earned him success. In 1901 he founded the German-Luxembourg Mining and Smelting Company. Before the outbreak of World War 1, this company had more than forty thousand employees and, under his leadership, combined efficient management with the most advanced technical machinery in mining, steel production, and transportation (Brinckmeyer 44).

The second pillar of Stinnes's growing fortune before the war was his involvement in the Rhine-Westphalian Electric Company, of whose board he became president in 1902. Sooner and more clearly than many others, Stinnes realized the wide-reaching impact of new technological innovations that allowed the long-distance transportation of electricity (von Klass 105). In Stinnes's eyes, electrical energy was a kind of transformed, converted coal, and he envisioned vast power plants fueled by coal from his mines. Under his directorship, the Rhine-Westphalian Electric Company soon supplied large parts of the Rhine/Ruhr region with electricity. Within a few years, several power plants had been erected in close proximity to his mines.

Hugo Stinnes's fortunes grew considerably during the war. His ships, mines, and steel mills were busy feeding the German war machine. Yet as the fourth year of the war began, Stinnes realized that Germany was economically and psychologically exhausted. As a vehement defender of laissez-faire capitalism, he was deeply concerned about the general anticapitalist climate that became prevalent during the tumultuous days of the fall of 1918. While other industrial leaders were paralyzed by the obvious imminent catastrophic collapse of their country, Stinnes met privately with members of the German trade unions. In order to forestall possible revolutionary actions such as Russia had experienced in 1917, he negotiated with Carl Legien, the leader of the trade union movement, an agreement that guaranteed many of the trade unions' central demands, such as the introduction of the eight-hour day and mandatory collective bargaining (Feldman, Disorder, 107). On November 15, 1918, barely a week after the collapse of the Kaiserreich, the Stinnes-Legien Agreement was signed. During the reparation negotiations in Spa in 1920, Stinnes was invited as an expert to speak on Germany's economic situation. He impressed especially his conservative contemporaries by his outspoken and straightforward resistance to the Versailles treaty and the demands of the Allies.

At the same time, Stinnes was actively rebuilding and expanding his empire. One secret to his success was the building of so-called vertical trusts. As Hermann Brinckmeyer explains, "The vertical trust is a complete and self-contained consolidation of all successive stages of manufacture from the production of raw material to the final distribution of the finished article. It is an industrial cycle completely protected at both ends, with every source of supply and every stage of production in the same hands" (60–61). His creation of the gigantic "Siemens-Rhine-Elbe-Schuckert Union" in concert with the industrialists Emil Kirdorf and Carl-Friedrich von Siemens was Stinnes's greatest and last masterpiece in that regard. This trust, consisting of many independently working plants and branches, included all stages of industrial production, from the production of raw material to the manufacturing of finished goods such as the electric trams and locomotives that were built in the Siemens plants. At the end of his life it was estimated that Stinnes had holdings and investment interests in about 1,650 companies, ranging from coal to newspapers, from the timber industry to airplanes (Benz and Graml 331). In addition to being closely tied to the relatively new process of vertical integration of different industries, the name Hugo Stinnes is also intimately connected to the rapid process of a horizontal industrial concentration, meaning the merging of companies within the same economic sector. The German iron and steel industry reacted to the loss of valuable mines in Lorraine, which resulted in a shortage of raw material, with an unprecedented concentration and consolidation of related companies. The liberal credit policy of the Reichsbank and the devaluating mark made industrial concentration, both vertically and horizontally, very attractive financially and led to "a degree of concentration . . . in just a few years that would have required decades before the war" (Kupzyk 75).

Yet his ingenious entrepreneurship can only partially explain Stinnes's economic success. While other industrialists, especially in heavy industries, also profited from the increasing currency depreciation, nobody understood the mechanism of inflation as well as Hugo Stinnes. He ruthlessly took advantage of credits, often from government and other official sources, and successfully speculated in the progressing depreciation of the German mark. In addition, he had major holdings abroad, which provided him with a considerable stream of highly valuable foreign currency. Stinnes never denied that he welcomed the inflation as an effective means to expand his industrial empire, and he legitimized his action by pointing out that the creation of employment through a booming inflationary economy had precedence over price stability and the security of savings. His sudden and untimely death at the age of fifty-four, only six months after the currency reform of November 1923, and the collapse of his industrial empire within a few years, suggest an ironic link between the endpoint of his life and the duration of the inflation. Yet it would be wrong to judge Stinnes simply as a gambler, a short-lived product of the inflation, someone whose fortune relied solely on the ups and downs of the stock market.

II.

In his autobiography Elias Canetti captures the enormous contemporary fascination with Hugo Stinnes:

> In those days, the name Stinnes often cropped up in the papers. . . . The way people talked about Stinnes, the envy I sensed in Herr Bemberg's voice when he mentioned his name, the cutting scorn with which Herr Schutt condemned him ("Everyone keeps getting poorer, he keeps getting richer"), the unanimous sympathy of all the women in the boardinghouse (Frau Kupfer: "*He* can still afford things"; . . . Fräulein Parandowski would have liked to work for him: "You know where you are with a man like him" . . . —they always talked about him for a long time. . . . And Herr Schimmel, mildest of all smilers, gave an unexpected twist to Fräulein Parandowski's comment: "Maybe we've already been bought up. You can't tell." (*Torch* 15)

In the first biography of Stinnes, written by Hermann Brinckmeyer and published in 1921, this wide array of opinions on Hugo Stinnes is also acknowledged: "For many people he is an idol, for others he is a terror abroad in the land. . . . Walter Rathenau characterizes him as a particularistic industrial baron whose work is destroying the present system as a step towards collectivism. Sentimental Rhinelanders speak of "Hugo" with the same respectful familiarity with which the Israelites may have used the name of their leader in the desert" (vii–viii).

The rivalry between the shy pragmatist Hugo Stinnes and the eloquent politician Walther Rathenau is the subject of a 1922 satiric drawing by Thomas Theodor Heine in *Simplicissimus,* entitled "Die Weitblickenden" ("The visionaries") (see Figure 18). "From here one overlooks the situation the best!" claims Rathenau. "No, from here!" argues Stinnes. Meanwhile, the German Michel—the symbolic common person— turns his pocket inside out. The intellectual Rathenau sits on a tower formed by his "Collected Works" while Hugo Stinnes addresses him from the smokestack of one of his many factories. Whereas both men seem to have little regard for the fate of the common person, we are left

Figure 18. "The visionaries." Illustration by Thomas Theodor
Heine, in *Simplicissimus* 26 (February 22, 1922).

with no doubt who is in power in Germany. The middle ground and the
horizon are dominated by Stinnes's vast industrial empire. Smoking
chimneys indicate full production. While Stinnes's power rests in his
many factories, the caricature highlights the difference between the two
men by proposing that Rathenau's power is based on nothing more than
his intellectual work—the compilation of his own writings.

    Of course, there were other industrialists, such as August Thyssen
and Alfred Krupp, whose economic might and influence were by no
means less impressive. All of them were legendary in their own right,

and their names are intimately connected with Germany's rise to economic world power during the early twentieth century.[1] Yet while Thyssen and Krupp confined their economic activities largely to coal and steel, Stinnes expanded his empire, often in silent partnerships, into almost all other sectors of the economy. His contemporaries grew justifiably suspicious that his secret influence reigned almost everywhere. The fear of a "Stinnes-ization" of Germany was widespread, especially during his ultimately futile attempts to take over the German railway system in the early 1920s. The leading left-wing journal *Die Weltbühne* predicted in its first issue of 1922, "During this year the German people will have to decide whether they want to live in the German Republic or the Kaiserreich Stinnesien" (Morus 20). On the other side of the political spectrum, the influential conservative journalist Maximilian Harden greeted Hugo Stinnes as a great savior. In his flattering, somewhat overbearing portrait of Stinnes he records some popular voices: "All over the world, [he has] houses, real estate, industrials, partnerships. He owns half of East Prussia, a large part of Southern Sweden. . . . He's going to modernize and complete France's canal system . . . , in the coalless lands, Holland, Italy and Austria, he will electrify the railroads . . . " (140).

During the last years of his life Hugo Stinnes had become a cultural icon occupying a space in the popular imagination that transcended his actions as a brilliant and ruthless industrialist. His larger-than-life stature, the many legends and fictional accounts circulating about him, lent him a dark and mysterious aura similar to that of Fritz Lang's figure *Dr. Mabuse*. Both invite projections and fantasies about an omnipotent man with control over the inflationary economy. In response, envious fantasies of power and wealth mixed with ideological and political assessments from both the left and right. Thus the persona, the "myth" of Hugo Stinnes created a complex discursive space that was an integral part of the culture of the inflation. In the remainder of this chapter, I will explore this space as a field for dreams, nightmares, and visions and will attempt to link the figure of Stinnes to a wider cultural context.

III.

It would be easy to describe Hugo Stinnes within the established cultural matrix of the 1920s as a greedy, ruthless, and power-hungry capitalist who amassed enormous amounts of money and used his financial assets to manipulate the stock market. Yet the public discourse around the figure of Stinnes was much more complicated and cannot simply be subsumed under the usual political and ideological positions of the time. Surprisingly, although the name Stinnes invoked big money and inflationary wealth, the man was simultaneously represented as a figure in opposition to inflationary excess. In fact, much of the public fascination with his persona was due to the shy behavior and inconspicuous appearance that belied his status as a powerful capitalist. His biographer Brinckmeyer stresses this popular impression: "He has the appearance of a worker and could go about in the clothes of a foreman or a miner without attracting attention" (1). Even at the height of his career, the richest man in Germany called himself simply "Hugo Stinnes, merchant from Mühlheim." Maximilian Harden adds that, in contrast to many of inflation's winners who led luxurious public lives, Stinnes "did not smoke, barely sipped a light wine, never noticed what he ate. . . . To this man luxury quickly became a burden, the fragrance of culture a wearisome discomfort, the most beautiful unreality remained to him the absolute zero" (145–54).

Any exploration of the "Stinnes myth" that merely linked this figure to the nexus of luxury, consumption, or monetary speculation would yield few results. Central to this myth was rather a quality that was closely linked to his disdain for luxury and ostentatious display of wealth: his almost superhuman, obsessive work ethic. In then-contemporary accounts, Stinnes always seemed to work, and his vision of "Stinnesien," a world ruled by Stinnes, was of an empire of total and relentless production with very little regard for the spheres of consumption, the arts, or the luxury of leisure. "Stinnes never stops working," asserts Hermann Brinckmeyer (2); and Maximilian Harden describes his work habits in more detail: "Every week he spent at least four nights on the road. [He was] in the office from seven in the morning until eleven at night" (148). What Stinnes demanded of himself, he asked from others. "Germany still works too little," he reprimanded his fellow countrymen in his pursuit of ever greater industrial production (158). Stinnes, the workaholic, was obsessed with one ultimate goal: to become the supreme employer for all Germans. Thus, it is not the discursive patterns of wealth that make Stinnes an interesting subject for a cultural analysis, but rather the multifaceted connections between Stinnes as a cultural icon and the notion of work.

The aspects of the culture of inflation I have thus far investigated belong primarily to the spheres of commodity exchange and consumption: the rise of prices, the rapid circulation of money, the increased value of *Sachwerte,* the display of extreme luxury amid widespread poverty. In contrast to this carnivalesque side, the inflationary economy was also characterized by full employment despite, or rather because of, the devaluation of the mark. Unemployment became rampant only during the height of the hyperinflation in the summer and fall of 1923 (see chapter 2). Money bought less and less, yet most people had a job. The orderly and methodical sphere of work and production stood in contrast to the anarchic side of inflationary culture, so aptly captured in *Dr. Mabuse, the Gambler* and many other sources contemporary to it. The space beyond the iron gates of the factories, beyond the doors of the large office complexes, must have provided at least some hours of refuge from the inflationary maelstrom.

Interestingly, among the many anecdotes and eyewitness accounts in Hans Ostwald's *Sittengeschichte der Inflation (Moral History of the Inflation),* we cannot find a single reference to how inflation affected actual working conditions. Instead, we find in his introduction a telling explanation of how Germans overcame the moral and cultural excesses of the inflation:

> Despite the apparent collapse of all the values that had guided human life for centuries, indeed for millennia, they were transformed or newly defined only to a very small extent. . . .
> That became evident as the inflation came to an end. The nightmare vanished. The German people resurrected itself. It created a new currency—on its own. And with that it rebuilt its economy, which was possible only because they were a people of work. Only through attention to work, only through work could it create values that became the basis for a new life.
> In a short time illicit trade and profiteering disappeared. This pestilence on the economy and on the entirety of the German people's intellectual and psychological life shriveled up and went away. (8)

This passage contains a powerful and widespread ideological dichotomy: it juxtaposes the long-held values of work against all that is connected to the "pestilence" of inflation, such as illicit trade and profiteering. Work becomes the antidote to inflationary monetary circulation, a refuge in which "the masses of German people" can stay "intact," "diligent," and "proper" (ibid.). Because Germans are deep down "a people of work," they are ultimately immune to the "pestilence" of inflation brought about by the destructive power of money. Ostwald's narrative is, from an economic point of view, complete nonsense. People's work ethic has very little impact on the coming and going of inflations. The belief that hard work can chase off the ghosts of currency depreciation is a powerful myth, yet it conveniently omits the pivotal role governmental monetary discipline plays in the restitution of a currency's value. Ostwald's creation of an ideological halo surrounding the concept of work that he sees as the ultimate weapon against the moral and economic confusions of inflation is all the more interesting.

In a larger context, Frank Trommler observes that the importance of work as a cultural concept that creates identity, even national identity, has risen since the late nineteenth century. Trommler argues that the concept of Germany as an *Arbeitsnation* competed with the traditional concept of a *Kulturnation*. Indeed, the notion of work became increasingly ideologically charged during the early twentieth century. Ostwald's assertion that Germans are a "people of work" resonates with a deeply felt and commonly held sentiment. The centrality of work, together with the embrace of modern technology, was crucial for the group of right-wing intellectuals Jeffrey Herf has fittingly called "reactionary modernists." They include Hans Freyer, Werner Sombart, Oswald Spengler, and others, yet it is Ernst Jünger who stands out as the most influential member of this group. His central theoretical work, *Der Arbeiter,* published in 1932, remains the most chilling and certainly most debated vision of a totalitarian society that embraces the principles of total production. His grandiose vision moves beyond the framework of a nation-state to that of a new order of a "planetary" magnitude.[2]

Jünger sees an epochal shift from an expired world of bourgeois culture with its *Scheinherrschaft* (false authority) and cult of individuality to a world that will be dominated by a new kind of human gestalt, the worker. He rejects liberal capitalism with its emphasis on individual agency and a sophisticated system of monetary capital circulation. Work for Jünger is more than simply an economic category; it becomes an all-encompassing structural principle of life: "Work does not have any opposite except itself; it resembles fire that consumes and changes all burnable material. Only its own principle, namely another fire, can contest it" (91). In Jünger's *Der Arbeiter* the dichotomy between work and leisure has been erased, as has any class difference and the bourgeois opposition between the individual and the masses. The centrality of work and production in his utopia stems from the hidden yet powerful dialectic between production and destruction, between Jünger's call for a *totale Mobilmachung* (total mobilization) for productive purposes and the author's pivotal experience of his own life, the encounter of modern warfare on the battlefields of World War 1. For Jünger, nowhere else is the existential dialectic between destruction and production better expressed than in technology. Technology destroyed the world of the nineteenth-century bourgeoisie in World War 1; at the same time it proves to be the driving force behind the new form of society that Jünger envisions in *Der Arbeiter*.

With regard to the postwar Germany of the 1920s, Ernst Jünger bemoans the fact that

> we live in a time of great consumption whose sole effect lies in the accelerated speed of wheels. . . . The peculiarity of our situation lies in the fact that our movements are controlled by the dictate of setting up records. . . . This fact prohibits the idea that life in any of its aspects is capable of establishing itself in secure and uncontested orders. . . .
>
> Therefore, capital in the old static sense ceased to exist; even the value of gold has become doubtful. . . . Traffic and production are inherently excessive and unpredictable—the faster one is able to move, the less one reaches one's goal. (178–79)

Economic competition is, in Jünger's mind, one of the forces that equally burden producer and consumer and waste valuable resources (184). Old forms of "hermetic and resistant" property such as the real estate of the aristocracy are regrettably transformed into more liquid and exchangeable forms of wealth (185). Such "feverish competition" leads to the "mobilization of money," which above all creates an ever larger system of credit. Jünger criticizes the fact that in contemporary Germany work is more and more defined by the obligation to pay debts. It is only in this context that he briefly mentions inflation by calling it an especially heavy "frontal attack" against all forms of economic security.

We would be mistaken to read any kind of nostalgia into such lines. Jünger wishes and predicts that the established capitalist system "will come to an end" by exhausting itself. Then the "excessive and unpredictable competition" will be brought back to a "natural competition" (186). Economic activity will not be regulated by an anarchic market, but rather by "guilds," large trusts, and state monopolies (ibid.). With the caveat that *Der Arbeiter* is not primarily an economic treatise, one can safely say that Jünger's envisioned economy is organized along military principles, that it stresses sacrifice, and that it is based on group action rather than individual activity. Above all, his economic vision is characterized by a deep longing for *Totalität, Konstanz, Rythmus,* and *Planung* (totality, constancy, rhythm, and planning). Such a one-sided economic world, with "heroes of works" engaged in gigantic "production battles," invocations of machine beauty, and the merging of nature and technology into an *Organ der Technik,* is obviously reminiscent of an ideological language that was used both in Stalinism and National

Socialism. Yet more important in this context is the fact that this vision ignores other sides of the economy: the intricate movements of the capital market, the sophisticated communications between a distribution system and a potentially international base of consumers—it denies most fundamentally money as the central medium of communication in an economy.

It is difficult to read Jünger's *Der Arbeiter* directly within the context of the German inflation. The constant reference to the experience of World War I determines this text and overshadows every other historical event. However, if one extrapolates on Jünger's economic critique, inflation appears to be an especially violent manifestation of an economy that is excessive, unpredictable, and present-oriented. Within Jünger's dialectic of destruction and production, inflation to some degree even speeds up the demise of the bourgeoisie—and is in that regard similar to that ground-breaking event World War I.

I have written earlier that war and inflation share many attributes. Both are unpredictable, create a general sense of destabilization and of presentness, disregard bourgeois values such as security and moderation, erase class and social background in the moment of danger, destroy all established moral and social order—the list could be continued. In that sense Jünger talks indirectly about inflation when he analyzes war and its many genuinely modern experiences and challenges that modern man has to reckon with. His strategy in *Der Arbeiter* is not to eradicate these fundamental aspects of modern life but rather to control them, to abolish the possibility of subjective agency, to channel their dynamic power into a system of *Konstanz,* of rhythm and predictability. With the help of technology and comprehensive planning, moments of "perfection" can be created in which, as Jünger writes, "power shows itself in its most unmitigated form" (191).

Inflation in Jünger's coming new world will not be an issue, because money will flow in an orderly, directed course. Indeed, I argue that Jünger has little regard for money at all; he must have sensed the inherently subversive quality of monetary circulation. Exchange, trade, and, as Georg Simmel stresses repeatedly in *The Philosophy of Money*, the potential for freedom that money gives to the individual—these qualities are not very compatible with a system that communicates through order and commands. *Der Arbeiter* is a fitting example of how inflation helped to bolster the powerful phantasm of a world divided between an orderly, hierarchical, yet communal and self-sufficient sphere of work and an immoral, unpredictable, "egoistic" sphere of monetary circulation and speculation.[3] To put this fateful dichotomy back into the frame of our textual analysis: the world of Dr. Mabuse is devoid of any work, the world of Stinnes knows nothing but work.

Let us now turn to three texts that provide special insight into the power of Hugo Stinnes as an icon within inflationary culture. The first perspective is a satirical account, a vision of "Stinnesien" come true: Heinrich Mann's novella *Kobes* (1925), a thinly disguised fictionalization of Hugo Stinnes's world. The second account reframes the vision of "Stinnesien" within the contemporary discourse of cultural modernism/ antimodernism of the 1920s. The small volume *Gott Stinnes: Ein Pamphlet gegen den vollkommenen Menschen (God Stinnes: A Pamphlet against the Universal Man,* 1922) by Eugen Ortner intertwines the hegemony of the Stinnes-type industrialist with an aesthetic and cultural vision of total production that in many respects foreshadows Jünger's *Der Arbeiter.* Finally, through a reading of Fritz Lang's *Metropolis* I will explore both the relationship between an inflationary economy and total production and the complex reenactments of the inflationary trauma in the guise of a machine culture and cyborgs.

IV.

In a 1941 manuscript, Heinrich Mann remembers the depressing picture of a culture corrupted by inflation. In one passage he describes the moral and economic desperation of a whole generation of left-wing intellectuals: "One could not expect that an inflation of such dimensions would be confined simply to the monetary sphere. Not at all; emotions, especially, rose and devaluated themselves: regret, anxiety, hate, and self-hatred. One degraded oneself and debauched; matters of the erotic became a public spectacle, every street corner . . . turned into a bar. Drunks staggered, starved people tottered, schoolboys making profits from the decay of the currency drove the most expensive cars, yet the corpses of inept intellectuals were picked up in the park at dawn" (*Gesammelte Werke in dreizehn Bänden* 3 : 490). For Heinrich Mann, the idealist and humanistic socialist, the impotence of intellectuals amid the moral chaos was painful to acknowledge. His belief in the intellectual as the moral conscience of society, and thus his belief in the special public responsibility of the "intellectual workers," lies at the heart of his own positioning as a writer. In a series of newspaper essays that he published during the inflation and later collected under the title *Die Tragödie von 1923,* he vehemently argues that any economic order depends on an intellectual, cultural, and moral order—and not vice versa: "The economy is not an end in itself" (98). Attacking the industrial concentration that is part of the inflationary economy, he warns his readers in May 1923, "Nothing else counts in this nation anymore except 'the economy'—which means the fortunes of the rich. . . . The intellectual workers apparently quietly starve to death or become office slaves. And what happened to the proud class of industrial workers in Germany? Meek as lambs and afraid for their lives, they cling to their all-powerful masters" (113). Not only did the rule of a few rich industrialists threaten the young German republic, but the inflationary economy was ruining the middle class and with it the existence of the *Geistig Schaffenden,* the "intellectual workers," who were, for Mann, the main producers of cultural work and the transmitters of culture (101). "We represent . . . values that are more important and less replaceable than coal mines and factories. An economy that never felt anything, and that allows fabulous wealth next to our own death is nothing more than a scandal. It simply calls into question the very idea of nation itself" (99). His essays reveal how much Heinrich Mann is a proponent of the concept of the *Kulturnation,* believing that a nation is held together first and foremost by its culture. He regards the predominance of the economic as the major antagonist and enemy of Germany as a *Kulturnation.*

In his novella *Kobes,* Heinrich Mann depicts his vision, his nightmare of a society that has turned from a *Kulturnation* into a barbaric *Arbeitsnation. Kobes,* he explains in a letter to Kurt Tucholsky, is a satirical "hymn of the inflation, a kind of Stinnes-transfiguration in the form of a novella, short, yet vehement" (*Gesammelte Werke in dreizehn Bänden* 3 : 543). Indeed, in *Kobes,* the kingdom of "Stinnesien" has come true: a mysterious coal and steel magnate rules the country through his vast industrial empire. *Kobes* is by no means the only literary text that thematizes the power of Hugo Stinnes, yet Mann's novella is certainly the most original and daring fictional account.[4] It first appeared in the journal *Neue Rundschau* in early 1925. That same year, the Propyläen Verlag published a book edition of the short story with illustrations by George Grosz that highlight the intensely satiric character of the story.

Kobes follows the same trajectory as Lang's *Metropolis* by extrapolating certain economic and social dynamics and pushing them to their extreme consequences, imagining a worst-case scenario, a science fiction story in negativo. In many respects *Kobes* could have been a screenplay for an expressionist movie of the early 1920s. The often puzzling and somewhat incoherent plot leads the reader through a series of distorted perspectives, long hallways, empty waiting rooms, and elevators that suddenly get stuck between floors.

The scene: a coal and mining city dominated by "monstrous, naked, blazing plants," the sky simultaneously "red and black." A man dressed in an elegant suit runs for his life, disregarding the muddy puddles and the drenching "black rain." His destination: an imposing house of "steel and glass, with five hundred wires on its rooftop," the center of power, the office of the industrialist Kobes (260). The reader learns that this runner, like the mythical messenger after the victory of Marathon, wants to convey an all-important note to his leader. Yet his attempt fails, he breaks down from exhaustion on the stairs, he dies without fulfilling his dearest wish: "To see him only once and die" (261). It is characteristic of the story that the overall expressionist, often surrealist atmosphere is mixed with moments of one-dimensional, crude realism when, for example, Mann refers to the dead runner as "the corpse of the petered-out middle class" (260).

Kobes has many different bureaucratic departments that control each sector of public life and politics. As much as the heads of these departments revel in their own power, they obediently bow to their ultimate authority. In a scene that foreshadows Lang's use of the radio in *The Testament of Dr. Mabuse* (1932–33), a radio voice coming out of a hole in the wall proclaims: "I have simple thoughts, simple goals. I am not high-class. Politics, I don't understand. I am a busy merchant, I am the symbol of German democracy, no one can fault me. I am Kobes" (265). As part of a ritual, all department heads respond to the voice of their master with a slogan that recurs throughout the novella and reiterates the popular sentiments about Stinnes's work ethic: "Kobes never indulges, Kobes never drinks, Kobes never dances, Kobes never fools around. Kobes works twenty hours a day" (ibid.).

An American woman enters the foyer and demands to speak to Kobes. She runs into Dr. Sand, an employee in the propaganda department. Dr. Sand had once been a university lecturer in philosophy before his position was cut. Mann portrays in him the bitter and resentful former "intellectual worker," a disenfranchised academic who has turned his intellectual energies into revengeful, omnipotent fantasies. The sudden opportunity to change his boring life by embarking on the dangerous quest to find the mysterious, all-powerful Kobes together with an attractive woman is not lost on Dr. Sand. They both enter the labyrinth of power; they manage to cross long hallways with secret trapdoors, outmaneuver several security guards, and pass a giant elevator moving end-lessly up and down.

Finally they enter his office. The legendary Kobes turns out to be rather unimpressive. They find a small, shabbily dressed man with a high-pitched voice. Surprisingly, he is not alone. The lady's husband, a rich American, is negotiating a loan with him that would enable Kobes to buy the German railway system. With this reference to a railway deal, Heinrich Mann mixes another bit of contemporary context into the story that links Kobes to Hugo Stinnes. The American woman embodies an overdrawn mixture of cynicism, candidness about her own immoral-ity, and sexual desire that blossoms in the vicinity of power. "What a wonderful man you are, Mister Kobes" (276), she shouts, and makes it no secret that she is determined to sleep with him. Initially, he refuses the indecent proposal claiming, "I am a family man" (280). Yet it is the hus-band, whose power seemingly diminishes in the presence of his wife, who urges him to obey: "We can't close the deal if you don't sleep with my wife" (ibid.). Driven by his "mad greed," Kobes finally succumbs. He leaves the room with the American woman as the radio voice begins to ramble again: "Kobes works twenty hours a day . . ." (281).

The expressionist, often nightmarish atmosphere of the short story is pushed to the extreme in its final part. Exhausted by the sexual demands of the unexpected female visitor, Kobes returns to his office. "Please help me," he moans to Dr. Sand, who sees his chance of a lifetime. In return for his promise to "take care of the lady," Sand is allowed to realize his ultimate power fantasy, the introduction of a new "religion," the "Kobes myth," under his leadership.

"World and factory as unity" and "the harmony between leadership and the masses" are two of the slogans of Sand's new "religion" (284–85). He plans a grand spectacle for the workers as a worship service in honor of the Kobes myth. Instead of the real Kobes, a hired actor repre-sents the enigmatic figure on stage. The curtain opens, and in a thun-dering voice the actor announces different exercises that celebrate the workers' total obedience to Kobes. This bizarre spectacle reaches its cli-max when a blazing furnace is rolled on stage. The Kobes actor, half se-ductive, half commanding, now asks for the ultimate sacrifice: all chil-dren must jump into the furnace. Willingly the audience complies, and soon the first children begin to jump into the furnace.

The story alludes here to the myth of the Moloch that originates in the Old Testament. The Moloch was a Canaanite idol, to whom children were sacrificed as burnt offerings. To the Jews, it meant a warning against idolatry. As the mythological icon that signifies the fall of a civilized society into materialistic barbarism, the Moloch reappears throughout the critical discourse on modern technology and society, perhaps most prominently in *Metropolis*. Heinrich Mann applies the biblical plot quite literally to represent the victory of a barbarous regime that expects total sacrifice for the sake of total production.

At last, anarchy breaks out when the actor on stage proclaims the end of all moral inhibitions. A sexual orgy ensues, as workers rip their clothes off and openly unleash their sexual desires. At this point, Sand has become an unpredictable risk for the Kobes trust. The department heads revolt against the "Kobes myth." The next day, the actor impersonating Kobes gets fired; Sand is stripped of all his power and commits suicide.

Mann's novella is a rather obvious exercise in unmasking the contemporary Stinnes myth. Kobes-Stinnes appears as an empty, regressive, slogan-stammering moron who has crushed German culture and civilization. Ironically, it is the job of a former "intellectual worker," the philosopher Sand, to push the Stinnes principle to the extreme. Inspired by Nietzsche's fervent critique of modern capitalist society, Sand wants to bring out the real truth underlying this regime: behind the veil of industrial order and business deals lies nothing but irrationalism and arbitrary cruelty.[5] Yet uncovering this radically immoral truth is ultimately too much for the Kobes trust: "Good business only takes place in the middle. Always stay sober" (289).

While the philosopher Sand unveils the morally empty idolatry of capitalist culture, the figure of the sex-driven American woman points to a widespread and long-held German reactionary prejudice about American culture and capitalism in general. The reader learns that behind the seemingly autonomous patriarchal capitalist stands a lustful woman who controls him. The American capitalist says to Kobes, "We [Americans] are like that. What our ladies want, we don't oppose. . . . We can't close the deal if you don't sleep with my wife" (280). Mann's attack on American culture is only sharpened by the racist description of the lady's husband, who has "a gray-white Negro face, broad, no forehead, grayed curly hair like weeds on fertile soil."[6]

It might be surprising that the novella takes almost no notice of the actual currency devaluation. As the representative of American capitalist greed, it is the American woman who brings up the topic briefly, yet blatantly: "Mister Kobes, . . . how did you hit upon that fabulous inflation scheme, which squeezed out your whole nation? Please tell me! This is the greatest hoax since Law" (278). Kobes's faint defense that he is an honest merchant and works for the greater good of the country only intensifies the story's position that the whole inflation is indeed masterminded by Kobes.

Rather than directly addressing the devaluation of the currency, Mann is more concerned with the effect inflation has on the triangular relationship between economic power, culture, and work. *Kobes* presents us with a world in which a workaholic and driven capitalist eradicates the uniqueness and interdependency of these three spheres. Yet the novella reaches such a drastic urgency and shrillness because Mann's own understanding as a writer and intellectual is drawn into the story. The economic and the cultural are diametrically opposed in Mann's worldview, which leaves the notion of work in between, a battleground for the two forces. Like many other leftist writers of modernism, Mann rejects the romantic notion of the artist as an unsociable outsider and genius. On the contrary, in many essays such as "Geist und Tat" ("Intellect and Action," 1910) he pleads for an active political and social role for artists and intellectuals. Art, and any other kind of intellectual pursuit, is for Mann not a form of Kantian disinterested "play," but rather a form of production, a form of work as a goal-oriented, socially directed activity. Intellectual production, therefore, participates in the context of work, a term that for Heinrich Mann is linked to both the economic and the cultural spheres: "It is evident that the health of the economy is ultimately dependent on the sophisticated feeling and thinking of the people" ("Tragödie" 99).

The traumatic vision of an *Arbeitsnation,* which Kobes and his industrial empire signify, eradicates this dual, dialectal notion of work as an activity of economic as well as cultural production. In fact, any critical artistic production in Kobes's empire has become an impossibility. The sphere of culture has collapsed into barbarism with the enactment of archaic rituals that even include human sacrifices. Work has taken on an ugly, dystopian face: structured by an excess of power and hierarchy, it has completely taken over people's lives and robbed them of all freedom. Dr. Sand, the former intellectual and Mann's ego in negativo, has turned into a propagandist of a powerful myth; his is a career not unlike that of Joseph Goebbels, who started out as a disgruntled Germanist. For Heinrich Mann, "the tragedy of 1923," the painful duress of German culture under the process of inflation, lies in the totalitarian predominance of the economic that eradicates all difference, that destroys the volatile balance between culture, economy, and work.

V.

"The name Stinnes signifies a whole epoch," exclaims Eugen Ortner jubilantly in a small book published in 1922 that attracted my attention not least by the expressionist pathos of its title, *Gott Stinnes: Ein Pamphlet gegen den vollkommenen Menschen (God Stinnes: A Pamphlet against the Universal Man)* (see Figure 19). Ortner (1890–1947) was a teacher and later a journalist and writer in Munich. He had some fleeting success as a dramatist during the 1920s. Ortner's oeuvre does not express much regard for the young German republic. He later sympathized with National Socialism without, however, ever belonging to the inner circles of Nazi artists. Neither Eugen Ortner nor his thin volume, *Gott Stinnes,* has thus far left any traces in scholarship on Weimar culture. Yet *Gott Stinnes* contains a fascinating and intriguing response to the cultural shifts during the early 1920s that are intimately connected to inflation. While, for Heinrich Mann, a German *Arbeitsnation* under the dictatorial leadership of a Kobes-Stinnes type represents the ultimate nightmare, Eugen Ortner considers such a scenario a positive grandiose vision for Germany's postwar future.

Two interpretative reference points guide my reading of this text. First, in an even more transparent manner than in Mann's novella, the notion of work serves in Ortner's volume as a counterdiscourse that covers up and offers an escape from the pains of the monetary depreciation, yet at the same time reenacts this trauma. Second, while certainly written in an expressionist tone, *Gott Stinnes* also contains an early type of *Verhaltenslehre,* a "code of conduct," which leads me to discuss Ortner's text in the context of Neue Sachlichkeit, or German Functionalism.

"God Stinnes," as Ortner writes, signifies not a person, but rather a set of principles that happens to manifest itself in the historical person of Hugo Stinnes. The spirit of "God Stinnes" rules over a new age of total production that leads to the transformation of Germany into a so-called *Weltfabrik.* "Money business is ultimately insignificant. Everybody can buy stocks. . . . At stake all over Europe nowadays is the formation of work," Ortner observes (22). To achieve these new forms of organizing work, Ortner enthusiastically supports the process of vertical industrial concentration. Only big trusts, he argues, can adequately respond to the needs of the masses and produce most effectively. In ad-

Figure 19. Book cover of *Gott Stinnes*, by Eugen Ortner.
Illustration by Schacht.

dition, vertical trusts eliminate the superfluous activities of trade and exchange: "We have to rely on ourselves and have to be producers, not
hucksters" (28).

The historical Hugo Stinnes possesses many characteristics that pre-
destine him to be the bearer of this new spirit. Ortner reiterates popular
sentiments and praises Stinnes for keeping a contemptuous distance
from the decadent and luxurious lifestyle of his fellow industrialists and

instead displaying an intimate relationship with the "rhythm of production" and his workers: "All these heads, all these hands are his head, are
his hands: the sheer force of this gigantic work rhythm 'hands—head—
hands' melts away all opposites and erases individuality, time-consuming
theorizing, political bickering and boring discussions about principles"
(10). Stinnes is both a leader and a man of the masses, "his goals are the
goals of the masses" (23); in this close affinity to the masses he is not unlike Lenin, Ortner observes. Next to his collectivist nature it is his ma-
chinelike, rational simplicity that determines his role as a leader. Says
Ortner, "He is like the creation of a machine" (10), and his *Sachlichkeit*,
his functionalism, is revered by his workers:

> Stinnes has a brain so well organized that his practical-organizational think-
> ing will process any problem in the shortest way and without disturbance. . . .
> No fantastic imagination, no emotional involvement, no superfluous distrac-
> tions interrupt this process, no metaphysical or artistic mood spoils the ex-
> actness of this apparatus. During a time of extreme political differentiation
> and enormous social problems this well-developed, one-sided modern brain
> throws his commands into the crowds of hundred thousands as if it could
> never err. . . .
>   And so he rises, every day anew, . . . and so the enterprise develops, each
> and every day newly equipped with all the inventions of technology and in-
> dustry. . . . Stinnes knows nothing other than the transformation of raw ma-
> terial according to human desire, the mechanization of life, the conquest of
> matter through itself. (17)

Half leader, half cyborg, Stinnes personifies and represents in Ortner's eyes the workers' love for the machine: "The beauty of the machine
and the beauty of rhythmic work are the fixed points in the inner life of
these masses. . . . Only during work can one gain an ethical and esthetic
experience of oneself" (60). Stinnes's organizational genius finds its most
fitting expression in Taylorism, the new system of industrial work organization that Ortner wants to see implemented in all industrial production: "This system is waiting for Stinnes, Stinnes is born for this system"
(37). Taylorism, with its division of labor into minute tasks, leads to new
levels of specialization. Future industries will no longer ask for all-round
talents, they rather will look for workers who have a special qualifi-
cation to perform one very specific task.[7] While most enthusiasts of Taylorism during the 1920s stopped short of thinking about its larger social
and cultural impact, Ortner accompanies his economic reflections with
an equally radical call for cultural change: "Our beginning is the machine, our principle is the mechanization of life, our moral base the col-

lective human being. What should perish is the individualistic occidental, the individual European" (68).

Ortner declares all of bourgeois culture, with its emphasis on individuality, an exhausted and empty construct. *Gott Stinnes* is full of rabid attacks against "bourgeois artists." They may be as different from each other as Fritz von Unruh, Ernst Toller, or Georg Kaiser—Ortner condemns them all as *Schöngeister* (decadent elites) who are not meeting the demands of the working masses (41). In this context, the mysterious subtitle, *A Pamphlet against the Universal Man,* unfolds its meaning. Central to the occidental concept of individuality is the idea of the "universal man" who is striving for personal completeness and a totality of experience. In his chapter "Farewell to D'Annunzio" Ortner exemplifies the change of epochs by contrasting Stinnes with Gabriele D'Annunzio, the latter being a towering example of a *Totalitätsmensch* (universal man) and a last representative of a dying bourgeois, romantic culture:

> Stinnes will destroy D'Annunzio, Stinnes will destroy all artists.
> Stinnes doesn't create playfully. He rather changes the world in an essential manner. . . . The equalization between the classes, the discipline of work, the systematizing of all aspects of life robs the artist of the tensions that were necessary for his production. Problems will decrease, and the most interesting part of life up to now, the fight for one's own perfection, will be regarded as an embarrassing hysteria which any decent person is best advised to suppress. (48)

The future, according to Ortner's prediction, will belong to so-called *Spezialmenschen taylorschen Musters* (63). Such "specialized men" will have given up the inappropriate search for the holy grail of individual completeness and instead will strive to perfect their highly specialized skills. Yet Ortner has not abandoned the idea of totality altogether. As a replacement for the bourgeois *Universalmensch* he advocates a *Kombinationsmensch,* a kind of virtual combination of several "specialized men" who are closely connected with one another. In small cultural communities the Taylor type regains his lost totality by being part of a communal endeavor. An example of such a *Kombinationsmensch* could be the combination of "a worker, a technician, a scientist, an organizer, and an artist—these five will form a unity which creates a new totality" (65). Only through such "planned solidarity," Ortner instructs his readers, can the "contingency, limitation, and brevity of our individual existence" be overcome (66).

At the beginning of the twenty-first century, as we read such lines we keep in mind the history of two bizarre and horrific attempts to erase in-

dividual freedom and autonomy through excessive forms of collectivism. We may shake our heads at Ortner's enthusiastic vision of a
"planned solidarity," of a society that no longer needs art, that finds its
social and ethical vision in the total mechanization of life. Yet one does
not have to look far in modern industrialized societies to discover a certain contemporary attraction for the same strange mixture of technological enthusiasm, an excessive form of work ethic, and the replacement of
social spheres such as family and neighborhoods by work-related, com-
pany-organized structures of social interaction.

Yet how does *Gott Stinnes* relate to the specific situation of the early
1920s? The text was written in 1922 when inflation was already in full
swing. It is striking that Ortner's economic and cultural utopia of a
German "nation of work" shows the complete absence of any monetary
circulation. Trade in general is seen as a superfluous activity that can be
mostly eradicated by huge trusts of vertical concentration integrating
every level of industrial production. What does a text that on the surface
seems to ignore the economic and social realities of monetary devaluation tell us about the event it so vehemently wants to suppress? *Gott
Stinnes,* I argue, presents an interesting case study of both the denial and
the reenactment of the trauma of inflation. Ortner's production- and
work-centered vision serves as an escape from the unpredictable, uncontrollable nature of monetary circulation and trade. At the same time
his utopia is a vocal, desperate mimicry that clings to the traumatic reality of inflation.

I have noted that massification, devaluation, and circulation, together
with the centrality of money, are the key parameters that signify inflation as an economic, yet also social and cultural, force. A closer look reveals that all these dynamics are at the heart of *Gott Stinnes.* The text
reenacts these traumatic processes yet promises at the same time either
agents of control or a radical, reverse reinterpretation. The loss of bourgeois financial and social autonomy that was vividly experienced by millions of Germans is celebrated here as a jubilant throwing away of a worn-
out mask. Yet the euphoric tone in Ortner's voice when he smashes the
porcelain figure of bourgeois culture actually betrays how much he imitates the grim cynicism of the culture of inflation. The traumatic process
of massification is displaced into its opposite: it suddenly becomes the
promise for a new social beginning, the creation of a new social subject
not on the basis of individuality but rather on collectivity. The destruction of bourgeois culture results not in anarchy but in a new structure of
ultimate order and predictability. And the circulation of money? It is dis-

placed by the abstract energy of work itself, a pre-monetary (or post-monetary, as Ortner would argue) form of exchange that he describes as "the sheer force of this gigantic work rhythm 'hands—head—hands' [that] melts away all opposites and erases individuality" (10). Nothing silences the shrill voices at the chaotic stock market better than the soothing "rhythm of the machine."

Gott Stinnes includes chapters on Stinnes's character, on his huge industrial trusts and vertical concentration, on Taylorism, on the end of "bourgeois art," and on the beauty of machines. Thus, Ortner takes a full swing at the contemporary situation of the early 1920s. His grand finale, however, is a short chapter entitled "Ethical Exercises for Beginners" in which he presents a behavioral guide that aims to prepare his readers for the coming age. Here is a selection of his advice:

> First, start doing sports, preferably soccer, boxing or car racing. Second, throw all your diaries in the toilet; your life should not be a story. Third, avoid ecstatic people, refuse to deal with them, they have no clue about life. Constantly test your ability to connect with all that is robust and healthy. . . .
>
> Learn to live boringly. Understand that you have to regard yourself more suspiciously, the more you attract the interest of other people. Recognize the moment when others find you interesting and inform them of your banality. . . .
>
> Refuse any resentment. Never react personally. Don't lash out against Frenchmen and Negroes. . . .
>
> Do not discuss ethics. Those who talk about it are choleric, power-hungry characters, they are ridiculous. The ethics of the collectivist are silent. Ignore arrogance wherever you may come across it. This is an ethical action, because arrogance is the pathos of the individual.
>
> Become a specialized man *[Spezialmensch]*, modest and industrious, and join together with others who are equally one-sided, modest and industrious. (69)

These codes of conduct are certainly noteworthy in themselves because of their cool, irreverent, and somewhat ironic concreteness. More important, however, they position Ortner's book within the sociocultural and artistic movement of Neue Sachlichkeit, or German Functionalism. Helmut Lethen in his 1994 study *Verhaltenslehren der Kälte: Lebensversuche zwischen den Kriegen* described such codes of conduct in the literature and culture of German Functionalism as distinct sociopsychological reactions to the social and economic disorganization of the 1920s. His analysis relies to a considerable extent on Helmuth Plessner's eminent study *Grenzen der Gemeinschaft* (1924). Plessner developed the parameters for such behavioral codes through his cultural anthropology: the reliance on form instead of authenticity, the embrace of tech-

nology and modernization, the soberness and mistrust of social radicalism, and an ironic distance from the mediated constructions of one's
self. The culture and artistic production of Neue Sachlichkeit is correctly
associated with the brief interlude of democratic liberal republicanism
during the mid-1920s. Yet German Functionalism was not inherently
democratic, and its rigid schemes of conduct codes were mainly geared
"to differentiate elemental things amid the complex territory of postwar
society with its economic insecurities and gliding social classes: One's
own and the Other, Inner and Outer, Male and Female" (Lethen 36).
Above all, they created an existential mode of distance—distance from
one's own emotions, from the unpredictability of the times, from other
people. They allowed people to save face and avoid the trauma of shameful, embarrassing experiences. In that sense Neue Sachlichkeit, with its
codes of conduct, served as a temporary painkiller, yet could not provide
a thorough therapy for the traumatized victims of war and inflation.

Central to Lethen's analysis of German Functionalism is the figure of
the "cold persona." The "cold persona" does not desire authenticity, but
rather strives for form and calculating behavior. It redirects, as Lethen
writes, the inner psychological qualities of guilt and self-responsibility
toward outer-directed, behavior-based schemes. One can hardly think
of a more fitting illustration of a "cold persona" than the highly stylized
descriptions of the *Spezialmensch* in Ortner's text: the willful preemption
of inner psychological agencies such as fantasy, conscience, and emotions; the sober realization of one's own limitations as the result of highly
specialized working conditions; or the radical presentness of experience
that has abandoned all eagerness to connect daily experience with a
larger story of one's own life. Inasmuch as Ortner's Hugo Stinnes also embodies all of these qualifications, he exemplifies in many ways the social
construction of the "cold persona."

In order to integrate the "cold persona" into the cultural context of
inflation, it is worthwhile to compare the two mythical, larger-than-life
figures of Hugo Stinnes and Dr. Mabuse. While the figure of Dr. Mabuse, with its intimate relation to the circulation of money, currency speculation, and the heat of the stock market, is constructed to signify the
chaos of inflation, the Stinnes myth offers just the opposite: the cool,
rhythmic, calculated, predictable, Taylorized world of work and production. Although Mabuse, too, may be calculating and coldly manipu-
lative, he is essentially Stinnes's opposite. A creature who is part of the
legacy of German Expressionism, Mabuse mostly manipulates the inner
psychological apparatus of his victims, creating emotional dependence in

some, inflicting overwhelming feelings of guilt or exploiting masochistic desires in others. Behind his actions stands the enormous self-centered force of his own ego. Ortner's Stinnes myth, by no means less totalitarian, rejects the kind of individualistic megalomania that signifies the figure of Mabuse. Instead, Ortner presents us with a leader type who is practically devoid of all individual desires and whose radical functionalism makes him subservient to the larger principles of efficiency and rationalism.

As important as it is to highlight the resemblance between the sociocultural strategies of Neue Sachlichkeit and Ortner's text, it is equally important to stress the limits of such a positioning. In its radical anti-individualistic and antiliberal gestures, *Gott Stinnes* clearly moves beyond the confines of German Functionalism, with its shaky, yet undisputed commitment to Weimar's republicanism.[8]

VI.

Our journey through different narrative and essayistic manifestations of the Stinnes myth finally leads us to an artifact that, like no other in Weimar culture, has captured the intricate relationship between industrial leadership, visions of relentless production, machines and modern technology, total massification—and the discontent with such a threatening, yet fascinating utopia. Fritz Lang's *Metropolis* (1927), as Anton Kaes writes, "extends over a large intellectual terrain, touching almost every debate of the Weimar Republic" ("Cinema and Modernity" 20). Our continuing fascination with this film lies in its abundance of intertextual references, both on its manifest level and in its deeper structures. Watching *Metropolis* is like riding on the huge elevator so prominently displayed in the film itself. We move up and down through this imaginary body of modernity: from the cool and calculating atmosphere in Fredersen's corner office high above the city, down to the hot and noisy generator rooms of the power plants, further down to the barren underground living quarters of the workers, and finally into the mythical depths of the secret caverns where the workers meet to pray for redemption and a better future. *Metropolis,* as Siegfried Kracauer writes, "was rich in subterranean content, that, like contraband, had crossed the borders of consciousness without being asked" (*From Caligari to Hitler* 163).

Accordingly, *Metropolis* has attracted an abundance of interpretations that focus on the film's many different discursive elements. It "displays the modernist dimension in fascism and the fascist dimension in modernism" (Kaes 20); in the figure of the cyborg Maria, the film signifies a modernist "synthesis of organic and technological elements" (Biro 71); it thematizes the complex relationship between technology, female sexuality, and male anxieties, as Andreas Huyssen argues. Many critics have remarked on the undoubtedly regressive politics of the film, which become most apparent in the final scene of the film, which reiterates screenwriter Thea von Harbou's main motto for *Metropolis:* "The mediator between the brain and the hand must be the heart." Most of the critics concentrate on the "lower half" of the *Metropolis* world—on the huge machine rooms and the workers' underground city that offer such abundant pictures, fantasies, and nightmares—and explore the relationship between technology, modern society, and its collective psyche.

Writing about Hugo Stinnes and the cultural iconography surrounding his persona, however, leads me to visit the "upper half" of the film's world in order to look for the Stinnes of *Metropolis:* the industrialist Joh Fredersen. For next to *Kobes* and *Gott Stinnes, Metropolis* offers another vision of a "Stinnesien come true." The similarities between Joh Fredersen and Hugo Stinnes are indeed remarkable. Just like Hugo Stinnes, Fredersen reigns over a vast industrial empire that rests, to a considerable extent, on the symbiotic relationship between coal and the production of electricity. The vertical spatial arrangement of the film and the workers' daily routine of moving down through deep shafts to their workplace imitates a mining environment. It is evident that the machines in *Metropolis* are huge turbines and generators that produce electricity. This is the visionary city of Hugo Stinnes, founder and chairman of the gigantic Rheinisch Westphälische Elektrizitätswerke (RWE) and owner of large coal mines in the Ruhr district. Even the end of the film, the handshake between Fredersen and foreman Groh, quotes a historical episode from Hugo Stinnes's life: the famous Stinnes-Legien Agreement from 1918. Labor and trade unions, represented by Carl Legien, shook hands with the corporate leader Hugo Stinnes and agreed to a treaty that brought at least for a brief time some peace to industrial relationships in postwar Germany.

In its basic ambivalence toward modernity, *Metropolis* displays the same aspects of the Stinnes myth that we have already explored in *Kobes* and in *Gott Stinnes.* Like the protagonist Kobes in Mann's novella, Fredersen is represented as a brutal industrial tyrant who sacrifices his workers for higher production goals, and who, without a moment's hesitation, fires his secretary, Joseph, knowing that his decision will result in

Joseph's suicide. Yet the figure of Fredersen also bears the unquestion-
ably attractive mystique of the "cool persona" in the tradition of Neue
Sachlichkeit. By no means an impulsive, irrational leader, he fascinates
us with his aura of cool, distant, calculating control; he radiates intellectual competence. His appearance is disciplined, even ascetic.

I could now follow the established parameter of the Stinnes myth and
explore how this film conceptualizes and represents the notion of work.
However, Matthew Biro and Anton Kaes have convincingly done this
and have emphasized that the film foreshadows and at the same time
criticizes Ernst Jünger's vision of a totalitarian synthesis of work and
technology. Instead, the rest of my analysis of *Metropolis* will be guided
by a question that is of greater concern for the larger project of this
book: if, as most critics indicate, *Metropolis* indeed incorporates so
many of Weimar's central cultural debates, does this film respond in any
way to the period of inflation beyond the apparent Stinnes-Fredersen
analogy?

Fritz Lang seemed to be mainly concerned with the fascinating and
nightmarish images of a machine culture, with class conflict, and certainly also with the oedipal revolt of son Freder against his father. At
first glance, the memory of the great currency devaluation that shook
Germany only four years before the premier of *Metropolis* seems to be
thoroughly absent from the film's fictional world, which addresses so
many other economic and social debates of the time. I will move into
uncharted territory by arguing just the opposite: *Metropolis* contains in
fact a hidden, subterranean reenactment of the inflation. To create a
sense of anxiousness, fear, confusion, and finally chaos in viewers at the
time, the film borrows from and reaches back to the traumatic repertoire
of the inflation.

To access this allegorized history, we have to look at the central event
of *Metropolis,* an event that sets off the dramatic narrative of the film
and causes a volatile situation to explode: Rotwang's counterfeiting of
Maria. To the extent that, in *Metropolis,* the real and the robot Maria
each appears to be a medium that circulates, we can interpret them, at
least in part, as allegorical figures of the circulation of money.[9] By splitting the signifier "Maria" into two entities, into a "before" and "after,"
a "moral" being and "immoral" being, a "mother" and "whore," the
film invokes male anxieties about the unpredictable powers of the feminine. At the same time, this split reenacts what we may call the "genealogy" of inflation. Rotwang's act is the primary deed that unleashes the
destructive force of inflation: he creates an immoral, a *scheinhafte* form

of a medium by imitating and mimicking its trusted, "integer" original. The two Marias are in essence the difference between hard currency and inflationary money. Lang furnishes Maria's original role as a trusted medium with the ultimate insignia of assurance and morality: In her first appearance, standing among the large group of children, she displays sheer, overwhelming motherhood. She speaks the truth about Metropolis by reminding son Freder of the desperate situation of the workers. Who would not believe her? Freder is so impressed by this encounter that he immediately runs out the door and wants to explore the miserable underground of the city.

Familial bonds, the trust children have that their parents will protect them, serve as an important criterion by which to measure the moral intactness of the community in *Metropolis*. Just as in Heinrich Mann's *Kobes,* the ultimate immorality of society is indicated by the fact that parents simply forget about their children. The central reference here is to the Moloch myth, in which parents are willing to sacrifice their children to the pagan idol. In descriptions of the culture of inflation that were contemporary with the time, such as Hans Ostwald's *Sittengeschichte der Inflation (Moral History of the Inflation),* this theme is explicitly formulated: "Mama danced with friends. The nanny took the opportunity and danced as well—and the children at home were all alone" (8). Similarly, the dramatic high point in *Metropolis* is reached when the workers leave their children behind to follow the false Maria into an orgy of destruction.

It is Fredersen's idea to send the robot Maria down to the workers in order to spread anarchy, yet it is the engineer Rotwang who plays the central role in its actual creation. To some degree, Rotwang himself is part of the robot. He has an artificial right hand as the result of some sort of accident during its construction; it is almost a kind of tribute to the machine. With respect to Lang's oeuvre, the links between Rotwang and Dr. Mabuse are quite apparent. Both are played by the brilliant actor Rudolf Klein-Rogge. They are similar characters: they both possess a peculiar mixture of intelligence, scientific ingenuity, and a mad sense of megalomania. Through many subtle and not so subtle devices, the films mark both characters as Jewish. In *Metropolis,* Rotwang's house signifies an anachronistic Jewish ghetto.

Thus, from the then-contemporary audience's point of view, *Metropolis* strikes a chord when it shows how an entire society is being ripped apart by the infiltration of a counterfeited, false medium. The staging of the initial inflationary act itself, the doubling of Maria, visualizes other

dynamics of the inflation mentioned earlier. Even if only one Maria robot is created, we know from Rotwang's plans that the cloning capacity of
his machine is potentially unlimited. He alludes to an existentially threatening form of massification when he indicates to Fredersen his desire to
create masses of work robots that would replace all human workers.

After the creation of the robot Maria, *Metropolis* goes into detailed
descriptions of how the dynamic of a devaluation rapidly infects every
segment of society. Lang uses established registers of sexual politics
when he furnishes the robot Maria with all the seductive female sexuality that is needed to destroy the moral fabric of society.[10] Exploiting the
trust people have in the real Maria, the false Maria is accepted as "currency" and circulates freely through all social classes. Up until this moment, Fredersen and Rotwang are still confident they have their creation
under control and are pleased that nobody detects her artificiality. However, after presenting us with so many austere images of technology and
work, the film suddenly switches scenery and displays an extravagant,
luxurious party. The robot Maria performs a nude dance that is reminiscent of Anita Berber's famous performance in *Dr. Mabuse, the Gambler.* The cyborg can cast an even stronger spell on the workers in the
underground of the city. She ignites an orgy of destruction and leads the
workers to the machine room, where foreman Groh tries in vain to bring
them back to reason. "And the children are home alone," Ostwald
might have commented.

Maria's sexual power to drive people into madness is culturally coded
through her identification as a "witch." The film targets her as the primary cause for the chaos. As I mentioned earlier in this book, and will
explain further in chapter 8, inflation was often called "the witches' Sabbat" to indicate its mad destructiveness. Lang alludes to the demonic
state of the bewitched workers when we see them in one scene frantically
dancing around the machines they are about to destroy.

The visual hallmarks of a culture of inflation become increasingly
vivid toward the climax of the film. The party above ground has turned
into a wild "witches' Sabbat," as Maria is throned on the shoulders of
one of the party guests, and shouts: "Let's watch the world go to hell."
It is hardly coincidental that the semiotics of destruction in *Metropolis,*
next to the visually impressive explosion of machines, concentrate on
the imagery of a huge flood.

We see its chilling beginnings when the water starts creeping into the
workers' quarters, and soon water pours in from all corners. A cartoon in
Simplicissimus contemporary with the film, entitled "Die Sintflut" ("The

Figure 20. "The flood." Illustration by Olaf Gulbransson,
in *Simplicissimus* 27 (August 13, 1922).

flood"), illustrates the powerful metaphoric link between inflation and
the image of the flood (see Figure 20). The traumatic experience of both
an uncontrollable massification and an uncontrollable circulation can
hardly be shown more convincingly. The illustration also carries the ugly
specter of anti-Semitism in it: the caricature of a Jewish man is sitting
safely on a secure boulder and is seemingly untouched by all this misery.[11] Throughout the film, the viewer is continually reminded that the
control of circulative forces such as electricity or water remains a constant challenge. We see the workers' terrified gaze at thermometers and
other instruments rising, and we do not forget the robot's diabolic pleasure when the gauges of the machines are rising and indicating an imminent explosion.

Finally, it takes the ultimate call from foreman Groh to bring the workers back to their senses: "Where are your children?" Then even Fredersen realizes that he has unleashed powers he cannot control anymore:
"Where is my son?" he shouts, echoing the desperation of the workers.

The burning of the witch Maria in the Gothic church grows out of the medieval discourse that is interwoven into the modern fabric of Lang's film. Yet at the same time the pile of wood with the false Maria on top invokes vivid memories of the end of inflation, when tons of worthless paper money were either burned or pulped.

At the end of the film, the world of Metropolis is cleansed of all remnants of inflation. The false Maria has been burned and Rotwang, even though only the executor of Fredersen's ideas, has fulfilled his role as a scapegoat. Fredersen has been forgiven; in fact, only the audience knows that the inflationary chaos was his idea in the first place. A new order sets in, when the workers march in a wedge formation toward the church and submit to the odd pact between labor and capital, mediated through "the heart."

"What remains," writes Anton Kaes, "is a transformed community that again embraces technology—a technology that is now free, the film insinuates, from 'Jewish control' and instead infused with German spirituality. What remains is the kind of community (Gemeinschaft, not Gesellschaft) reactionary modernists such as Werner Sombart, Oswald Spengler, and Ernst Jünger had valorized in their writings throughout the 1920's" ("Cinema and Modernity" 32). Indeed, Joh Fredersen will carry on the vision of "Stinnesien" in Metropolis. For it is clear that the final embrace of technology and work serves to cover up the hidden, painful story of the currency devaluation. Yet a fundamental question remains open at the end of the film: through what kind of medium will the society of Metropolis convey its economic and social information? Through "the heart"?

Fritz Lang called this a "fairy tale" answer (Bogdanovich 15). Lang and so many others underestimated how successfully National Socialism would work such "fairy tales" into its ideological fabric. Blurred lines between regressive sentimentality, organic social fantasies, and a resulting brutal biologism would be at the center of National Socialist ideology that only six years after the premiere of Metropolis would rule the country. And in that ideological context "the heart" would have a new meaning. The circulation of money would be replaced by the circulation of blood that would pulse through the German Volkskörper, with Adolf Hitler as its "heart," its medium, and its mediator at the same time.

PART FOUR

Accounts

CHAPTER SEVEN

Cultural Capital in Decline

Inflation and the Distress of Intellectuals

I.

In his 1923 essay "Wirtschaft, Kultur, Intellektuelle," the leftist writer Kurt Kersten proclaimed: "The 'economy' rules. And German culture, as much as it existed, is perishing. . . . The German intellectuals are part of the middle class. . . . This middle class is worn out—economically and intellectually" (583). For Kersten, the alternatives were clear: "If one doesn't want to become subjected to the 'economy,' one has only two choices: either slowly perish or join the revolutionary party" (ibid.). While Kersten's call to join radical leftist politics had only a limited appeal to most German intellectuals, his analysis of their economic and social situation was shared by many. As members of the middle class, and largely unprotected by trade unions or other powerful professional organizations, writers, artists, journalists, professors, and scientists saw their economic status drastically deteriorating during the inflation.

World War 1 had destroyed the fabric of Wilhelmine culture and had left intellectuals with a wide range of reactions: shock, confusion, defiant denial, quiet relief, cautious optimism, and even exuberant hope at the prospect of building a democratic society. Their role in the turbulent social changes that came with the inflation years was by no means clear. Heinrich Mann, as we saw in the previous chapter, regarded the "intellectual workers" as the guarantors of the survival of a German *Kulturnation*. Yet, to put it in Pierre Bourdieu's terms, what real value did their "cultural capital" have during the period of inflation? The devaluation of *Geld* was about to destroy their economic status; was the inflation thus also destroying the foundations of German *Geist?* And if so, what was to follow? Irreversible damage to German *Kultur,* or even a civilization without *Kultur?*

The perceived attack of *Geld* on *Geist,* the "unprecedented self-consciousness among intellectuals" (Kaes, Jay, and Dimendberg 285) about their function and role in society, is an essential aspect of German culture during the inflation period and is the focus of this chapter. Intensified and heightened by the inflation, the discussions about the role of intellectuals indicate in hindsight, as Anton Kaes writes, a radical turning point in modern German cultural history: the cultural dominance of the educated bourgeoisie *(Bildungsbürgertum)* ended, and a new economically oriented modern mass and media culture began to emerge ("Ökonomische Dimension" 308). Many essays, speeches, and pamphlets illustrate this cultural change. Yet how did this shift affect the psychosocial situation of individuals? In Thomas Mann's *Unordnung und frühes Leid (Disorder and Early Sorrow)* of 1925 we find a masterful fictional account that can provide us with a microcosmic view on the changing social and cultural status of the German *Bildungsbürgertum* during inflation.[1]

II.

The historian Gerald Feldman calls *Disorder and Early Sorrow* "certainly the most famous but also the most detached and even Olympian work of fiction dealing with the inflation" (*Great Disorder* 11). When compared with Heinrich Mann's shrill and expressionist story *Kobes,* Thomas Mann's *Disorder and Early Sorrow* seems indeed to lack the moral outrage about inflation's destructive power that characterizes his brother Heinrich's passionate writing. Both short stories thematize the crisis of an intellectual class, yet their approaches could not be more different. While *Kobes* is a stark woodcut with sharp and exaggerated contrasts, *Disorder and Early Sorrow* resembles a realist tableau full of painstakingly detailed character portraits.[2] The elements Feldman describes as "detached" and "Olympian" are actually part of the ironic perspective that enables Thomas Mann to illustrate the complexity of the protagonists' network of personal relations. Mann does not thematize the social and cultural dimensions of the inflation within the parameters of social marginality or the milieus of crime or prostitution; his protagonists are neither socially uprooted nor unscrupulous loners like Dr. Mabuse and Kobes. Rather, the psychological upheaval caused by the inflation unfolds within the milieu of Thomas Mann's own social reality, the struggling educated bourgeoisie.[3]

The story describes a day in the life of the Cornelius family during the winter of 1922–23. The third-person narrative is interspersed with observations from the perspective of the protagonist, Abel Cornelius, a successful forty-seven-year-old professor of history.[4] He and his wife reside with their four children, Ingrid, who is eighteen, Bert (seventeen), Ellie (five), Beisser (four), and a staff of servants in an elegant yet somewhat run-down villa in one of Munich's more affluent neighborhoods. The inflationary prices prohibit some much-needed repair; "it is still the proper setting of the upper middle class, though they themselves look odd enough in it, with their worn and turned clothing and altered way of life. The children, of course, know nothing else; to them it is normal and regular, they belong by birth to the 'villa proletariat'" (*Disorder* 142). As prototypical members of the *Bildungsbürgertum*, Professor Cornelius and his wife try to uphold the dignified and cultivated lifestyle of their class, albeit with increasing difficulty.

The story begins with a detailed description of the family's lunch, exemplifying how the family can barely adapt to the economic circumstances, which present the professor with a million-mark salary, yet also require his wife to buy 8,000-mark eggs. "The principal dish at lunch had been cutlets made of turnip greens [*Wirsing-Koteletts*]. So there follows a trifle [*Flammeri*], concocted out of one of those dessert powders we use nowadays, that taste like almond soap. Xaver, the youthful manservant, in his outgrown striped jacket, white woolen gloves, and yellow sandals, hands it round, and the 'big folk' take this opportunity to remind their father, tactfully, that company [*Gesellschaft*] is coming today" (139; translation slightly altered). Here we are immediately introduced to the economic reality of the year 1922. The Corneliuses' lunch consists mostly of substitutes. Money has lost its value and become deceptive and so has the food: the substance of *Wirsing-Koteletts* has nothing to do with real meat and the *Flammeri* is not made of milk and cream, but of a rather watery substance that tastes likes soap. Xaver with his yellow sandals and outgrown jacket looks more like a clown than a servant. Still, the members of the parent generation take their social status and obligations seriously. For the upcoming evening party, which the two older children host, Cornelius shows "bourgeois ambition" (142) and wants to serve good food despite the numerous shortages.

A remarkable lightness and tenderness pervade this story; all sharp edges are softened through Mann's mixture of irony, humor, and melancholy. Yet *Disorder and Early Sorrow* is by no means a sentimental family idyll. Rather, Mann masterfully weaves the ongoing societal changes of the inflation period into the intimacy of family life. He achieves this by building his narrative around the social construct of the bourgeois household. The term *household* expands on the socio-psychological meaning of family, and stresses the economic and cultural interplay between a family and its surrounding community. For example, the Cornelius household includes several servants: Xaver Kleinsgütl, the ladies Hinterhöfer, and Kinds-Anna (Kids-Anna), the churlish nurse of the "little folks." These figures are not mere decoration; each of them represents a segment of German society and indicates how the demise of the traditional *Bildungsbürgertum* affected other social classes.

The figure of Xaver Kleinsgütl allows Mann to describe the subtle breakdown of cultural hierarchies and class differences. The narrator tells us about the strong resemblance between Xaver and Cornelius's bohemian son, Bert: "Both lads wear their heavy hair very long on top, with a cursory parting in the middle, and give their heads the same characteristic toss to throw it off the forehead" (139–40). Bert wants to become either a dancer or a cabaret actor; the servant Xaver, "a child and product of the disrupted times, a perfect specimen of his generation, follower of the revolution, Bolshevist sympathizer" (160), similarly wants to fulfill his ultimate passion by joining the world of cinema. He serves dinner with great elegance, yet he also makes liberal use of the professor's bicycle; he is genuinely good-hearted, he loves to play with Ellie and Beisser, yet he simply refuses to do certain household chores; in short, the traditional relationship between servant and bourgeois master is more acted than real. The ladies Hinterhöfer, however, "two sisters once of the lower middle class, who, in these evil days, are reduced to living *au pair* as the phrase goes" (150), suffer severely under the breakdown of the Wilhelmine social codex. The inflation has wiped out their savings, and they have found asylum in the Cornelius household. Their worst hour comes once a week, when they have to substitute for Xaver and serve dinner to the family.

The atmosphere within the Cornelius family is relaxed and friendly despite their economic difficulties. Bert and Ingrid joke with their parents and call them lovingly "the ancients." The narrator recounts more with amusement than misgiving all the different little pranks the older children play. There are generational differences, and the narrator leaves no doubt about the professor's worries and misgivings regarding the future plans of Ingrid and Bert. Yet at the same time the parents more than willingly help with the preparation of the party. Mann conveys that a genuine sense of tolerance, of friendship and mutual respect, characterizes the daily life of the Cornelius family.

This democratic and egalitarian atmosphere extends also to the party. The detailed account of this party is the novella's longest section and includes the portrayal of a cross section of Weimar Germany's middle-class youth culture. The young people use the informal *Du* and interact cordially yet with little formality and gallantry. The inflation has effectively helped to break down social borders. The working class and the bourgeoisie do not unite in Professor Cornelius's house, but it is Mann's intention to present us with a "non-homogeneous, mixed and pluralistic middle class of young people," as Werner Hoffmeister writes (169). Significantly, Mann calls the gathering a *Gesellschaft* to highlight, with the double meaning of the word ("party" and "society"), its doubled narrative function in the story as a festive private party and as the symbolic tableau of a newly emerging German postwar society.

One after the other, the guests arrive and are introduced to the reader. Young Herr Zuber is in business and works in his uncle's brewery. Fräulein Plaichinger, "a perfect Germania, blonde and voluptuous" (153), will later impress Cornelius with her skilled dancing. An especially welcomed guest is the actor Iwan Herzl, who performs quite successfully in expressionist roles at the local theater. Professor Cornelius detects with some surprise and consternation that the rouge on his cheeks is undoubtedly of cosmetic origin. Then Max Hergesell arrives; he is an engineering student, jovial yet polite, slightly eccentric but full of reasonable plans for the future. Mann's introductory portrait of another guest, young Herr Möller, shows how subtly and skillfully he makes his point about the new cultural amalgamations. Möller is a typical *Wandervogel,* a member of the German Youth Movement, "who obviously neither owns nor cares to own the correct bourgeois evening attire (in fact, there is no such thing any more), nor to ape the manners of a 'young gentleman' (and, in fact, there is no such thing any more either). He has a wilderness of hair, horn spectacles, and a long neck, and wears short pants and a belted blouse. His regular occupation, the Professor learns, is banking, but he is also an amateur folk-lorist and collects folk-songs from all localities and in all languages" (154; translation slightly altered). As a bank employee who dresses after hours as a sort of rebel-folksinger, Möller in many respects has more in common with a young professional of today who slips into his tie-dyed T-shirt on the weekend than with a Wilhelmine bank teller, who would never dare to be seen without his stand-up collar. In other words, the story stresses the shift from the rigorous traditional bourgeois society, with its set of strict social codes, to a modern society of lifestyles that are individually chosen and do not necessarily coincide with one's social background.

Mann does not forget to intersperse the *Gesellschaft,* the evening party, with a genuine inflation character: "There is a tall, pale, spindling youth, the son of a dentist, who lives by speculation. From all the Professor hears, he is a perfect Aladdin. He keeps a car, treats his friends to champagne suppers and showers presents upon them on every occasion, costly little trifles in mother-of-pearl and gold" (162). These are strange times: for the young speculator, throwing such a party would mean a minor expense; for Professor Cornelius and especially his wife, who often appears worn out by the "fantastic difficulties of the housekeeping" (142), providing some Italian salads, sandwiches, and drinks represents a major economic undertaking. The party is a great success, and soon dancing starts: "The young people appear to be absorbed in their dancing— if the performance they are carrying out with so much still concentration can be called dancing. They stride across the carpet, slowly, according to some unfathomable prescript, strangely embraced; in the newest attitude, tummy advanced and shoulders high, waggling the hips. . . . Two girls may dance together or two young men—it is all the same. They move to the exotic strains of the gramophone, played with the loudest needles to procure the maximum of sound: shimmies, foxtrots, one-steps, double foxes, African shimmies, Java dances, and Creole polkas, the wild musky melodies follow one another" (162). *Disorder and Early Sorrow* highlights the fact that the inflation and the emergence of a popular Americanized mass culture were experienced as two closely intertwined events. Amid the subtle irony that accompanies the description, the observer concedes that as a result of the "disorder," new expressions of freedom are possible. Even established gender codes begin to break down: young women dance together, young men dance together, and the unfamiliar jazz movements indicate a different body language. The narrator quietly applauds this newly found freedom from the stifling conventions of the Wilhelmine era, yet Professor Cornelius remains much more reserved toward these changing times.

While the term *disorder* in the title points to the rapid cultural changes that become apparent in the portrayal of the party, *early sorrow* addresses the story's second narrative strand and relates to five-year-old

Ellie, Abel Cornelius's sunshine. There is a "deep tenderness" between father and daughter, a love that, "like all deep feeling," conceals a "melancholy strain" on the father's side (144). Besides its realist, descriptive level, *Disorder and Early Sorrow* contains a second narrative mode that, as we will see, evolves to a somber and complex reflection on the relationship between time, history, and the unfolding of inflations.

The course of events seems to start quite innocently. During the party, little Ellie is invited to the dance floor by Max Hergesell, the dashing young engineering student. After a short dance, Ellie is completely taken by Max and seems to have lost all interest in her father, who observes the scene from the sideline. The story culminates when Ellie is crying heartrendingly in her bed that night because she wants Max to become her brother. Nothing can ease her pain, her "early sorrow," and Professor Cornelius's "fatherly heart is quite torn by it, and by a distressful horror of this passion, so hopeless and so absurd" (167). It is, in the end, servant Xaver who comes up with the saving idea. He drags Max Hergesell from the dance floor and brings him upstairs to little Ellie's bedroom. Max understands the situation immediately. With all his charms he approaches her bed. "Ellie sits struck mute. She smiles blissfully through her tears. A funny, high little note that is half a sigh of relief comes from her lips, then she looks dumbly up at her swan knight with her golden-brown eyes" (168). What father Cornelius has failed to accomplish even with his greatest promises, Hergesell is able to do with a few words. "And you'll lie down and go to sleep like a good girl, now I've come to say good-night? And not cry anymore, little Lorelei?" (169). Ellie blissfully lies down, ready to go to sleep. Professor Cornelius brings Max Hergesell back to the party downstairs, feeling toward the young student "a most singular mixture of thankfulness, embarrassment, and hatred" (ibid.). On the surface, it may seem that this short scene has little significance, except for its portrayal of the sudden powerlessness of a loving patriarch. Yet Ellie's infatuation with Max Hergesell destroys, as we will see, one of Professor Cornelius's most cherished illusions.

During the evening, curiosity prompts Professor Cornelius to shuttle back and forth between the party and his "peaceful kingdom" (156), his quiet study on the second floor where he prepares tomorrow's lecture. "First he reads Macaulay on the origin of the English public debt at the end of the seventeenth century; then an article in a French periodical on the rapid increase in the Spanish debt towards the end of the sixteenth" (151). In his seminar he plans to compare "the astonishing prosperity which accompanied the phenomenon in England with its fatal effects a hundred years earlier in Spain, and to analyze the ethical and psychological grounds of the difference in results" (ibid.). The issue of currency depreciation resulting from public debt and its concurrent social and cultural changes are thus historized.[5] Cornelius deals with the disorderly present by transforming its essential dynamics into a distant past. He is aware that his passion for history emerges from a deep psychological disposition: "He knows that history professors do not love history because it is something that comes to pass, but only because it is something that *has* come to pass; that they hate a revolution like the present one because they feel it is lawless, incoherent, irrelevant—in a word, unhistoric; that their hearts belong to the coherent, disciplined, historic past. For the temper of timelessness, the temper of eternity . . . —that temper broods over the past; and it is a temper much better suited to the nervous system of a history professor than are the excesses of the present" (146). This reflection on time as a prerequisite for experience appears at different points in the text. In a wonderful vignette, we read that Cornelius repeatedly tells Xaver Kleinsgütl to leave the professor's calendar alone when cleaning the office, because of Xaver's tendency "to tear off two leaves at a time and thus to add to the general confusion. But young Xaver appears to find joy in this activity, and will not be deprived of it" (161). The distortions and even breakdown of a common time horizon that characterize the inflation could not find a more fitting symbolic representation.

More important, Cornelius also links his boundless love and "melancholic tenderness" for little Ellie to his deep longing for a stable time horizon: "It is this conservative instinct of his, his sense of the eternal, that has found in his love for his little daughter a way to save itself from the wounding inflicted by the times. For father love, and a little child on its mother's breast—are not these timeless, and thus very, very holy and beautiful?"[6] Yet Cornelius himself realizes how much his boundless love for Ellie originates in his defensiveness against a disorderly present. He imagines their love as being positioned outside the *geschehende Geschichte,* outside the unfolding history, and thus eternal, timeless, and mythical. Max Hergesell, who embodies this present with his dancing, his slang language full of neologisms and references to popular culture, will destroy once and for all this illusion. At the moment Ellie enters the dance floor and takes the shimmying steps with Max, she becomes a social being, a *gesellschaftliche Person,* and has forever left behind the mythical, timeless bond with her father. It is not accidental that Max's last name is Hergesell connoting both "fellow," *Gesell,* and "society," *Gesellschaft.*

Thus, the wounds that the "lawless and incoherent" times inflict upon Professor Cornelius are not just economic ones. The overwhelming presentness of time, its unpredictable flow and liveliness during the inflation, insults his sense of order and meaning. Yet he also realizes that history, with its demand for structure and coherence, ossifies human experience; even the most chaotic revolution will one day present itself in the history books as another piece in a great coherent narrative. Cornelius finds this ultimately reassuring. As often occurs in Thomas Mann's prose, a philosophical subtext underlies the professor's position, in this case Friedrich Nietzsche's vehement criticism against historicism. For Nietzsche, this gagging of the immediate present by the forces of historization represented a most visible sign of the fatigue of nineteenth-century bourgeois culture, of its false sense of security, of its hostility toward life.[7]

The story ends with Cornelius's hope that a night of good sleep will erase all traces of Hergesell in Ellie's memory. We know better: Ellie is as much a child of her times as she is an object of Cornelius's desperate longing for a "holy" and "eternal" order. This "eternal" order is also part of a romantic idea of patriarchy; it points to the larger cultural subtext contained in the influential dichotomy between a modern "society" *(Gesellschaft)* and the timeless bonds that constitute a "community" *(Gemeinschaft).*[8] The dynamics of the inflation may forcefully rip apart such bonds, and indeed create in the end a heterogeneous, more egalitarian society, yet they also intensify a seductive nostalgia for the seemingly timeless bonds of a "community."

In his 1926 commentary on *Disorder and Early Sorrow,* Thomas Mann stressed that his story was written in hindsight, two years after the inflation. The ironic and humorous tone of the novella creates a conciliatory atmosphere in which Mann distances himself from his earlier conservative positions that are inscribed in his protagonist. At the same time he cautiously welcomes the arrival of a more heterogeneous, pragmatic German society. In that sense, his novella participates in the cultural movement of Neue Sachlichkeit (New Sobriety, New Functionalism) that characterizes the middle years of the Weimar Republic. Mann's ironic position in his short story has much in common with New Sobriety: an aversion to ideology and radicalism, a tendency toward pragmatic, technocratic solutions to social problems; it is an antiromantic gesture that is coupled with a reserved and shielded form of individualism. While the inflation challenges Professor Cornelius and his generation, it is not represented as a traumatic event. On the contrary, despite the description of its unsettling aspects, the novella depicts a side of the inflation that authors such as Elias Canetti and Stefan Zweig have also noted: its disorder created new spaces of freedom. It resulted in a more egalitarian society that brought people together who were once separated by a strict cultural code.

But we should not forget that Thomas Mann wrote this story after the currency reform and from his position as an economically well-established author. His *Magic Mountain* had been a great success. By 1925, he had fully recovered from the economic perils of the inflation. For most intellectuals, however, the inflation did not evoke such conciliatory memories. Their economic and social misery had been profound, and their recovery after the inflation took much longer and resulted in a rather modest standard of living. Thus, it is important to place *Disorder and Early Sorrow* within the larger economic and social context of intellectual life during the inflation.

III.

During the early 1920s, many overlapping terms such as "intellectuals," "intellectual workers," *Bildungsbürger,* and *freie Berufe* (professionals) were used to identify those who were seen as the bearers of Germany's cultural and intellectual life.[9] This broad range of terms is not surprising; it mirrors the differing positions of intellectuals within German culture and is linked to the relationship between a cultural center and positions of marginality, between high culture and popular culture, and the role of state institutions such as schools and universities in the creation and dissemination of cultural practices. The concept of *Bildungsbürger* is strongly linked to a traditional, nineteenth-century bourgeois culture and relates to those groups who achieved their middle-class status primarily through *Bildung,* through education: lawyers, doctors, teachers, professors, and to some degree the technical elite, such as engineers. The notion of *Bildungsbürger* is often used to differentiate this group from another pillar of the German bourgeoisie, the *Wirtschaftsbürger,* who gained their status primarily through success in business-related activities. The term *intellectual* points less to an economic situation than to a specific position within a cultural and political context. It stresses autonomy, individuality, nonconformity, and above all the social and political responsibility of writers and artists. The notion of the intellectual originated in France in connection with the Dreyfus affair as a summary designation for all of those who publicly fought for a revision of the Dreyfus trial (Stark 15–16).

In his brief essay "Intellektuellendämmerung" ("Intellectuals' Twilight," 1920), the critic Michael Charol stresses a distinction among intellectuals that became of great economic importance during the inflation: "Economically, intellectual workers [geistige Arbeiter] can be divided into two groups: those with salaried positions [Festbesoldete] and those with free-lancing positions [Freie]" (6). The first group consists of scholars, professors, teachers, and artists who had salaried positions with the state and of those who received a regular monthly income from private businesses, such as journalists, theater directors, and editors at publishing houses. While the economic situation of this group grew increasingly difficult, those who made a living as freelance authors, artists, or actors were often hit even harder during the inflation. All freelancers and many professionals, such as lawyers and doctors, suffered especially because payment for their goods or services was often delayed considerably, which resulted in an even further devaluation of their income (Wittmann 316). The distress of many independent authors was highlighted by a spectacular trial in February of 1921, when the well-known expressionist writer Georg Kaiser was sentenced to one year in prison for burglary. Kaiser defended himself during his trial by claiming that sheer physical survival had necessitated his act.[10] Yet it is very difficult to make generalizations about the experiences of the various members of this group, because, on the one hand, their position as freelancers allowed them to react more flexibly to the inflation, but on the other hand, their economic vulnerability often put them at great risk of ending up in total misery.[11] It is somewhat easier to draw a clearer picture of those intellectuals who received their main income through a salaried position. To be more specific, I would like to look here at a subgroup within that cluster.

If Professor Cornelius had been a real faculty member at the University of Munich in the early 1920s, what would his actual living and working conditions have been like? In 1923, Dr. Georg Schreiber, a professor and a delegate of the Zentrum Party in the Reichstag, published the detailed survey Die Not der deutschen Wissenschaft und der geistigen Arbeiter (The Distress of German Science and Intellectual Workers) to steer public attention to the alarming "decline of our intellectual culture" (5). Schreiber focuses especially on the situation of German universities and research laboratories. He provides ample evidence of how seriously the work of researchers and scholars in both the sciences and the humanities was threatened by rising prices, which could no longer be covered by the budgets of their academic institutions. For example, the price for a microscope that had cost 1,000 marks before the war had risen to 400,000 marks in December of 1922. The price for a liter of pure alcohol had risen over the same period from 50 pfennig to 1,500 marks, making it difficult to undertake even basic experiments (18–19). Budget amendments usually came too late to account for the rising costs of maintaining a laboratory. The paralyzing difficulties scientists had to face during the height of the inflation came in often unexpected forms. Schreiber quotes Professor August Wassermann, director of the Friedrich-Wilhelm Institute for Experimental Therapy in Berlin-Dahlem, who reported that his laboratories had to cancel most of their experiments because the institute was unable to secure a supply of lab animals. The situation became so worrisome that Wassermann approached the German government with the unusual request to issue an export ban on lab animals such as rabbits, mice, and guinea pigs (21–22).

The conditions in the social sciences and humanities were equally dire. The library of the Department of Canonical Law at the University of Munich had a budget of 2,000 marks in 1922. Yet the subscription price for a single scholarly journal was already 10,000 marks (22). The purchase of foreign journals had become nearly impossible for any German library. "Before the war," writes Schreiber, "the library of the University of Hamburg subscribed to about five hundred foreign journals, in 1923 it carried only five" (29). But even the purchase of German books and journals was hampered, primarily as a result of the exorbitant cost of paper. Schreiber also notes a consequence of the inflation that is easily forgotten nowadays. Not only were German scholars and researchers increasingly cut off from access to foreign journals, the almost worthless mark made traveling abroad prohibitively expensive. The inability to travel outside Germany in order to attend conferences or conduct research in foreign archives contributed to a strong sense of isolation and to the fear of quickly falling below the international standards of research. In 1920, leading German scientists and scholars founded the Notgemeinschaft der deutschen Wissenschaft (Emergency Society for German Science and Scholarship), with the hope that sponsorship from German industry and business would help to alleviate the situation. Unfortunately, these efforts had only limited success (Feldman, *Disorder*, 542–44).

At the same time, German universities experienced a flood of new students when tens of thousands of demobilized soldiers enrolled after the

war. During the summer semester of 1918, 80,000 students were studying at German universities; by 1923 this number had increased to 112,000
(Ringer, *Decline*, 65). Many of them worked while studying to ensure a
most rudimentary standard of living. Their prospects for a future career
in academia or education looked dim. There were far too few positions
available for university graduates. "For the first time, a kind of academic
proletariat grew up in Germany" (ibid.).

The hardest blow for professors and researchers during the inflation
was the rapid devaluation of their income. In Wilhelmine and Weimar
Germany, a professor's total compensation consisted of two parts: his
basic salary as a higher civil servant *(höherer Beamter)* and a fee students
had to pay for attending lectures, seminars, or to take exams. In addition,
some added income resulted from scholarly publications or consulta-
tions. As many of the students were already impoverished, fees were held
at a relatively constant level after the war. In addition, the salaries of
higher civil servants increased only slowly during the inflation. The effect was more than the fact that a professor's income in 1922 had shriv-
eled to one-third of his real prewar income (Weber 42): what often proved
to be the greatest humiliation was the decline of the salary in comparison to those of other social groups. In 1913, the salary of a higher civil
servant was 7 times that of an unskilled worker. In 1922, a professor
earned only 1.8 times more than an unskilled worker.[12]

For some left-wing intellectuals, the economic destruction of the intellectual classes was the logical consequence of the crisis of capitalism.
The economist Emil Lederer argues, "We cannot solve the crisis of intellectual work without at the same time opening up the question of how
social labor is at all possible at higher levels. We have to deal with the
crisis of capitalism if we want to do away with the crisis of intellectual
labor" (quoted in Feldman, *Disorder*, 551). Lederer envisioned a socialist society in which the role of intellectual work would be reposi-
tioned and "manual and intellectual labor [would] be treated as con-
stituent parts of an entire socio-economic system rather than as totally
separable and possibly antagonistic elements" (ibid.).

Yet for the majority of intellectuals, especially members of German
academia, the frightening compression of income differences between
salaried intellectuals and workers was not greeted as a call for solidarity with the working masses against capital, but rather as an "immoral
perversion of conditions," as a contributor wrote in *Die Weltbühne* of
June 21, 1923. Under the pseudonym "Meridionalis," he complained
that a school director was now earning less than a janitor, and that en-

gineers and architects made less money than locksmiths and bricklayers. He concluded that the inflation had brought about "a reversal of means and end. For the mental labor of the master builder is the precondition for the bricklayer's manual labor and not the other way around. He who draws the plan, creates a new mental value *[Geistwert]*; he who builds a wall with bricks and cement, creates a new material value *[Sachwert]*. And this is the key point: the creation of material values today is without exception more highly valued than the creation of mental values— and this exclusivity is the difference from past times. The currency devaluation, the 'flight into material values' . . . did not cause this perversion of values, but certainly enlarged and poisoned it" (711). This assessment points to a fundamental shift that goes beyond the quantifiable comparison of different incomes. It declares an end to a culture in which mental and intellectual work enjoyed a privileged niche, a sanctuary. The author believes that the primacy of economic production has become total and has pushed mental and intellectual work into a subservient position catering solely to limited economic goals. Interestingly, he argues that the reversal of the position of means and ends *(Umkehrung von Mittel und Zweck)* brought about by the inflation leads to a situation of immoral perversion in society.[13] Only intellectual workers can draw up the great social and cultural master plans that contain a primacy of ends over means. Economic activity, which for the author is primarily industrial and manual production, should be only a means and never in and of itself an end that forces intellectual workers into compliance.

This short essay in *Die Weltbühne* is symptomatic of a basic discussion that emerged from the concrete economic circumstances of intellectuals during the early 1920s. The inflation fundamentally rearranged social relationships, and almost all participants in the discussion realized that even after a currency reform, things would never be the same. It was thus all the more urgent for intellectuals to reflect on their role in this newly emerging society.

IV.

On September 21, 1922, the sociologist Alfred Weber (1868–1958) gave the keynote address at the yearly general convention of the Verein für Sozialpolitik in Eisenach. Founded in 1872 and celebrating its fiftieth anniversary at this convention, the Verein für Sozialpolitik was the most important and respected scholarly association for social scientists in Wilhelmine and Weimar Germany. Alfred Weber, the brother of Max

Weber, had long been an active member in the Verein and was well known not only as a cultural sociologist but also as a political figure, being one of the founders of the left-liberal Deutsche Demokratische Partei. His convention address, *Die Not der Geistigen Arbeiter (The Distress of Intellectual Workers),* was the most widely discussed document on inflation's impact on German intellectuals at the time.

Alfred Weber's keynote address has a programmatic character and is in many respects an important contribution to the sociology of intellectual culture. Reading this text of 1922, I am struck by the many instances in which it echoes the cultural sociology of Pierre Bourdieu. Thus, interpreting *Die Not der Geistigen Arbeiter* through a dialogue with Bourdieu's work will link this text to modern cultural studies and at the same time elucidate the historical specificity of Weber's reflection on the status of intellectuals.

Just like Alfred Weber in *Die Not der Geistigen Arbeiter,* Bourdieu is concerned with the social and economic parameters that shape cultural production. Besides his pathbreaking study of French culture, *Distinction: A Social Critique of the Judgement of Taste* (*La Distinction: Critique sociale du jugement,* 1979), Pierre Bourdieu has published widely on such topics as the French art-market in the nineteenth century, the relationship between high culture and popular culture, and the role of intellectuals.[14] In *Distinction,* Bourdieu investigates the ways in which high culture helps to reproduce power relations, "why art and cultural consumption are predisposed, consciously and deliberately or not, to fulfill a social function of legitimating social differences" (*Distinction* 7). Bourdieu's most influential analytic term is probably "cultural capital," which he defines as "a form of knowledge, an internalized code or a cognitive acquisition for or a competence in deciphering cultural relations and cultural artifacts" (Johnson 7). Such cultural capital is "accumulated through a long process of acquisition or inculcation which includes the pedagogical action of the family or group members (family education), educated members of the social formation (diffuse education) and social institutions (institutionalized education)" (ibid.). Like economic capital, cultural capital is not equally distributed throughout society, yet equally important is the fact that the "possession of economic capital does not necessarily imply possession of cultural or symbolic capital, and vice versa."[15]

Important to my analysis of Alfred Weber's speech is the specific relationship between cultural production and its surrounding society that Bourdieu developed in his article "The Field of Cultural Production: The

Economic World Reversed" (1983). While in this article he refers mainly to artistic production (paintings, poetry, novels), the same principles hold largely true for the works of scholars and scientists. For Bourdieu, the field of cultural production in general is structured by the opposition between two subfields. The first one is the field of "restricted production" and is largely synonymous with "high culture." Bourdieu characterizes this field as "production for producers": poets who write largely for an audience that consists mostly of connoisseurs and other poets, scholars who usually address their specialized works to a small audience of other scholars. The goal is not economic profit but rather different forms of "symbolic profit," such as prestige and artistic or scholarly celebrity, that result paradoxically from "the profit one has on seeing oneself (or being seen) as one who is not searching for profit" (Johnson 15). A whole network of cultural institutions such as museums, libraries, and the educational system sustain the existence of this field. The other subfield is defined by "large-scale production." It contains popular culture, the worlds of television, of large-scale cinematic productions, of lifestyle magazines, of the best-seller book market. Here, economic capital and monetary profits play a dominant role and products are geared toward a wide audience; and while formal experimentation is rare, this field does sometimes borrow from avant-garde concepts developed in the field of restricted cultural production (16).

Bourdieu regards these subfields as the result of two principles of hierarchization that struggle with each other: "the heteronomous principle, favorable to those who dominate the field economically and politically (e.g. 'bourgeois art') and the autonomous principle (e.g. 'art for art's sake'), which those of its advocates who are at least endowed with specific capital tend to identify with [a] degree of independence from the economy, seeing temporal failure as a sign of election and success as a sign of compromise" (*Field* 40). However, the heteronomous and the autonomous principles are both ideal types. At one extreme, a cultural product that would be completely subordinated to external economic forces would eventually become unrecognizable as a cultural product. At the other extreme, a radically autonomous work or art that disregards any institutional setting or a response by an audience would run the risk of being denied any reception at all and would soon be forgotten. In reality, each cultural product contains a unique mixture of both principles. Bourdieu points out that the field of "restricted cultural production" is marked by the constant effort of its members to exclude those whose work is considered to be compromised by economic profits.

Yet as much autonomy and critical distance as the producers of "restricted cultural productions" may claim from the dominant economically and politically powerful class in a given system, and as much opposition as intellectuals and artists may voice—and despite their actual low degree of economic capital—Bourdieu nevertheless considers them members of the dominant class because of their possession of symbolic capital. Thus, he refers to intellectuals and artists as a "dominated fraction of the dominant class" (Johnson 15).

It is remarkable how Alfred Weber's speech of 1922 unintentionally employs Bourdieu's theoretical parameter. *The Distress of Intellectual Workers* is a spirited defense of "restricted cultural production" and, at the same time, a tacit avowal that new social conditions have radically called into question the possibility of intellectual independence. At the beginning of his address, Weber tries to define intellectual work. Is all work that requires intellectual means therefore intellectual work? Are white-collar workers such as insurance agents, salespeople, and lower-level civil servants intellectual workers? Obviously not, and he legitimizes the special status of real intellectual workers by invoking the same principles of cultural capital that Bourdieu describes. Intellectual work for Weber is not entangled in any kind of functional relationship leading to an economic goal. "The intellectual and artistic endeavor is . . . first and foremost a mental unloading *[seelische Entladung]* of productive intellects whose thinking is naturally anchored in the general public *[im Allgemeinen]*" (7). And foreshadowing Bourdieu's principle of autonomy, Weber writes: "Such work, as much as it comes in contact with ruling social forces, may not be directed towards money. . . . Economic matters may only provide a provisional footstool on which such work can rest in a moment of exhaustion. Intellectual work is distorted and devalued, when it is being done for monetary gain *[ein Geldberuf wird]*. The artist or the scholar who strives for money becomes a scoundrel; and even the writer, the journalist, the physician, and the lawyer— all those for whom money plays an important role are, in my opinion, jeopardized. . . . The value of intellectual work for the society as a whole cannot be calculated, it is not quantifiable, not measurable." Most of art, literature, and basic science may appear to be not essential to life, but may appear instead to be something that one could demolish or let deteriorate without being disturbed in one's comfort (ibid.).

Weber establishes here a strong demarcation line defending pure cultural production against the intrusion of those heteronomous forces that would submit intellectual work to economic factors. He vehemently disavows that such intellectual work has any measurable economic value, thus defining it as part of what Bourdieu calls "restricted cultural production." Yet like Bourdieu, Weber also observes that there are "gradual differences," starting from the purest intellectual work of writers, artists, scholars, professors, and priests, progressing to the work of physicians and lawyers, and finally to those whose intellectual work is most directly "economically measurable," such as the work of engineers (8). Bourdieu stresses that despite the lack of economic capital, intellectual work creates a strong cohesion among the dominant class in a given society. Weber is equally aware of this mechanism. He identifies the dominant class as the main consumers of intellectual work and the main providers for the next generation of "intellectual workers." And finally, to point out another important similarity, Weber shares with Bourdieu the same understanding of the paradoxical position of critical high culture within capitalism.

In the course of two or three generations, economically successful bourgeois families had amassed so much capital that the next generation could to some degree live off this capital. A new group emerged that Alfred Weber calls *Rentenintellektuelle,* rentier intellectuals.[16] Weber considers this group to be a "last independent island outside strict class interests, an asylum for ideas and arguments that were not linked to the economic." And he continues, "The social-reformist and socialist critique of capitalism . . . during the second half of the nineteenth century would not have been possible without their existence; the proletariat would probably have been without leaders" (14). Karl Marx and Friedrich Engels as examples of such rentier intellectuals come to mind here. Like Bourdieu, Weber places the position of the critical intellectual not at the margins of capitalist society, but rather at its very core. A critical stance that assumes a position of disinterestedness and that claims to speak for a social totality is possible only because of the accumulation of capital that assures a certain independence.

Yet all of this describes a world that in June of 1922 had largely vanished. The inflation, Alfred Weber points out, had destroyed the capital savings of the rentier intellectuals, had led to the rapid decline of salaried incomes for intellectual workers, and had caused the decline of universities, museums, libraries, and theaters. Weber warns his audience not to naively believe that things would return to the old situation after the inflation: "These changes have been too deep, and they have affected the fundamental relationship between the intellectual sphere and the rest of life, especially the economic sphere" (26). Weber's main fear very much coincides with Heinrich Mann's pessimistic view of the future that I discussed in the previous chapter. Both foresee that as a result of the inflation, with its trend toward industrial concentration, Germany would enter an era of a "limitless reign of the economic" (27), in which all intellectual life would be swallowed up by business interests. Cultural life would simply become an "appendage" of the economic sphere (23).

Nevertheless, Weber's thoughts on how to rescue intellectual life imply an embrace of the economic realities. He predicts that a new type of intellectual will replace the rentier intellectual. The *Arbeitsintellektuelle* (worker intellectual) will combine his intellectual education with a practical training that will allow him to earn a steady income. He will be part of the newly emerging class of educated white-collar workers who will take over the role of the disappearing *Bildungsbürgertum* and become his main audience. Weber also advises intellectuals to organize themselves in unions, even though he realizes that the very nature of their product would make it difficult to fight for such goals as common wage structures. In his speech, Weber indicates that he himself doubts whether he has the strength to become such an *Arbeitsintellektueller,* combining practical work and intellectual pursuits. The discussion that followed his address raised serious questions about the feasibility of his concept.

Weber's desperate attempt to give some practical advice to his audience indicates how helpless he and many other intellectuals were in the face of the unfolding inflation. As an economic force it destroyed their material livelihood, yet there is an additional, a partially hidden level to this traumatic experience that must be analyzed: inflation called the very existence and worth of restricted cultural production into question.

First of all, the currency devaluation exposed, attacked, and devalued a core principle of restricted cultural production. As Alfred Weber puts it, "The value of intellectual work . . . cannot be calculated, is not quantifiable, and cannot be measured" (7). This definition declares intellectual work to be incommensurable with the basic functions of money: it appears to be the complete opposite of money. It implies that intellectual work possesses an immunity against the forces of monetary circulation. In short, intellectual work is "invaluable." On the one hand, this "invaluable" quality of intellectual work, according to the paradoxical principle of an "economic world reversed," predestines it as a source of cultural capital. On the other hand, with the destruction of a class that once needed this cultural capital for its cohesion and identity, the term *invaluable* unveils its other, ugly meaning: because it cannot be measured in monetary terms, it is suddenly not worth anything. Figure 21

Figure 21. "Starving Germany: 'Well, you give me your old painting, and I'll give you my old lard.'" Illustration by Eduard Thöny, in *Simplicissimus* 24 (November 12, 1919).

plays on this difference of meaning. The scene takes place against the distant backdrop of the Brandenburg Gate in Berlin. A shabbily dressed German, probably a member of the *Bildungsbürgertum*, holds a truly invaluable piece of art under his arm: Rembrandt's *Man with the Helmet*. He is approached by a stereotypical American who brings with him a barrel labeled "American bacon." [17] The drawing depicts a typical scenario in postwar Germany: economic misery forces the middle class to sell their possessions for food. The cartoon's shock effect lies in the suggestion that anybody in his right mind would ever trade a Rembrandt painting for food. It is heightened by the crudeness of the barter situation. By claiming that the main quality of the painting is its oldness, the American legitimizes his offer of trading an old painting for old lard. It is interesting how the illustration plays here with the principle of a "reversed economy" inherent in the field of high culture. As a work of art, the painting is so valuable in part because of its age. The age of *The Man with the Helmet* proves that it harbors an immaterial, timeless, almost spiritual value that has survived throughout the last centuries. Within the sphere of economic production, age indicates just the opposite: the older an object, the less value it has—old lard being a quite drastic example. Obviously, the illustration allows for a further interpretation: the viewer may decide that the American knows all too well that the age of a painting cannot be compared to the age of lard, that he is just pretending to be an "uncultured American" in order to strike a great deal.

The scene exposes a brutal invasion and annexation: it depicts the dominance of economic capital with the goal of profit over the sphere of art. In that sense, the Rembrandt painting stands for all other products of "restricted cultural production": the work of avant-garde artists, and of writers and scholars. In a culture of inflation in which everything is drawn into the circulation of money and consequently becomes calculable and exchangeable, even an invaluable painting turns into just another object to be bought, sold, or bartered. Repudiating its artistic, its "intellectual" value, the worth of the painting is determined by the crudest form of materialism: it is old, therefore, it is not worth more than old lard.

Inflation called a second important aspect of intellectual work into question. Weber repeatedly stresses in his speech that such work is oriented toward the general public. Intellectuals have the freedom and responsibility to critically think in generalizing terms. They assume a position of disinterestedness; their work, according to Weber, is not connected to particular interests or groups in society.[18] Weber's notion of intellectual work was broadly shared and explains why the state, with its many different cultural institutions, played such an overwhelming role in the production of German cultural goods. The idea that the interest of the society as a whole coincided with the interests of the state originated in Hegelian philosophy and was put into practice most visibly in Prussia. Intellectual work carried out by state-salaried scholars within the walls of state institutions thus promised to guarantee a position free of any particularism. The intrusion of private, monetary forces into this sphere was seen as an invasion of particular interests. Weber, for example, rejects in his speech the idea that large-scale private sponsoring of the arts and sciences could take over the role of the impoverished state (24).

In that sense, the inflationary dynamic that fragmented German society and drastically weakened an already unstable state can be seen as a most radical form of particularism and an aggressive attack on the concept of the general public. Consequently, Weber warns his audience that the disappearance of autonomous intellectual work could in the end also result in the disappearance of the state itself: "One has to tell the state that its own existence is at stake when it somewhat tepidly observes the battle of the primacy of the intellectual over the economic. In reality, the battle is about its own existence. Once the intellectual background of the general public has broken apart the state will perish as well and become the booty of competing economic forces" (40).

While Alfred Weber's speech is an in-depth analysis of the fate of "restricted cultural production," he remains silent about the sphere of "large-scale cultural production," although the period of inflation was accompanied by an unprecedented rise of a new mass culture, with its dance revues, sport events, and, above all, new medium of film. Could it be that this emerging mass culture that exemplifies Bourdieu's "heteronomous principle" of economic profit was conceived by Weber and his audience as part of the problem, as simply an extension of the economic forces, even as "cultural inflation"?

V.

Bourdieu's quite complex analysis of cultural production starts from a simple insight: the creation and existence of a cultural good is fundamentally shaped by the triangle of production, circulation, and consumption. The three parts of this triangle relate to each other in varying and historically unique ways. Bourdieu is careful not to introduce any kind of economic determinism into his investigations; literature, art, and intellectual life do not "reflect" the economic situation of a certain group or society, but rather constitute a field that "is relatively autonomous from the demands of politics and economics" (12).

Using Bourdieu's differentiation between "large-scale cultural production" and "restricted cultural production," we can conclude that both fields represent quite different models of a "cultural economy." In general, high culture tends to idolize the producer and his product, especially within the tradition of the romantic artist-genius, while downplaying the distributive and consumptive side that involves the censoring or supportive force of publishers and gallery owners, audience reception, the role of critics, and so on. Popular culture, on the other hand, tends to be more concerned with the distributive and consumptive sides of cultural products.

It is significant that in the critical discourse of the 1920s two very different concepts of consumption were applied to high culture and mass culture. The enjoyment of high culture was believed to leave the consumer with an asset of lasting value. The two operative terms here are *Sammlung* (collecting, saving) and *Bildung* (formation, education, accumulation, growth). The very concept of high culture was organized around these principles; it was regarded as a savings account of (national) culture that would accrue a steady amount of interest over time. Popular culture, on the other hand, was believed to be consumed without any "savings" accumulating. Here, the operative terms are *Zerstreuung* (entertainment, dissemination, distraction) and what I may call, for lack of a better term, *Vergessen* (forgetting, escape from reality).[19] Within these two cultural economies, money had a very different status and function. Mass culture fully integrated money through its reliance on wide circulation and consumption. High culture, as we have seen, tended to suppress or even deny its ultimate reliance on money.

It becomes apparent that as a cultural economy the field of "large-scale production" was much better suited to survive the cultural onslaught of an inflation. Its consumption was instantaneous, and it could adapt itself well to the present-oriented atmosphere during the inflation. Because it did not rely on the investment of cultural capital, it was not related to an idea of formation and saving. Because it did not deny the centrality of money for its formation, mass culture provided, in a sense, the most suitable cultural economy for the period of inflation. One can push this point even further. From the perspective of high culture it can be easily argued that mass culture was so eminently suitable for the times of inflation because it presented in itself an "inflation of culture." It was closely intertwined with monetary circulation, it "devalued" cultural goods by orienting itself toward quantity rather than quality, its operative elements were the massification and circulation of cultural products. Its sense of time was "here and now," its relationship to cultural tradition eclectic. Like the young speculators on the stock exchange, mass culture's producers and heroes often came socially out of nowhere and reached almost instantaneous fame overnight or were forgotten within a few months. My point is that the heated debate about

Figure 22. "Gutenberg and the billion-[mark] printing press: 'I didn't intend this.'" Illustration by E. Schilling, in *Simplicissimus* 27 (November 15, 1922).

the power and the dangers of mass culture during the 1920s received some of its intensity from the strong analogies between inflation and popular culture. For a member of the traditional *Bildungsbürgertum,* the attempt to integrate popular culture as a legitimate part of the over-all spectrum of German cultural life was hampered by the simultaneous experience of inflation and the emergence of modern mass culture. Figure 22 presents a superb visual representation of this remarkable amalgamation between the dynamics of mass culture and inflation. This illustration from *Simplicissimus* encapsulates all three dynamics of inflation that apply to both the cultural and the economic nature of the currency devaluation. The ongoing massification is strikingly apparent as the printing machine is spewing out an uncontrolled stream of paper money. With its huge mouth and the two gauges that look like eyes, the printing press invokes the iconography of the Moloch machine that I described in the previous chapter. Closely related to the dynamic of massification is the aspect of devaluation captured in the way the paper money flows haphazardly out of the machine. The rapid circulation that characterizes inflation is encoded both in the greedy hands that grip the money and in the big transmission wheels of the printing press.

The overriding thematic tension in this picture is created by the contrast between the running money-printing press and Johannes Gutenberg, who stands next to the machine holding his head and moaning in a mixture of consternation and panic: "I didn't intend this." The illustration depicts the two different kinds of cultural economy. The figure of Gutenberg holds a single, valuable book in his hand—it may well be one of the priceless Gutenberg Bibles. This book symbolizes the field of "restricted cultural production" and the domain of high culture. What makes this illustration so insightful is the fact that the printing press contains two layers of meaning: it symbolizes both the inflation and the field of "large-scale cultural production," for we can easily imagine that the next printing job of this machine will be another artifact of mass circulation such as a *Groschenheft*, some pulp fiction or an entertainment magazine.

It is important to realize that the two different domains of cultural production are, nevertheless, linked by certain commonalties. These commonalties ensure that the Gutenberg figure is not just a perplexed bystander from a different century, but rather is thematically related to the unfolding mass production on the right side of the illustration. First of all, both domains share paper as a common material base. The big rolls of paper on the machine can be used to print books, paper money, or a mass-circulating magazine. Second, they share a common production technology, the printing press. Third, the illustration depicts Gutenberg as an inventor with doubts and self-accusations, and the picture poses the question: to what extent can he and his technology be held responsible for the inflationary printing of money?

The question is framed within an interesting historical constellation by placing a fifteenth-century figure next to a modern printing press. This historical and cultural discontinuity urges the viewer to reflect on a common parameter that may bridge the apparent gap. What I see at the core of Gutenberg's seemingly shocked recognition concerns the fundamental character of reproduction and is closely related to Walter Benjamin's arguments about the effect of reproduction technologies in modern societies that he describes in his "Das Kunstwerk im Zeitalter seiner technischen Reproduzierbarkeit" ("The Work of Art in the Age of Mechanical Reproduction"). Printing has been certainly the most revolutionizing technology of reproduction in history and has been followed in modern times by photography and film.

Benjamin argues that the social and cultural effects of reproduction technology become especially apparent in art's loss of aura, in its loss of authenticity: "The authenticity of a thing is the essence of all that is transmissible from its beginning, ranging from its substantive duration to its testimony to the history which it has experienced." The reproduction of a work of art "detaches the reproduced object from the domain of tradition. By making many reproductions it substitutes a plurality of copies for a unique existence" (221). It is important to mention that "aura" is not just an attribute of a work of art. It denotes in general a "unique phenomenon of a distance, however close it may be. If, while resting on a summer afternoon, you follow with your eyes a mountain range on the horizon or a branch which casts its shadow over you, you experience the aura of those mountains, of that branch" (222–23). Modern mass societies, Benjamin concludes, are characterized by a decay of aura that is caused by the desire of modern masses "to bring things 'closer' spatially and humanly, which is just as ardent as their bent toward overcoming the uniqueness of every reality by accepting its reproduction" (223).

The book that Gutenberg holds in his hand still seems to radiate an "aura," especially if we interpret this book as the Bible. And yet the illustration forces us to partake in Gutenberg's belated and painful recognition: by inventing the technology of printing he has started a process of reproduction that invariably destroys the auratic qualities of the reproduced products, as the right side of the picture strikingly indicates. Benjamin registers this loss of aura, but he also has great hope for the formative power of reproduction technologies. For him, they create the potential for a new alignment between art and progressive social change, especially with the increasing importance of film in modern society.

In our context, however, a different scenario emerges. The illustration establishes a powerful link between reproduction and the creation of money that Benjamin does not mention in his essay. In many ways, we can understand the medium of money as the most anti-auratic force in modern society. Money, as Simmel observes, takes away the uniqueness of all objects; it functions as a powerful agent that indeed brings things closer but also rips them out of a context of tradition. It is equally important to realize that money in its very essence is always a reproduced entity. New money must be printed constantly within a functioning monetary system, yet this process of reproduction has to take place under strict control. Thus, money always embodies both the potential and the danger of reproduction. Walter Benjamin correctly states that modern societies communicate largely through symbolic and cultural forms that emerge from techniques of reproduction. What he fails to acknowledge is the hidden inflationary aspect that lurks within any process of reproduction: the fact that, as inflation shows, reproduction can become a limitless, an out-of-control process that utterly devalues the product.

We can conclude that the analogy between inflation and mass culture is by no means accidental, but rather is based on a number of subterranean links. Thomas Mann's novella *Disorder and Early Sorrow* provides insight into how the inflation affected the sphere of social interaction, how it caused certain breakdowns of class barriers that made sudden and unexpected moments of liberation and freedom possible. Culturally, these moments were often linked to and expressed by the symbolic field of an emerging mass culture. In particular, the young generation, which stood in front of the ruins of an old political and economic order, was attracted to this new and decisively American-influenced modern culture, as Thomas Mann describes with such acute observation in his story. Anton Kaes writes, "Especially Jazz music that was widely circulating through records, became in Germany during the inflation period the sign of a modern, ahistorical, respectless and nonliterary culture that, with its hectic rhythm and irregular syncopes, was seen at the height of its time" ("Ökonomische Dimension" 318). Records, films, and entertainment journals with large photo sections became the hallmarks of this decisively nonliterary culture, which was at the same time based on the newest reproduction technologies. This culture was linked to a "traditionless mass audience that was skeptical of cultural goods that were associated with education and instruction" (320). It was a culture that was accessible but without much cultural capital: pragmatic, sober, and distrustful of those who once maintained that culture and money could be held strictly separate.

CHAPTER EIGHT

Witches Dancing

Gender and Inflation

I.

It is inevitable that the grand narratives of modernity employ the dichotomy of gender as a powerful rhetorical strategy to mark basic structures of difference such as the private and the public, authenticity and alienation, nature and society, desire and rationality. Within an intellectual tradition that emerged with the process of industrialization during the nineteenth century and that spans from Hegel to Marx and Max Weber, modernity is perceived as a dynamic economic development of unlimited growth and, at the same time, as one that caused new forms of bureaucratization, alienation, and libidinal repression. Not surprisingly, as Rita Felski points out, this narrative of modernity often encoded industrial production, the public sphere, rationality, bourgeois individuality, and the idea of progress as male. The female sphere was mostly defined as a nurturing environment within the family. Femininity in general served as a symbolic space that remained essentially outside the dynamics of modernization and indicated the nonalienated, the genuine nonmodern, the ahistorical (18–19).

An essential feature in this discursive tradition was the overwhelming dominance of the sphere of production as the primary motor for economic development and progress. However, around the turn of the twentieth century a different yet not unrelated narrative of modernity emerged. The big cities became the harbors for the enticing dreamworld of modern mass consumerism.[1] The economic sphere of consumption moved into the center, and with it the figure of the female consumer. New department stores provided an urban public space for women; new advertising strategies catered to female buyers.[2] A feminized form of modernity appeared; its narratives stress the role of the unconscious, of desire, of a certain passivity, of the object as fetish. Georg Simmel was one of the first to center his view of modernity on distribution and consumption by reflecting on the increasing commodification of modern culture that emerged with the circulation of money and a specific modern urbanity. Charles Baudelaire and Walter Benjamin discovered that the dreamlike, often surreal aspects of this "feminized modernity" led to a reenchantment of modern urban experience.[3] At the same time, this feminization of modernity was often "synonymous with its demonization," as Felski notes. "Women are portrayed as buying machines, driven by impulses beyond their control to squander money on the accumulation of ever more possessions. The familiar and still prevalent cliché of the insatiable female shopper epitomizes the close associations between economic and erotic excess in dominant images of femininity" (62).

How does the phenomenon of inflation fit into these two different narratives of modernity? I have argued in previous chapters that inflation can be conceptualized as a violent rupture, a rift that opens up between the spheres of production and consumption. An inflationary economy often provides full employment while the sphere of consumption runs havoc. The fluctuation of money requires people's full attention; it relentlessly commodifies every aspect of life; it forces quick and instantaneous acts of buying. Thus, the crisis of inflation is conceptualized predominantly within a narrative of modernity that stresses the distributive and consumptive sphere. And it is here that we have to place the question of how gender and inflation intersect. If this "feminized modernity" is saturated with the iconography of the feminine, which has its sources in certain essentialist assumptions about women, how does this symbolism enter the representation of inflation?

II.

"Mothers begging for their starving children, and all these prostitutes on the streets!" In the memory of many Germans, in countless diaries and contemporary reports, the human misery that came with the hyperinflation is clearly gender coded.[4] While the topic of prostitution will be of central concern in a later part of this chapter, Figure 23 exemplifies

Figure 23. "Paper money? Paper money! Bread! Bread!" Artist
unidentified; illustration in *Simplicissimus* 28 (June 11, 1923).

how the abundance of paper money was linked to the lack of food that
resulted in widespread starvation and malnutrition among children. A
mother with a hungry child is probably one of the most prevailing symbolic representations of undeserved misery. Much of the inflationary dynamic directly affected the daily workings of the family household. In
many ways, it was women who were most immediately confronted with
the unpredictable price swings. The food shortages after the war came
to be represented by the frequent scenes of lines of women standing for
hours to receive some rationed portions of bread or meat.

If we look at Figure 24, for example, we will not detect a single man.
The photo allows for several interpretations. Obviously, it depicts a
specific form of women's hardship during the early 1920s. The scene
links a strong impression of powerlessness and dependency to the sight

Figure 24. Women standing in line in front of grocery stores. Photo by
Sennecke, Berlin, in Ostwald, *Sittengeschichte der Inflation*, 254.

of women. As a representational strategy, it permits men to literally
"stay out of the picture" and to distance themselves from social decline
and its related shame.[5] As a source of a sociohistorical analysis it forces
us to ask questions: Are these women all of the same class? How many
of them are interrupting their jobs? How many are standing in line for
a whole family? Thus, the photo cautions us not to operate in this sociohistorical context with a generalizing term such as *women*. Only a
detailed historical study could examine the very diverse experiences
women of different ages, marital status, and class background had during the early 1920s.[6] An analysis of inflation's economic and social impact on women still remains to be done; it certainly poses a challenge
that is beyond the scope of this book.

There are, however, several fundamental historical developments that
had a lasting impact on gender relationships in postwar Germany.
Women had played a significant role in the German war economy. Ute
Frevert reports, "By 1917, over 700,000 women worked in the engineering, metallurgical, iron, and steel, chemical and mining industries—

six times more than in 1913. The firm of Krupp, which had employed
only 2,000–3,000 women before the war, had 28,000 on the payroll on
1 January 1918" (156). Many women had to leave these jobs after 1918
to make room for the returning soldiers of a beaten, demoralized army
and tried to find new work in other areas of the economy. Almost 2 million German men between the ages of sixteen and sixty had been killed,
and about 4.2 million had been wounded and crippled, in World War 1
(Schrader 7). Consequently, in the postwar German population there
was a disproportionately high percentage of women who had been born
between 1875 and 1900.[7] Many of them had been widowed or had remained single, and were forced to struggle economically on their own.
At the same time, cripples—men maimed by warfare, men psychologically damaged by their traumatic experiences in the trenches—were an
all too common sight on the streets of German cities. It is hard to comprehend this misery nowadays; it is even harder to weigh the social and
emotional costs of a war that psychologically (and sometimes literally)
emasculated men and estranged them from women, that provoked all
sorts of male anxieties, yet that also opened up ambivalent spaces of
freedom and liberation for women. The history of women's struggle for
equality and emancipation would retain that profoundly ambivalent
character throughout the 1920s. The Weimar Republic had brought
women the right to vote; in the first Weimar National Assembly 9.6 percent of the delegates were women (Frevert 169). Yet certain fundamental
demands such as equal pay, access to higher education, and reproductive rights remained largely unfulfilled during Germany's first democracy and were finally rendered impossible with the rise of National Socialist power.

   A significant development that coincided with the unfolding of the
inflation was the emergence of the so-called New Woman that provoked
a whole set of new female images: the young, "liberated woman" wear-
ing short hair and casual clothing, smoking cigarettes, and pledging
never to get married.[8] The emergence of these images that belie the economically often precarious situation of these young women is strongly
linked to changes in the forms of female employment. The overall percentage of women employed full-time had actually not changed much
between the beginning of the century (34.9 percent in 1907) and the
mid-1920s (35.6 percent in 1925). What caused so much discussion
about the changing role of women in postwar Germany was the rapid
rise of female clerical workers, such as secretaries, typists, and sales-
women. The percentage of these predominantly young, female white-

collar workers among all working women rose from 6.5 percent in 1907 to 12.6 percent in 1925.[9] By 1925 almost 1.5 million women were employed as white-collar workers.

Hans Ostwald's ambivalent comments on women's changing roles in his *Sittengeschichte der Inflation* express a fairly typical view of the culturally conservative majority of Germans. In the introduction to his book he notes that during the inflation "the family seemed to be in rapid decline" and "an ecstasy of eroticism whirled the world around. . . . Especially women in many respects completely transformed themselves. They asserted their demands, particularly their sexual demands, much more clearly. In every conceivable way they intensified their claim to experience life more fully and intensively. . . . If during the war women were forced to take over many male jobs, they did not allow themselves afterward to be pushed quite all the way back into home and family. That had its effect on relations between the sexes as well. And, as the last stage of this development, there arose the female bachelor—the woman in charge of her own life, whether unmarried, divorced, or widowed" (7). Ostwald then reports that in hindsight these phenomena were just "temptations" and "temporary symptoms" that had largely disappeared after the inflation or were securely integrated into German society—a proof that the German people had not forgotten traditional values and gender roles after all. Yet he shares the widespread conception that at least temporarily the inflation severely damaged the moral fabric of German society as much as its economic base. While his descriptions address to a certain degree the actual social changes in the early 1920s, his observations are far more interesting within the context of inflation's conceptual representation. It is significant that he and many of his contemporaries cite, next to the increase in crime and corruption, women's changed behavior as evidence for the moral decay of society during the currency devaluation. The extent to which women begin to deviate from traditional gender norms becomes an indicator that measures the loosening of society's moral fabric.

Thus, the conceptual link between gender and inflation exists not only through the symbolic coding of misery as feminine but also through a second aspect of feminine representation, one that concerns women's role as alleged agents of the inflationary chaos. Asserting an immediacy of experience, driven by their sexual demands, women were believed to live out an "ecstasy of eroticism" during the inflation, as Figure 25 suggests. While the coding of economic misery as feminine receives its suggestive power from countless scenes of everyday life, the symbolic rep-

Figure 25. "Gallant drawing from the time of inflation."
Illustration by Kamm; reproduced from Hans Ostwald,
Sittengeschichte der Inflation, 143.

ertoire of a feminine, sexually charged force that causes an unpredictable social and moral chaos is rooted in a web of male fantasies and
anxieties. The iconography of feminine evil is certainly not unique to the
inflation. Rooted in a long tradition of mythological symbolism, it accompanied the conception of a "feminized modernity" all along and
gained artistic prominence especially during fin de siècle culture.[10] Many
symbolic representations of the inflation built on this tradition. I have
chosen three female figures that recur with particular urgency throughout the symbolic discourse of inflation: the witch, the woman as symbol
of decadent luxury, and the prostitute.

III.

The symbolic representation of inflation itself as a demonic female force has already come up at a prominent place in this book. In one of the most memorable scenes in Elias Canetti's *Auto-da-fé,* the housekeeper Therese Krumbholz gains access to the testament of the novel's protagonist, the sinologist Peter Kien. She forges Kien's handwriting and adds three zeros to his will, thereby changing his personal wealth from 12,650 crowns to the inflated sum of 1,265,000. The scene is part of a series of vicious private battles between the scholar and his housekeeper and later wife. In his creation of Therese Krumbholz as an allegorical figure who represents the destructive forces of inflation, Canetti resorts to frequent referencing of a specific misogynist discourse that flourished in turn-of-the-century Vienna. In many respects, both Kien and Krumbholz are caricatured figures illustrating Otto Weininger's central theses about the ontological difference between male and female. Weininger's influential book *Geschlecht und Character* (1903) is both a compendium of misogyny and a testimony of male anxieties about female sexuality. Weininger assumes that the actual male or female identity of individuals is the result of a unique mix between an "ideal" set of male and female character traits. Therese Krumbholz, however, seems to lack any balancing male character traits. As a Weiningerian *femme pure,* not only does she display an insatiable erotic desire and a compulsive lust for material objects, but the simplicity and naïveté of her worldview stand in stark contrast to the intellectual "genius" Peter Kien.

While Therese Krumbholz is part of the unique fictional world of Canetti's *Auto-da-fé,* one finds other feminine-coded images for the inflation. One frequently used image in accounts of the time is the figurative expression of the inflation as a *Hexentanz,* " a witch dance," or a *Hexensabbat,* a "witches' Sabbat." [11] This expression is visualized in Figure 26. Simply titled "Inflation," the illustration presents us with a dense allegory capturing different traumatic aspects of the unfolding economic and social catastrophe. In the center of Heine's caricature we see a corpse with a literally "inflated" belly—indicating not pregnancy but a painful symptom of prolonged hunger. The illustration plays with the grimly paradoxical nature of this symptom: the swollen belly is not the result of a grotesque act of overeating but indicates ultimate starvation. It parallels the paradoxical character of inflation itself: the more inflated money becomes, the more diminished is its actual value. Cir-

Figure 26. "Inflation." Illustration by Thomas Theodore Heine, in *Simplicissimus* 27 (November 8, 1922).

cling over the dying body is a group of vultures symbolizing the "vultures of inflation," the profiteers and speculators who feed on the overall misery of the population. The illustration captures a tense moment, because the viewer expects that in the next moment the corpse's belly may pop open like a pierced balloon. Thus, the upper half of the drawing clearly encodes the economic misery of the inflation in a quite overdetermined way. What makes this illustration disturbing—and interesting—are the naked women dancing around the corpse. The drawing obviously depicts a witches' Sabbat and symbolically addresses a third dimension of inflation besides misery and ruthless profiteering: a Dionysian, amoral celebration of sensuality and chaos.

The collective imagination about witches—their secret orgiastic dancing, their supposed devil worship, and their threatening sexual powers—constitutes one of the most fascinating intersections between cult and culture in the Western tradition, and caused terrible consequences for thousands of innocent women between the fourteenth and seventeenth centuries. A church-organized witch-hunt started all over Europe after publication of the legal codex *Malleaus malificarum,* or *Hexen-hammer,* in 1487. This church-legitimized codex allowed for brutal torture to force an accused woman into "confessing" that she was a member of a coven of witches and had had sexual relations with the devil.[12] Many such women were burned alive. The last witch trial in Germany took place in 1749. The persecution and murder of these women have their roots both in the deeply misogynist teachings of the scholastic Catholic tradition and the drastic, often catastrophic social changes during the late medieval period in Europe.[13]

To complement Heine's drawing I have included an illustration that depicts a witches' Sabbat and summarizes the major characteristics of witches in medieval mythology (see Figure 27). Medieval popular mythology tells us that on certain dates such as the *Walpurgisnacht,* the night before May first, witches gather in deserted places for the cultic celebration of their Sabbat.[14] This illustration, from 1669, shows one of the most famous of such supposed meeting grounds, the Bocksberg (Brocken) in the Harz Mountains. The witches fly on brooms or goats; they dance and are about to have intercourse with different devil figures; they can transform themselves into animals. In the middle of the picture, one of them kisses the devil's behind as a sign of her devotion. On the right, a witch creates an aphrodisiac drug, probably from the body of a stillborn child or the bones of a hanged criminal. There is a striking formal similarity with Heine's drawing with regard to the big boulder in the upper half of the picture, signifying a place where demonic ritual sacrifice takes place.

In medieval mythology witches are forces that attack and confuse God's natural order. They are allied with the devil; their dark magical powers are expressions of the "unnatural." As symbols of the unnatural, they engage in all kinds of "perverse" sexual practices with the devil, which the *Hexenhammer* and other medieval treatises describe in vivid detail. In short, they symbolize a chaos that is strongly coded as feminine, as Ines Brenner and Gisela Morgenthal convincingly argue (214). Within medieval mythology, this notion of chaos finds its ritualistic expression in the spectacle of the Sabbat, the dance of the witches. Although medieval imagination about the witches' Sabbat and the German inflation are historically separated by hundreds of years, the following description of such a Sabbat by the Frenchman Pierre de Lancre in his *Tableau de l'Inconstance des Mauvais Anges et Démons (Description of the Inconstancy of Bad Angels and Demons),* from 1613, reveals striking similarities to a traumatic inflationary scenario: "The sabbat is like

Figure 27. *Witches' Sabbath on the Bocksberg, Bockes-Berges Verrichtung,* 1669. Woodcut by J. Praetorius. Reproduced from Gerhard Zacharias, *Der dunkle Gott.*

a market of randomly assorted, raging, and crazy merchants who have come together from all sides. It is a meeting and a mixture of a hundred thousand things, sudden and transient, that are new, but their novelty is repulsive and insults the eye and offends the heart. Among these things[,] one sees those that are real and those that are mere appearance and fake. Some of them (only a few) are pleasing. . . . The others are distasteful, full of ugliness and horror, and they serve only dissoluteness, depravation, ruin, and destruction." [15]

Uncontrolled circulation, the anxiety that the shockingly new causes, the horror that the "real" and the "fake" are uncomfortably close to each other—these are deeply rooted ingredients of the chaos that is characteristic of the inflation and that makes the allegory of the witches' Sabbat especially powerful.

The symbolic significance of the dance creates an additional nexus between this medieval allegory and inflation. Far from being an orchestrated, studied, and harmonious motion of bodies, the witches' dance symbolizes an orgiastic expression of powerful female sexuality, a sign that the patriarchal order is in danger of being overcome by anarchic, feminine forces. When Klaus Mann, for example, tries in his memoirs to capture the cultural essence of the inflation, he resorts to a seemingly endless string of vignettes related to dancing:

> Why should we be more stable than our currency? The mark is dancing, so we dance along.
>
> Millions of malnourished, corrupted, desperately horny people staggered and tumbled along in a jazz delirium. Dance was a mania, an *idée fixe*, a cult. The stock market danced. The members of the Reichstag hopped about as if mad. Cripples, war profiteers, film stars and prostitutes, retired monarchs . . . and retired teachers . . . —all of them threw their limbs in gruesome euphoria. . . . The "Girls" of the new dance revues shake their behinds. People dance fox-trot, shimmy, tango, the old-fashioned waltz and the chic St. Vitus' dance. They dance hunger and hysteria, anxiety and lust, panic and horror. Mary Wigman—every inch angular sublimity, each gesture a dynamic explosion—performs something solemn with music by Bach. Anita Berber—her face frozen to a shrill mask, her hair all in horridly purple curls—does the keitus dance. . . . Fashion becomes obsession and spreads like fever, uncontrollable, like certain epidemics and mystic compulsions of the middle ages. (132)

For Klaus Mann, the inflation transformed Germany into one gigantic witches' Sabbat. The irrational character of the currency devaluation— when the money starts dancing—leaps over into the social sphere and causes everybody regardless of social background to dance deliriously. Prominent in his list are the names of two famous dancers, prototypes of modern "witches" who seem to incorporate the anarchic forces of inflation: Mary Wigman, the founder of expressionist dance *(Ausdruckstanz)*, and especially the scandalous Anita Berber, who enticed the German public throughout the early 1920s with her naked dancing.

The dark side of medieval witch mythology lay in its exercise as a scapegoat mechanism for a variety of catastrophes ranging from large-scale epidemics and drought to personal misfortunes such as miscarriage and male impotence. The public burning of witches throughout the Middle Ages became a sacrificial ritual by which the cause of these misfortunes could be eradicated. In the cultural context of Weimar modernity, such a ritual sacrifice reappears in one of the most telling fictional narratives of the time: Fritz Lang's film *Metropolis*. I argued in chapter 6 that the "witch" Maria symbolizes the inflation as she incorporates the dangers of uncontrolled duplication. Lang resorts to the context of medieval mythology when the "witch" Maria is burnt at the stake toward the end of the film. Only the sacrifice of the demonic female force will ensure the stable patriarchal harmony that the problematic ending of the film promises.

IV.

One of the most disturbing aspects of the inflation, especially for the status-conscious middle class, was the emergence of the so-called *Raffkes*, a class of nouveaux riches: speculators, black marketeers, and profiteers, whose sudden wealth seemed to have arrived overnight. Their ostentatious display of wealth was as much a part of the scenery of inflation as the long food lines that indicated the general misery of most other Germans. At the same time, the *Raffkes* were the target of many jokes that were based, as Bourdieu would describe it, on the apparent large gap between their economic and their cultural capital. To establish themselves as affluent in the eyes of society, the newly rich utilized those symbols that strongly and unambiguously signified wealth to the outside world: elegant clothes, lavish parties, expensive cars, cigars.

Probably the most powerful and culturally pervasive symbolic representation of wealth takes place within a gender scenario: the wealthy man appears with young, beautiful women in elegant clothing and precious jewelry at his side. Figure 28 gives us a sociological analysis of a prototypical *Raffke*.[16] The bottom right alludes to his past: The same man who appears in the upper half with elegant mistresses was a short time ago just a shabby guy from whom women tried to escape. Then inflation brought him wealth and catapulted him into the lifestyle of the rich and famous. As a sign of his newly acquired economic fortunes, he is presented with two lavishly dressed young women who are obviously not his daughters. This scene violates the code of bourgeois morality, and at the same time it reveals with piercing clarity the commodification of women. The *Raffke*, living out his fantasy, with a woman on each arm, makes no pretense to any kind of "romantic" involvement.

Figure 28. "*Raffke*'s nightly entertainment." Illustration by
Kamm; reproduced from Hans Ostwald, *Sittengeschichte der
Inflation,* 166.

The force of a brutish commodification could not be clearer: the more
women, the better. The illustration also seems to indicate that the relationship between the *Raffke* and these women mirrors the amorality of
the inflationary dynamic itself: having an (inflationary) multitude of
women thus symbolizes the opposite of the stable bourgeois, monoga-
mous marriage.[17] Instead of commenting further on the obviously sex-
ist character of these fantasies, I would like to historically contextualize
woman as a symbol of luxury, a symbol that gained such notoriety as a
sign of decadence and amorality during inflation.[18]

In 1913 the economist and social theorist Werner Sombart, one of the towering "mandarins" of the Weimar Republic, published *Luxus und Kapitalismus,* which he initially called *Liebe, Luxus, und Kapitalismus.* In this richly documented study, Sombart proposes an account of the origins of capitalism that is radically different from Max Weber's classic analysis in *The Protestant Ethics and the Spirit of Capitalism* (1904). Weber locates the inner dynamic of capitalist development in the asceticism and work ethic of Calvinism and Protestantism, which led to capital accumulation and eventually to the emergence of industrial production. Sombart does not reject Weber's thesis; indeed, he agrees with him that modern capitalism is imbedded in the value system of "bourgeois propriety" (65). But he proposes an alternative beginning. Sombart believes that the rise of capitalism was due to an emerging desire for luxury that began with the Italian Renaissance and then spread from Italy to France and England. The aristocracy and a nascent class of rich merchants in the cities longed for refined goods that could rarely be produced within a local economy, and thus they spurred a far-reaching trade supplying exotic and expensive goods. Sombart has a surprising explanation for the rising importance of luxury. He argues that with the end of the Middle Ages a liberalization of gender relationships took place that created a new role for women within the aristocratic classes: the *cortigiana,* courtesan, or *maitresse* entered the stage. According to Sombart, these women were the main force behind, the principal organizers of, and the visible bearers of an emerging capitalist culture of luxury. This became especially apparent with the growth of big cities between the seventeenth and nineteenth centuries. Sombart shows quite convincingly that it was not production but rather "the accumulation of consumption that led to the formation of the first big cities" (47). And as such, he argues, they harbored a large contingent of courtesans and mistresses; in eighteenth-century Paris, for example, there were about ten thousand such women. As consultants on luxury and lifestyle, they were in a powerful economic position, and, besides giving sexual favors, they often educated the nouveaux riches in the art of luxurious living. "Thus it was luxury, the legitimate child of illegitimate love, that engendered capitalism," he concludes his book (194).

One may disagree with Sombart about the degree to which the emergence of a luxury culture organized by women outside traditional marriages was consequential for the overall development of capitalism. The significance of Sombart's *Luxus und Kapitalismus* lies in the fact that it provides us with a view of capitalism that enriches and contextualizes the model of a feminized modernity that I mentioned at the outset of this chapter. In contrast to Weber's analysis, Sombart's genealogy of capitalism proceeds from the centrality of consumption in its most pronounced sense, namely, in the form of luxury. Within this genealogy women initialize and steer economic development without, however, owning the means of production. Women become associated with the underlying forces of luxury: sensual pleasure and excess. Within the context of the inflation, it is excess that becomes especially important. Women are not only presented as commodified objects of luxury, but they also embody excess, the "unreasonable" and the "unnecessary" use of economic resources. Luxury as feminine excess originates within the private sphere and demonstrates publicly the success of an individual. In its excessiveness it contains an anarchic quality: it represents an affront against the social whole, in particular against the Prussian ideology of the (male) state, with its ideals of moderation, obedience, and order. It stresses a radical, self-sufficient yet also self-centered individuality as an extreme form of the atomized, "egoistic" society during inflation.

Thus, the iconography of consumption includes two images of women that are diametrically opposed: the traditional image of housewife and mother as the careful guardian of economic resources, and the image of the *Luxusweib*, the mistress whose sexual permissiveness is mirrored in her excessive forms of consumption. We can interpret the figure of the *Luxusweib* as a capitalist, secular version of the precapitalist witch. The pervasive dualism in the Western religious tradition of witch and saint, so strikingly illustrated in the doubling of Maria in *Metropolis*, finds its new rendering in economically defined images: the virtues of the female saint, above all the Virgin Mary, are translated into the economic order of the bourgeois household, with its prerogatives of saving and unlimited, sacrificial support of the male producer. The witch finds its contemporary iconography in the *Luxusweib* indulging in excessive consumption. The *Luxusweib*, and in an even more pronounced way, the prostitute, signify the other, alluring, yet often repressed side of a seemingly irrational and amoral capitalist development.[19]

V.

While the mistress and the courtesan are part of the nexus of wealth and luxury (even though they themselves may not have become rich), the prostitute, especially in the socioeconomic context of the inflation, signifies sexual permissiveness coupled with economic and social misery.

There is little doubt that the inflation caused an increase in the already widespread prostitution that characterized most modern European capitals in the early twentieth century.[20] It is estimated that the number of prostitutes in Berlin around 1910 was about 40,000 (Frevert 87).

Oskar Dreßler and Hugo Weinberger, two officials of the Viennese city administration, compiled the following numbers on the impact of the inflation on prostitution: Before World War 1, about 1,700 to 1,800 legally registered prostitutes in Vienna were subject to mandatory regular examination by a physician (324). During the war, prostitution decreased: in 1918 the number of surveyed "official" prostitutes had dropped to 1,070. With the unfolding of the inflation, however, this group increased to 1,387 women in 1920. Yet of real concern for public health officials was the drastic increase of secret, illegal prostitution. The Vienna police statistics show that in 1918, 5,540 women were charged with illegal prostitution. This number rose to 7,637 in 1920, with a dramatic increase of women (about 900) who were infected with venereal diseases. While these police reports give some indication about the rise of prostitution during inflation, they say little about the actual number of prostitutes, which was many times higher. In their interpretation of these statistics, Dreßler and Weinberger stress the strong link between the economic dispossession of the middle class and "serious moral damages" (325) within the Austrian postwar society. They also note the overall corruptive influence on society caused by speculation, black marketing, and the display of luxury by the newly rich. This ostentatious luxury, note Dreßler and Weinberger, lured many, especially young, women into prostitution.

The link between prostitution and urban poverty is important, yet the discourse about the figure of the prostitute contains many aspects besides the socioeconomic perspective. At the beginning of the nineteenth century, the prostitute became the object of intense discussions within the fields of science, sociology, medicine, and social policy. As Foucault has shown, these discourses attempted to differentiate and define sexuality along the categories of "normal" and "deviant." Alexandre Parent-Duchalet's *De la prostitution dans la ville de Paris* from 1836 is one of the early landmarks in this endeavor.[21] Throughout modernity the figure of the prostitute continued to be one of the most densely inscribed discursive spaces.[22] Within the patriarchal discourse of feminine identity, it has served as the embodiment of a threatening and fascinating "other" that stood in stark contrast to the traditional construction of an exclusively reproductive female sexuality (Bell 41). For Marx, the figure of the prostitute is a symbol of commodification and exploitation. In the third of his "Economic and Philosophical Manuscripts" he remarks, "Prostitution is only a *specific* expression of the *universal* prostitution of the worker, and since prostitution is a relationship which includes both the one who is prostituted and the one who prostitutes . . . , so the capitalist, etc. comes within this category." [23] Walter Benjamin, in his reading of Charles Baudelaire's *Les fleurs du mal*, stresses that the emergence of widespread street prostitution, in which the prostitute appears as a commodity and mass-produced article, constitutes a signature of a new urban modernity ("Zentralpark" 668). The construction of male and female sexuality; the dynamics of exchange and circulation; the urban experience of the street with its mix of anonymity and momentous experience; and questions of moral relativism, autonomy, and repression—all these overarching themes that define modernity come together in the figure of the prostitute.

If the prostitute appears to some degree as an allegorical figure of modernity, in what way can this figure then be linked on a conceptual level to inflation? I have defined inflation as the simultaneous process of uncontrolled massification and devaluation taking place in an ever faster circulation of money. These dynamics are, at the same time, constitutive for the experience of modernity. In that sense I have called inflation a "modernity out of bounds." The extent to which the figure of the prostitute incorporates these dynamics is remarkable. The process of massification, for example, is embodied in this figure on several levels. Benjamin points out that like the *flâneur,* the modern prostitute is linked to the emergence of a mass society in the cities of the nineteenth century. Different from the mistress in an aristocratic or bourgeois environment, the prostitute is a creature of the urban masses that provide both anonymity and opportunity.

More fundamentally, we can think of prostitution itself as a "sexual inflation." If we consider for a moment sexuality within the terms of economic analogies and understand the sexual act as a currency, then prostitution resembles the inflationary dynamics because it is based on the potentially unlimited duplication of the sexual act. The sexual act during prostitution defies the concepts of both uniqueness and individuality; rather, it stresses quantitative sameness and multiplicity: it is defined by the very fact that other men came before and will come afterward. Thus, prostitution is regarded as devaluing the sexual act by violating the very rules that make the act valuable within a patriarchal society; namely, it is a noncirculating, unique, qualitative, not quantitative event between two people. The third characteristic, circulation, is also a constitutive moment of prostitution and becomes symbolically coded in the site of the street.

The (inflationary) sexual economy of prostitution, in other words, operates on "devalued money": in its characteristics of immediate exchange and consumption, its rapid circulation, its presentness that comes with the inability to provide for future investments, and its curious imitation of valued money, it resembles the quality of an inflated economy. Thus, prostitution can be seen as a kind of "shadow economy" that always lurks in the background of an otherwise rigidly controlled sexual economy within the framework of bourgeois society. During inflation, prostitution moves out of the shadow and occupies the public imagination not only because there are in fact more prostitutes roaming the streets but also because inflation and prostitution share so many fundamental characteristics and mirror each other.

At this point it becomes apparent how difficult it is to even conceptualize prostitution without linking it to the domain of money—which is another reason for the elective affinity between inflation and prostitution. In his *Philosophy of Money* Georg Simmel writes, "The indifference as to its use, the lack of attachment to any individual because it is unrelated to any of them, the objectivity inherent in money as a mere means which excludes any emotional relationship—all this produces an ominous analogy between money and prostitution" (377). Money, as Simmel observes, corresponds to the fleeting relationship between the prostitute and her customer, it does not leave any traces, and it stresses the quantitative, exchangeable nature of the act.[24] In addition, Simmel calls prostitution "the most striking instance of mutual degradation to a mere means," and he concludes that "this may be the strongest and most fundamental factor that places prostitution in such a close historical relationship to the money economy, the economy of 'means' in the strictest sense" (ibid.). Simmel regards sexuality above all as a means to express the most personal and intimate self.[25] This view incorporates the traditional division between a regulated, "ends-oriented" reproductive sexuality and a nonreproductive sexuality, with its sources of desire and potential excess, which was criticized, especially within church doctrines, as merely "means-oriented." Prostitution, then, appears as the most drastic form of such a "means-oriented" sexuality.

For Simmel, the potential domination of "means" over "ends," of *Mittel* over *Ziel,* is a constant threat to modern culture as a whole, which tends to conform more and more to the attributes of money. During inflation, these tendencies reach their extreme manifestation. In fact, as we saw in the previous chapter, the cultural atmosphere during the inflation can be described as an extreme reversal of means and ends.[26] The rapid circulation of deteriorating money emphasizes the act of buying and blocks out any goal-oriented planning, and it severs the present from a larger meaningful context. Thus, the social relationship between the prostitute and her client stands for a traumatic view of inflation society as whole, a society devoid of trusted relationships that stand outside the mediating force of money, a society without moral direction, engulfed in the immediacy of both hunger and excess.

In summary, the figures of the starving mother, the witch, the mistress, and the prostitute, with their wide-ranging cultural, economic, and historical contexts, offer an ensemble of *personae dramatis* who illustrate and symbolize the cultural impact of the inflation. The final part of this chapter will briefly look at these *personae dramatis* "in action." G. W. Pabst's famous film about the impact of inflation on Viennese society, *Die Freudlose Gasse* (*The Joyless Street*, 1925), convincingly portrays this turmoil through a fictional world that is predominantly feminine, and in which women play a surprisingly wide range of roles: as victims, as mediators, and as calculating agents.

VI.

In the movie's literary source, Hugo Bettauer's novel *Die Freudlose Gasse* (*The Joyless Street*, 1924), the plot centers on a detective story in which Otto Demel, an investigative reporter for the *Wiener Herold,* solves the murder case of Lia Leid, the beautiful young wife of the successful Viennese lawyer Dr. Leid. While pursuing this case, Demel takes lodging with the Rumfort family, falls in love with Grete Rumfort, and in the end saves her from the clutches of Frau Greifer, the lesbian procuress and owner of a secret nightclub on Melchior Street. The novel, with its hero-savior perspective, has a strong biographical flavor: Bettauer himself was a well-known reporter in Vienna in the early 1920s.[27] In contrast to Bettauer's novel, Pabst's film contains two melodramatic strands: The story of Grete Rumfort (Greta Garbo), daughter of a caring, honorable civil servant, illustrates the victory of virtue over economic misery and amorality. The tragic story of Maria Lechner (Asta Nielsen), who comes from an impoverished working-class family being terrorized by her unemployed, brutal father, exemplifies the destruction of a young woman's life by the forces of economic and social destitution. The difference in plot development and character arrangement between Bettauer's novel and Pabst's film is striking. It shifts from a male-centered murder story to a female-oriented social drama of inflation.[28] The guiding question for my discussion of *Joyless Street* arises from this change in perspective: In what way does this shift to a strong female presence in the film relate to the topic and representation of inflation?

Within current film criticism, G. W. Pabst's film *Joyless Street* has become almost synonymous with questions of female spectatorship in Weimar cinema and the role that the melodramatic form plays in establishing a specific relationship between film and a female audience. Especially the film melodrama, with its insistence on everyday life, the ordinary, and the private, as Patrice Petro points out, "frequently addressed women's experience in Weimar" (*Joyless Street* 34). Petro argues that while many Weimar films displayed a destabilized male identity, Weimar cinema also often addressed in a quite open way women's dissatisfaction with their traditionally defined gender roles (35–36). Melodrama as a form charges the experience of the everyday with exaggeration and excess, it has the desire "to say it all" and, therefore, typically resorts to cliché, overstatement, and sentimentality (200).

Petro convincingly argues that *Joyless Street* is a melodrama sui generis in its display of unambiguous identities and relationships, in its clear separation between villainy and virtue.[29] Lotte Eisner, in her classic study *The Haunted Screen,* has already observed that Pabst's seemingly "realistic" portrayal of a society under the reign of hyperinflation was interspersed with melodramatic clichés and types rather than complex characters. She criticizes that "everything is too studied, too arranged, too emphatic" in Pabst's film (256).

Because inflation hit most dramatically the private sphere and the ordinary routine of people's lives, one can also argue that the melodramatic form, combined with *Joyless Street*'s female protagonists, provided an ideal framework for a strong rapport with a female spectatorship. Inflation's own tendency to exaggerate the once trivial and ordinary, to charge a society both with staggering, seemingly random social injustice and material excess, and to undermine established gender relationships almost invites a melodramatic fictionalization. The stark contrasts that characterize the culture of inflation indeed shape the cinematographic style of Pabst's film. *Joyless Street* is full of drastic cuts between luxury and misery. Pabst uses the iconography that I have discussed in this chapter when he cuts back and forth between boisterous dancing in the luxurious ballrooms and emaciated women waiting in front of the butcher's store. For example, the film comments on the toast of the Argentinean millionaire Cunez to "all happy Viennese" with a juxtaposition of two close-ups, one showing young women dancers drinking champagne, the other focusing on the exhausted faces of the women waiting in line. Accordingly, the mise-en-scène of *Joyless Street* displays almost no social "middle ground." Most scenes take place either in lavishly decorated clubs or in the shabby, dimly lit environment of Melchior Street, indicating strikingly the disappearance of the middle class. The last social space of the middle class is the apartment of the Rumforts, which is, however, endangered. As a visible sign of their economic despair the Rumfort family decide to start renting out part of their apartment.

With the emphasis on current discussions of melodrama, one easily forgets a strong cultural-historical tradition that is also very much present in *Joyless Street*. Linked to Grete's destiny, and resonating with the experience of many contemporary viewers of the time, is the humiliating social decline of the bourgeois middle class that her father, the councilor and civil servant Rumfort, embodies to the point of cliché. The situation is "classical" in a literary sense: Pabst reiterates a constellation that is at the core of eighteenth-century bourgeois tragedy, of the *bürgerliche Trauerspiel*. These dramas, such as Lessing's *Emilia Galotti,* depict an emerging bourgeois identity in contrast to that of the aristocratic class by insisting on the catalogue of bourgeois virtues such as fidelity, prudence, frugality, and honesty. The daughters of bourgeois fathers become the showpiece for these virtues, but they are also vulnerable to aristocratic seduction.

In contrast to the eighteenth century, when the bourgeoisie sought to construct an identity that separated it from the aristocracy, in the twentieth century it is against the *Lumpenproletariat* and social decline that the bourgeoisie seeks to define itself. In *Joyless Street,* the Rumfort family can barely manage to uphold their comfortable lifestyle. Councilor Rumfort had chosen early retirement with a lump-sum pension payment, which he quickly loses on the stock market. They feed themselves on cabbage soup, while Grete's young sister dreams about a meal with some meat. At the same time the film exposes the bedrock of their identity: bourgeois virtue. By narrating the parallel stories of two daughters— Grete inherently bourgeois, Maria shaped by her proletarian background, and both endangered by the demoralizing forces of inflation— Pabst effectively reconstitutes a powerful construct of bourgeois identity: what separates the Rumforts from the proletarian Lechner family is a long tradition of bourgeois virtues that becomes manifest in the virtues

of their daughters. While Lessing's Emilia Galotti stands at the beginning
of this tradition, *Joyless Street* represents almost a nostalgic view back.
Neither Germany's nor Austria's postwar and postinflation society remains structured in this tradition. Instead, a much more diffuse concept
emerges that is no longer centered on bourgeois virtues but rather on social mobility and income differentials: the concept of the middle class,
which offers alluring opportunities for upward mobility, even though accompanied by the anxiety-inducing possibility of moving downward into
a lower class.

The invocation of bourgeois family values explains the close father-
daughter relationship in the Rumfort family (and, in contrast, the abu-
sive relationship between father Lechner and Maria). Yet Grete Rumfort
and Maria Lechner are not the only vital female characters in *Joyless
Street*. There are Regina Rosenow, who makes no secret of her greed in
her relationship with Egon Stirner; Lia Leid, who pays for her adulter-
ous desire with her death; and last but not least Frau Greifer, who lures
young women into her brothel. To be sure, Pabst does not break gender
stereotypes: on the contrary, whenever it comes to big business, to back-
room deals and stock market manipulations, the film displays an exclusively male universe. *Joyless Street* is primarily concerned with the
consequences of these deals; it shows us how clever, seemingly coldly
calculated (male) business strategies during the inflation result in an av-
alanche of both excess and misery that sometimes engulfs these men
themselves: Stirner becomes accused of murder; the butcher, "the tyrant
of Melchior Street," is murdered by an enraged woman; and even the
otherwise sympathetically treated councilor Rumfort loses his pension.
Thus, the film presents us with a quite different view of inflation than,
for example, Fritz Lang's *Dr. Mabuse, the Gambler,* which reacts to the
unraveling of social positions and identities by erecting an oversized,
megalomaniac male individual who promises relentless action in times
of acute powerlessness.

Because the film intends to portray the psychosocial impact of the
inflation, it almost automatically succumbs to the strongly gendered typology of misery and moral decay that I have outlined in this chapter. In
other words, the strong female presence in this film is as much the result
of genre structures as it is inscribed by the collective imagery of inflation
itself. This explains, for example, the clichéd characters lacking psychological depth, whom Lotte Eisner criticizes. Thus, when the film wants
to show economic misery it resorts first and foremost to the imagery of
female misery, to the angry and exhausted women lining up in front of

the butcher store, to the fate of Maria Lechner, who succumbs to prostitution, commits a murder, and falls terminally ill of a lung disease. Similarly, the trio of Regina Rosenow, Lia Leid, and Frau Greifer covers quite well the territory of feminine excess and sexual permissiveness captured in the typology of the *Luxusweib* and the prostitute.[30]

Furthermore, as a portrait of the social and cultural impact of inflation, *Joyless Street* is a fitting representation of what Rita Felski broadly calls "feminized modernity"—and not only on the level of female roles in this film. While *Metropolis,* with its relentless display of production and male industrial performance, represses the impact of inflation, Pabst is almost obsessed with displaying one of inflation's most important features, one that at the same time characterizes a "feminized modernity": the hectic and seemingly never-ending circle of exchanges. While in *Metropolis* almost everybody works, *Joyless Street* shows people enslaved not by work but by a constant chain of exchanges. There are more than fifteen such exchanges that the film displays very consciously, be it the overdetermined exchange of "meat" for "flesh" when the women go down into the butcher shop, be it the incriminating money sticking out of Grete's skirt when she comes out of her boss's office or the seemingly harmless gift of cans of food to the Rumfort family by the American Red Cross official Davy—the film creates an overwhelming sensation that everybody and everything is sucked into this whirlpool of exchanges.

Women are obviously subject to commodification in this sphere, and the struggle of resisting or gliding into the different levels of prostitution is a major subject in *Joyless Street.* Yet at the same time there is a subversive dimension, because women themselves are active negotiators. Young Egon Stirner, for example, becomes an object of Lia Leid's desire, and she pays for sex with him by handing him her pearls. The end of the film simultaneously shows us the rescue of Grete from Frau Greifer's brothel by her father and the American official Davy and the startling killing of the butcher by an enraged woman who is part of a female mob in front of his store. With such an ending, Eric Rentschler notes, the film engages "both the male anxiety of the *Angestellten* class as well as acknowledging female rage, supplying in the end two resolutions, one comforting in its patriarchal logic, the other transgressive in its expression of repressed female desire" (*Films of G. W. Pabst* 6).

In *Joyless Street,* as well as in many popular texts of the time, the representations of inflation are deeply interlinked with such outbursts of repressed female desire. Repressed desire becomes the witches' Sabbat that destroys male order and rational calculation; it is the site where female excess and luxury triumphs over frugality and modesty. Both threatening and alluring, the female iconography of inflation expresses and reveals much of the deep ambivalence that characterizes so many then-contemporary accounts of the social and economic turmoil during the early 1920s.

PART FIVE

Epilogue

CHAPTER NINE

Aftershocks

Inflation, National Socialism, and Beyond

I.

The German inflation ended in November 1923 with the introduction of the provisional *Rentenmark*. The Dawes Plan, initiated by the American government, brought a solution to the war-reparations conflict in early 1924. Later that year, the German government introduced the new *Reichsmark*, which was tied to the gold exchange standard. Although the German economy stabilized during the mid-1920s, a structural unemployment of about 10 percent and poor economic growth were visible symptoms of a fundamentally weak economy.[1] Then, beginning in October 1929, Germany's already fragile economic system was crushed with enormous force by the world economic crisis. Industrial production plummeted. Between 1929 and 1930 the index for capital goods production fell from 103 to 81, and in 1931 to 61. In 1932, the index dropped to 46, which was below the prewar level. Unemployment rose from 8.5 percent in 1929 to 14 percent in 1930 and continued its dramatic rise to 21.9 percent in 1931 and 29.9 percent in 1932.[2]

Both inflation and depression caused tremendous economic misery and existential anxieties. But whereas the impact of inflation, as we have seen in examples throughout this book, varied depending on the individual's response to the currency devaluation, the repercussions of the depression were overwhelmingly linked to massive unemployment. In addition to their economic hardship, the more than 5 million Germans who were out of work in the early 1930s bore the psychological burden of having to spend their days without the discipline and temporal structure that a job had given them (Peukert, 254). Consequently, long-term unemployment often led to widespread apathy and disorientation. In contrast, the inflation period provided, for the most part, full employment that gave people the sanctuary of order and rhythm in an otherwise chaotic world (see chapter 6). There is no question that the rise of right- and left-wing extremism, the hollowing-out of a democratic center in German politics by the early 1930s, and finally Hitler's coming to power in January of 1933 are much more directly related to the depression than to the hyperinflation of 1923.

Yet one of the most interesting and most frequently posed questions concerns the link between inflation and National Socialism. If the inflation did not directly "cause" Hitler's success, in what way did it facilitate National Socialism's rise to power? In what way did the experience of the inflation compel Germans to sympathize with radical right-wing politics? How did National Socialist ideology incorporate this experience, especially in its anti-Semitic agenda? These questions themselves indicate that the link between inflation and National Socialism has to be viewed from two perspectives. German fascism, in our context, must be understood both as a response to the inflation and as an ideology that in itself was being shaped and marked by the inflation.

II.

I will preface my discussion by addressing a fundamental, historically persistent attitude toward capitalist development that has pervaded modern German culture since the mid–nineteenth century and that seems to have only recently changed. In his study *Das Schicksal des deutschen Kapitalismus (The Fate of German Capitalism,* 1930), the economist Moritz J. Bonn writes that the inflation shed new light on the "old opposition between debtor and creditor that pervaded all social revolutions of the past" (16). With a critical eye, he observes that throughout German cultural history the position of the debtor was privileged in relation to that of the creditor: "The debtor is the productive one, a man whose labor and creation of material goods are for the benefit of the social whole. The creditor is a parasite who feeds on his blood. The debtor has tangible, visible pieces of property: the factory, the estate; the creditor has only an abstract legal title. . . . Thus the owner of a 'substance' has to be compensated, the owner of a legal title only if there is a surplus" (ibid.).

Bonn concludes that the German inflation of the early 1920s proved to be one of the most pronounced discriminations directed against creditors and in favor of debtors, against "finance capital" and in favor of "industrial capital." "Banks in particular," writes Bonn, "willingly allowed their assets to be diminished by aggressive industrial leaders who paid back their credits with devalued money" (18). He argues that this behavior destroyed a foundation of capitalism, the "sacredness of contracts" that is the prerequisite for saving money and the accumulation of liquid, "nonmaterial" capital.

The privileging of industrial debtors and the slant against financial creditors who have to rely solely on abstract legal titles are also contained in an ideological tradition in which anti-Semitism and an illiberal anticapitalism merge. Otto Glogau, in a 1874 article on the stock market and financial speculation in the journal *Gartenlaube,* introduced the opposition between *schaffendes Kapital* and *raffendes Kapital,* between "productive" capital and the "greedy" capital that is merely interest oriented. Glogau identifies the Jews with the latter and writes, "The Jew doesn't work, but rather lets others work; he speculates and makes deals with the products of the manual and intellectual labor of others. The center of his activities is the stock market" (quoted in F. Raphael 109). This view was echoed by the anti-Semitic preacher Adolf Stoecker around the turn of the twentieth century, and found its most ardent voice in the right-wing economist Gottfried Feder, whose views influenced Hitler in the early 1920s. Feder, who became one of Hitler's earliest supporters, also preached on "breaking the slavery of interest" *(Brechung der Zinsknechtschaft),* which became as much a slogan in Nazi rhetoric as the division between *raffendes* and *schaffendes* capital.[3] Avraham Barkai notes that Feder's distinction "permitted the Nazi party to assume an anticapitalist stance without frightening that part of the business world whose financial and political support it sought" (23).[4]

In addition to this strategic aspect, it is important to emphasize that the Nazis' economic view of idealizing production and describing elements of the finance sector as "Jewish" and "parasitical" originates from two separate yet interlinked sources. One is, obviously, the already mentioned historical tradition of anti-Semitism, which contains the figure of the Jew as usurer and profiteer. The second strand is more opaque, yet becomes visible in Bonn's observation.

One can argue that Bonn's important insight about discrimination against the creditor points to the overall weak foundations of German civil society in the aftermath of World War 1. A civil society is based on

the trust its citizens have in the many levels of mediation and representation embodied in civic associations, in parties, in the legal system, and
last but not least, in its monetary system. By allowing, even encouraging,
a legitimate bias against creditors, the inflation undermined the trustworthiness of the economy's contractual net and thus further damaged
Germany's civil society. The German government did not intervene, because this inflationary dynamic worked to its advantage. I see National
Socialism's contempt for the basic foundations of civil society and the
unscrupulous casualness with which the Nazis broke agreements, promises, and even international treatises as the direct outgrowth of the cynical nature of the inflationary process.[5]

In this context, National Socialism's characteristic as both a product
of and a response to inflation becomes especially evident. As a reaction
to the chaos the inflation had caused via the medium of money, the Nazis
promised a return to immediacy: Hitler *was* the will of the German
people; there were no differing interests among the German people, because their essential Germanness united them: the slogan "Ein Reich—
ein Volk—ein Führer" meant to stress the virtual identity of these three
terms. In many ways, the Nazis envisioned a German culture and society that was the complete opposite of the culture of inflation: a tightly
controlled, anticapitalist (at least in its rhetoric) society, an economy
with fixed prices that centered on German production and sought to
make itself independent of "international Jewish capital." As I mentioned before in this book, the "blood and soil" ideology thus contains
a powerful countervision to the circulation of "Jewish" money and internationally operating capitalism.[6]

And yet, National Socialism also bears the direct imprint of the inflation, especially in its cynical attitude toward legal agreements and the
social networks of trust. The circulation of worthless paper money during the hyperinflation was a deeply cynical act in itself. Such inflated
money only imitated the function of valued money; it circulated, yet did
not hold its promised value. This situation created an almost schizo-
phrenic double standard. If we look at the political practice of National
Socialism, we can find a similar double standard. I believe that the longing for order, and at the same time the acceptance of unpredictable terror that characterized National Socialism, was shaped in part by the
inflation. The inflation and National Socialism bear many resemblances
as fundamentally Janus-faced phenomena. Just as inflation money participated in the rational conduct of business transactions and yet simul-

taneously betrayed the fundamentals of these transactions, so the ideology and practice of National Socialism combined planned rationality with a set of irrational visions about Germany's destiny. Many Germans emerged from the inflation period with a cynical tolerance for contradictions and a mistrust of the functioning of a civil society that may explain why so many were willing to accept the many obvious discrepancies in National Socialist ideology and practice. During the inflation, as Thomas Mann noted, Germans "learned to look on life as a wild adventure, the outcome of which depended not on their own effort but on sinister, mysterious forces" ("Inflation" 63).

Hitler's first public appearances occurred during the hyperinflation. His leading participation in the ill-fated putsch attempt in Munich on November 9, 1923, the so-called Bierhallen-Putsch, gave him much national prominence. On that day, Hitler proclaimed a national revolution and announced a provisional "German National Government." After the putsch collapsed, Hitler was arrested and sentenced to five years imprisonment. Yet after only eight months he was released. He used much of this time writing his *Mein Kampf*.

In a speech given six months before the putsch, he proclaimed, "Thousands of old rentiers, middle-class people, scholars, and war widows sold their last gold marks for scraps of paper money, which is not even worth a hundredth. That way, the last remaining national wealth of the entire people, almost in a 'playing' fashion, changes into the hands of the relentlessly grabbing Jews! The result of the outrageous fraud are the tears of millions of people. Millions of livelihoods, founded on frugality for an entire generation, are being destroyed in this swindle" (von Kotze 54). Not surprisingly, Hitler identifies the ruthless inflation profiteers as Jewish, and his rabid anti-Semitism was certainly fueled during the currency devaluation.

Examining Hitler's speeches from a rhetorical angle, it is interesting to note how the inflation left its mark in his repeated use of large numbers, especially his constant mentioning of "millions." Elias Canetti, as well as Victor Klemperer in his study on fascist language, *LTI*, has observed how much the language and ideology of Hitler in particular and of National Socialism in general are characterized by an almost obsessive lust for big numbers with many zeros. "In all his threats, self-congratulations and demands he [Hitler] used the word *million*," writes Canetti (*Crowds and Power* 185). In a similar vein, Klemperer writes of the Nazis' and Hitler's obsession with superlatives that bear no reference to reality

(275–86). For Klemperer the very concept of the "1,000-Year Reich"—
a reign with three zeros—indicates a fatal mixture of both mindless
grandiosity and a *hasardeur*-like attitude toward time.[7]

Hitler's rhetoric and his thinking were indeed inflationary: there were
millions of soldiers he was moving back and forth in his war scenarios
in the Berlin bunker (millions of soldiers he was counting on during the
last days of the war, who were no longer alive), millions of Germans he
planned to resettle in Eastern Europe, and millions of Jews he wanted to
eradicate. Like inflation, Hitler's thinking seemed to center on the rapid
and potentially unlimited growth that the number zero represents. The
discussion about the signifying potential of the number zero in chapter 4
allows us to explore this link further. Hitler's love of the zero, his tire-
less work for "millions of *Volksgenossen*," indicates a special position
of power: he is the one who counts. His use of big numbers wants to convey, on the one hand, a sense of control and rationality. Yet Hitler's fascination with the number zero is, on the other hand, related to its dialectical quality signifying both multiplying growth and void. It betrays
a deep undercurrent inherent in National Socialist ideology: a longing
for annihilation (and self-annihilation), for void, for "nothing," for a cult
of death. His vision of Germany's destiny was one of either unlimited
power and glory or total annihilation. In his boundless anti-Semitism,
Hitler's declared goal was not to just decimate the Jewish people, but to
eradicate them to "zero."[8] It is on this relationship to the Holocaust that
Elias Canetti has written his most thought-provoking reflections on the
German inflation.

III.

In *Crowds and Power,* Canetti ends his essay on inflation with the following remarks:

> No one ever forgets a sudden depreciation of himself, for it is too painful. . . .
> And the crowd as such never forgets its depreciation. The natural tendency
> afterwards is to find something which is worth even less than oneself, which
> one can despise as one was despised oneself. It is not enough to take over an
> old contempt and to maintain it at the same level. What is wanted is a dy-
> namic process of humiliation. Something must be treated in such a way that
> it becomes worth less and less, as the unit of money did during the inflation.
> And this process must be continued until its object is reduced to a state of ut-
> ter worthlessness. Then one can throw it away like paper, or repulp it.

Figure 29. "Bank business." Illustration by Wilhelm Schulz,
in *Simplicissimus* 28 (November 19, 1923).

The object Hitler found for this process during the German inflation was
the Jews. . . .

In its treatment of the Jews National Socialism repeated the process of
inflation with great precision. First they were attacked as wicked and dangerous, as enemies; then they were more and more depreciated; then, there not
being enough in Germany itself, those in the conquered territories were gath-
ered in; and finally they were treated literally as vermin, to be destroyed with
impunity by the million. The world is still horrified and shaken by the fact that
the Germans could go so far, that they either participated in a crime of such
magnitude, or connived at it, or ignored it. It might not have been possible to
get them to do so if, a few years before, they had not been through an inflation during which the Mark fell to a billionth of its former value. It was this
inflation, as a crowd experience, which they shifted on to the Jews. (187–88)

I was reminded of Canetti's analogy between the inflation and the Holocaust when I saw a chilling illustration from November 1923. (See Figure 29.) In looking at this picture, one can scarcely avoid making the
connection to a scene in a Nazi extermination camp—except that, as

Canetti's scenario suggests it, the roles are exactly reversed. In the 1923 illustration Germans are entering a bank, and a (Jewish?) bank official robs them of all their clothing. The illustration emphasizes the same central theme that Canetti assumes as the driving energy behind the Holocaust: the dynamic of depreciation and utter humiliation. The nakedness of the victims in the concentration camps is etched into our memory—the nakedness that took away all their individuality, that signified their powerlessness, that marked them as living corpses.

What makes the illustration so eerie is the density and intensity with which the destructive transformation from something economic into the sheer physical is depicted in this drawing. When I read the illustration's title, "Bankbetrieb," "Bank business," I was reminded of the cynical motto the Nazis inscribed over the entrance gate of Auschwitz I: "Arbeit macht frei," "Work gives freedom." Work in this concentration camp meant with few exceptions almost certain death; for the people in the illustration, conducting *Bankbetrieb* did not lead to prosperity but rather to the loss of all possessions.

I continue to be mesmerized by Canetti's explanation of the Holocaust. Was the extermination of 6 million Jews indeed a monstrous *Wiederholungszwang,* a repetition compulsion that reenacted the dynamics of the inflation?[9] One balks at the frightening determinism in Canetti's observation. Could an explanation of the unspeakable crimes of the Holocaust be that simple?

Let us move one step back and then carefully reapproach Canetti's text. The fact that the inflation spurred a prevalent anti-Semitism in Germany is abundantly evident.[10] As far back as the early 1920s, for example, random street protests in Munich against price rises contained such slogans as "Death to the profiteers! Down with the Jews!" (M. Geyer 280). Many of the stereotypes of Jews—the profiteer, the capitalist, the banker—are intimately connected to the inflation.[11] To give just one example of the countless and repetitive accusations that the Jews were the main beneficiaries of the inflation, the National Socialist Curt Rosten wrote that the inflation represented a disastrous waste of German property that coincided with the emergence of the *Raffke,* which he describes as "the unscrupulous profiteer, the nouveau riche, a class of people consisting mostly of culturally inferior Eastern Jews, who migrated in masses across the border after the war and swamped our big cities" (7). It was easy for anti-Semites to attribute the inflation to the activities of the Jews. The hostility toward money, with its fluctuations and unpredictabilities,

and the resentment against the inherently somewhat disorderly development of capitalism in general, found in the Jews a target, a scapegoat, an
ideologically powerful screen on which to project such feelings.

Thus, Canetti's argument that National Socialism found in Jewish
people fitting victims on which to unleash a "dynamic process of humiliation" can hardly be contested. Furthermore, Canetti rightfully reminds
us that the Holocaust was not only an act of mass killing but was organized as an intricate system of humiliations, beginning with public
discrimination in 1933 and ending with torture and killings in the concentration camps.[12] And the dynamics of humiliation indeed mark both
the inflation and the persecution of Jews. The extent to which the Holocaust was organized around the interlinking dynamics of devaluation
and massification is also striking. The establishment of concentration
camps with thousands of prisoners may fall within the operational logic
of the persecution of Jews; at the same time it is important to emphasize
that these camps were organized as yet another way to humiliate
people—a humiliation that came from crowding them by the thousands
in the barracks of Bergen Belsen or Auschwitz.

I believe one would be seriously misreading Canetti if one interpreted
his strong link between the inflation and the Holocaust as deterministic,
as if Germans were almost forced to reenact the inflation as an act of
genocide. Canetti points out the hidden forces of humiliation and depreciation that unleash the desire for revenge, but his interpretation of the
causes of the Holocaust has to be strictly shielded from accusations that
it implies any sort of empathy for the perpetrators. The reverberations of
the inflation in National Socialism need to be explored further; they are
complex enough to become the topic for another study. What I find especially persuasive in Canetti's argument is the stress it places on the subterranean interplay between economic devastation and social violence.
According to Canetti, the Holocaust was not so much the outcome of
the idea of racial Darwinism as it was of the way in which Jews were
forced into a role and identified with a specific development in a capitalist system that humiliated large parts of the German middle class. The
organic imagery that saw Jews as "parasites" who infected the "body"
of the German folk gained its vicious power, its dangerous allure, and
its persuasiveness primarily within the economic sphere, and specifically
in the form of such stereotypes as the Jewish war and inflation profiteer.
Thus Canetti stresses an additional, perhaps even more primal force
than modern racism in the unfolding of the Holocaust: the mechanisms

of revenge and scapegoating for a humiliation that can be very precisely
located historically.

IV.

Rainer Werner Fassbinder's masterful film *The Marriage of Maria Braun*,
a social analysis of Germany's immediate postwar period, starts by visually re-creating a typical scene around 1946 or 1947. We are introduced to a situation not unlike that after World War 1. We see a defeated
and devastated country: war widows, cities in ruins, starvation—and an
economy that once again had deteriorated into black marketeering and
bartering. The *Reichsmark* had become increasingly worthless. The actual valued currency between 1945 and 1948 was the cigarette. Fassbinder himself plays the role of the black marketeer who sells Maria a
black dress for cigarettes. In repeated close-up shots, the film captures
the magic power of a box of Camel cigarettes. Cigarettes brought into
circulation by the Allied forces were the yardstick of value in a society
whose financial system was once again defunct.

This situation changed drastically when the currency reform in the
Western Allied zones was enacted on June 20, 1948. The *Deutschmark*
was introduced and the worthless old *Reichsmark* was replaced at a rate
of 1 to 10. Each West German was allowed to exchange up to 400 *Reichsmark* and received in return 40 *Deutschmark*. Later an additional 200
Reichsmark could be converted into 20 *Deutschmark*. Within days,
stores were suddenly filled with goods, the black market quickly re-
ceded, and industrial productivity began to rise. For many West Germans, it was not the introduction of German constitutional law or the
establishment of the Federal Republic on May 23, 1949, that marked the
beginning of a new era, but the almost mythical event of the *Währungs-
reform*. For Germans living in the Russian-occupied zone, the currency
reform in the West was another visible sign of the further widening gap
between East and West.

The first half of the twentieth century left most Germans anxious and
fearful—fearful as a result of war, inflation, and political dictatorship,
but also fearful of themselves as a society that had participated in aggression and unspeakable crimes. Ironically, both West German democracy and East German Communism responded, in their respective ways,
to this deep longing for security. The extent to which a Stalinist regime
could relatively successfully take hold in East Germany for forty years
can be understood only if one takes into account how much this regime

catered to those who longed for, above all, some kind of economic stability. The centrally planned economy of the GDR, with its system of fixed prices for basic goods (that proved economically disastrous in the long run), responded to this longing. Just as no unemployment was supposed to exist in the GDR, so inflation was a phenomenon that supposedly had been solved once and for all in Communist East Germany.

In West Germany, the longing for security was equally well understood by all political forces that formed the Federal Republic after 1949. The concept of the *Soziale Marktwirtschaft,* of the "social market economy," provided a buffered form of capitalism. For almost forty years it delivered on its promise: economic development and middle-class prosperity, without the pains of much mobility, without rapid and unpredictable changes that could leave citizens in the cold. Economic and social changes were negotiated and controlled by large corporate institutions under the axiom of *sozialer Friede,* social peace: an immensely powerful state, accommodating both large labor unions and employers' associations who realized how existentially important a sense of security was for Germany's postwar society. Economic development was steered by a few powerful banks that were intimately connected to the industrial sector. Their overall attitude can be characterized as paternalistic; their mistrust of the new and yet unproved was considerable. Conservatism in all financial matters was pervasive throughout West German society during the postwar period. Although West Germany became one of the most passionate consumer societies, people remained eager to save. The fact that until recently only about 5 percent of Germans had money invested in the stock market has to be seen as the result of deep-seated mistrust of the workings of the financial markets. Even today, millions of Germans, especially of the older generation, continue to deposit their entire life savings in simple savings accounts—an attitude that has, of course, worked to the considerable advantage of banks. All of this cannot be adequately understood without the trauma of the German inflation of 1923. A new attitude toward investing as an individual choice and responsibility is, however, gradually emerging. Lately, Germans have begun to discover the stock market, and German banks are increasingly beginning to cater to a new sort of middle-class investor.

The inflation continued to reverberate, of course, most strongly in the monetary and fiscal policies of the Federal Republic. A cultural history of Germans' relationship to money has still to be written and would, I think, contribute much to an overall understanding of German postwar culture both in the East and West.[13] Serious inflationary pressure seemed to recur in the mid- and late 1970s as a result of the global oil crisis. Yet as in the United States, Germany has been spared any serious inflationary increases since the mid-1980s. As a result of its rigorous anti-inflationary course and its fiercely defended independence from political pressures, the Deutsche Bundesbank became probably the most highly regarded and trusted public institution in Germany.

The 1990s have brought drastic changes to Germany, not only as a result of the end of the cold war and German unification but also because the model of the Rheinische Republik that was widely shared by the main political forces seems to have come to an end, for reasons that include, but are not limited to, German unification. International competition and a quickly changing global financial market had considerable influence on contemporary German society. With regard to monetary policies the introduction of the new European currency, the Euro, is opening a new chapter in monetary and economic history. The newly established European Federal Reserve in Frankfurt protects this new currency against inflation as vigorously as the Bundesbank. Yet for many Germans this change still constitutes a huge leap of faith.

I am optimistic that European financial experts and politicians have learned from history. Most of them have become aware that a serious inflation is more than a short-lived economic crisis. As John Maynard Keynes noted, debauching a currency is a powerful means to overturn the existing basis of a whole society; and indeed, inflations have sometimes led to political revolutions. The example of the great German inflation teaches us that inflation affects the most valuable fabric that holds groups and societies together. It damages, even destroys, the trust we have in others and in our government. As Elias Canetti writes, trust that has been betrayed creates traumatic humiliation, a wound that rarely heals completely. Thus, fighting inflation means more than developing a set of economic policies; it means more than keeping financial markets stable. Fighting inflation always means first and foremost protecting the basic foundations on which our modern civil societies are built.

Notes

NOTES TO CHAPTER 1

1. For an assessment of *Sittengeschichte der Inflation* within the context of Hans Ostwald's work see Fritzsche, "Vagabond in the Fugitive City," 388.

2. T. Mann, "Inflation," 63. Translation from *Encounter* slightly altered.

3. See, for example, Holtfrerich, *German Inflation,* 332–33.

4. And, on a side note, his thinking in "millions" shows how easily inflation seems to infect the thoughts of those who reflect on the phenomenon.

5. The economic literature on inflation is obviously immense. See, for example, Trevithick, *Inflation;* Sargent, *Rational Expectations;* Hall, ed., *Inflation.*

6. See also Feldman, *Great Disorder,* 8–11.

7. For a summary of the book that places it into the larger economic and historical debates of inflation, see Theo Balderston's article "Gerald D. Feldman Analyzes the German Inflation."

8. For further information on *Simplicissimus,* its history, and political positions over time, see the exhibition catalogue *Simplicissimus: Eine satirische Zeitschrift München, 1896–1944.*

9. From his essay "Erfahrung und Armut," in *Gesammelte Schriften,* vol. 2, pt. 1, 214.

10. On other aspects of changes in time perception during war see Bernd Hüppauf's article "Der Erste Weltkrieg und die Destruktion der Zeit."

11. It should be noted, however, that there are obviously limits to the structural analogies between war and inflation. While the war experience was to a large degree an exclusively male experience, the inflation affected the entire population. The relationship between gender and inflation will be explored in more detail in chapter 8.

12. This is, for example, of central importance for the individual and collective memories of Holocaust survivors and raises crucial questions about how

to represent the Holocaust from the perspective of its victims. See Friedländer, ed., *Probing the Limits*.

13. See Eksteins, *Rites of Spring;* or Fussell, *Great War and Modern Memory*.

14. For a contemporary context see, for example, Erwin Loewy Hattendorf, *Krieg, Revolution, und Unfallneurosen;* or Sandor Ferenczi et al., *Zur Psychoanalyse der Kriegsneurosen.* Recent research on what is called today "traumatic stress disorder" concentrates mainly on Holocaust survivors and Vietnam veterans.

NOTES TO CHAPTER 2

1. Lester Thurow even argues that, within the context of the American economy, inflation has become an "extinct volcano" (185–93).

2. For this brief overview of different inflations throughout history I relied mostly on Richard Gaettens, *Geschichte der Inflationen.*

3. Gaettens quotes from the letters of Liselotte von der Pfalz to Gaugräfin Louise. The letters of von der Pfalz from December 3 and December 7, 1719, read in part:

> Es ist Etwass unbegreiffliches, wie Erschrecklich reichtum jetzt In frankreich ist. Man hört Von nichts alss millionen sprechen, ich begreiffe nichts In der welt Von der sach, wen Ich Von allen den reichtum höre, denck Ich dass der gott mamon jetzt Zu paris regirt. . . .
> Hir wirdt alles abscheülich thewer, alles doppelt wass Es auch sein mag, auss Engellandt schickt man alle demanten Juwellen undt bijoux her, alle die so Erschrecklich In den actionm gewonnen haben, Kauffen alles auff ohne handtlen noch marchandiren. (Gaettens 112)

4. For a financial analysis of the relationship between changing political circumstances and inflationary pressures, see Steven B. Webb, *Hyperinflation and Stabilization in Weimar Germany.*

5. The *Goldmark* contained .35 gram of gold (Tormin 111).

6. An insightful and concise overview of the situation of European economies during the interwar period is offered by Charles H. Feinstein, Peter Temin, and Gianni Toniolo in their book, *The European Economy between the Wars.* Regarding the impact of the inflation, see especially pp. 38–99.

7. Kroner's essay was published in *Berliner Illiustrirte Zeitung* on August 26, 1923. This translation by Don Reneau appears in Anton Kaes, Martin Jay, Edward Dimendberg, eds., *Weimar Republic Sourcebook,* 63.

8. The inflation was especially advantageous for foreigners because for most of the early 1920s the depreciation of the mark's exchange rate advanced faster than the rise of internal prices.

9. For a detailed analysis of costs of living during the inflation, see Niehuss, "Lebensweise und Familie in der Inflationszeit," 3–45.

10. In 1925 the Verein für Sozialpolitik published a wide-ranging analysis on the impact of inflation on Austrian economy, society, and culture. See Bunzel, ed., *Geldentwertung und Stabilisierung.*

11. I will concentrate my remarks on the Austrian postwar development. Through the treaty of Trianon (1920), the newly established Republic of Hungary

lost 67 percent of its former territory. As did Austria, Hungary had to fight internal political unrest and considerable inflation. For a detailed account see Horsman, *Inflation in the Twentieth Century,* 55–57.

12. See Paul Ufermann, *Könige der Inflation.*

NOTES TO CHAPTER 3

1. This chapter appeared in a earlier version, in German, in *Merkur: Deutsche Zeitschrift für europäisches Denken* 48, no. 11 (1994): 985–97.

2. On the astonishing boom of doctrines of salvation and spiritualist religions during the inflation, see Ulrich Linse, *Barfüßige Propheten.*

3. This distinction, expressed in French as that between *pudeur* and *honte,* can also be found in the ancient Greek terms *aidos* und *aischyne: aidos* is the demand for sexual modesty, expressed in, for example, the prohibition against displaying the genitals, which in German, not without reason, are also referred to as *die Scham. Aischyne,* in contrast, refers to disgrace, the shame incurred by an individual who has transgressed certain cultural norms; it arises through the disapproval of others. See Neckel, *Status und Scham,* 18–19.

4. It is noteworthy that Canetti's *Crowds and Power* finds one of its earliest receptions in Marshall McLuhan's *Understanding Media: The Extension of Man* (1964). McLuhan not only mentions Canetti's *Crowds and Power* at a time when the book was barely known, he also acknowledges the fundamental role of money in modern societies, comparing it to language:

> Language, like currency, acts as a store of perception and as a transmitter of the perceptions and experience of one person or of one generation to another. As both a translator and storehouse of experience, language is, in addition, a reducer and distorter of experience.... Money, like language a store of work and experience, acts also as translator and transmitter. Especially since the written word has advanced the separation of social functions, money is able to move away from its role as store of work.... As money separates itself from the commodity form and becomes a specialist agent of exchange (or translator of values), it moves with greater speed and in ever greater volume. (139–40)

5. For an analysis of Nietzsche's mass concept see Renate Reschke's article "'Pöbel-Mischmasch' oder vom notwendigen Niedergang aller Kultur," 14–42. For a general overview on the concept of masses see Bernd Widdig, *Männerbünde und Massen.*

6. In that respect one can read Fritz Lang's cinematic epos *Nibelungen,* with its centrality of the Nibelungenschatz, as a fitting reaction to the experience of the inflation.

7. Canetti, *Auto-da-fé,* 131–32. The text of the novel makes quite clear in another passage that Kien and Therese operate in different semiotic systems. Their argument about how exactly the money should be divided is an example: "'Und die 265 000?' sagte sie, auf jeder Zahl verweilend, mit deutlichen Blicken. Jetzt muß man sie rasch und endgültig erobern. 'Die zweihundertfünfundsechzigtausend gehören dir allein.' Über sein mageres Gesicht stülpte er einen fetten Gönner, er schenkte ihr was, den Dank nahm er schon vorher und gerne an" (147). In repeating the figure the text insists, once again, on the different systems in which

the sum of money is expressed: Therese speaks in numbers, Kien expresses the same sum in words.

8. See my discussion in *Männerbünde und Massen,* 197–204; see also El-friede Pöder's contribution "Spurensicherung," 57–72.

NOTES TO CHAPTER 4

1. For a brief history of usury and its condemnation see the chapter "Money Lending, the Church, and the Jew," in Angell, *Story of Money,* 179–99.

2. This becomes especially apparent in the correspondence with his father. See Mazlish, *Meaning of Karl Marx,* 49–53.

3. In his critique of money, the many ideas that influenced Marx's philoso-phy merge: his indebtedness to German idealist philosophy (not known for a par-ticularly sympathetic view of money), his studies of the British economy, but cer-tainly also his own struggle with his Jewish heritage that resulted in a vehement rejection, even hatred, of his own roots. This becomes especially apparent in his early essay *On the Jewish Question,* where he simply equates the "everyday Jew" with money: "What is the profane basis of Judaism? Practical need, self-interest. What is the worldly cult of the Jew? Huckstering. What is his worldly god? Money" (34).

4. A modern society with a functioning monetary system certainly does not guarantee freedom and justice, but the absence of money often indicates a sys-tem of totalitarianism and oppression. James Buchan gives a moving example of this in his account of the *Theresienstädter Kronen.* In a cynical attempt to de-ceive the public about the true conditions of concentration camps, the Nazis de-cided in the early 1940s to "beautify" the concentration camp Theresienstadt and give it a kind of small-town appearance. Shops were opened where the per-sonal items of those who had been killed were sold, and even a café was built. Yet the Nazis were well aware that this illusion of "normality" was not perfect without money. They decided to create a currency for the concentration camp Theresienstadt, the *Theresienstädter Kronen,* which inmates had to use for their purchases. The notes in different denominations displayed the signature by Jakob Edelstein, the Chief Elder, and showed Moses with the Ten Command-ments (Buchan 258). For several years, this money was handed out to the pris-oners and used within the confines of Theresienstadt, a strange reminder of life outside the barbed-wire fence for those who had to play their part in this cruel game of deception.

5. For a comprehensive introduction to this book see Gianfranco Poggi, *Money and the Modern Mind.*

6. For an insightful discussion of the role of trust and morality within dif-ferent monetary theories see S. Herbert Frankel, *Money.*

7. For an excellent discussion that contextualizes the tense relationships be-tween countryside and city see Martin Geyer, *Verkehrte Welt,* 217–70.

8. For a detailed analysis see Otto Pfleiderer, "Das Prinzip 'Mark = Mark' in der deutschen Inflation, 1914 bis 1924"; and Feldman, *Great Disorder,* 567–68.

9. During my archival research in Berlin, I had the chance to look at many photos in the daily newspapers of the early 1920s. In his *Sittengeschichte der*

Inflation, Hans Ostwald has collected some of these photos and other visual material. My visual examples remain necessarily selective, yet they express quite typical themes and arrangements.

10. It should be noted that Marshall McLuhan had already observed the link between the introduction of the zero and the introduction of the vanishing point in his *Understanding Media:* "The need was to have a sign for the gaps between numbers. It was not until the thirteenth century that *sifr,* the Arab word for 'gap' or 'empty,' was Latinized and added to our culture as 'cipher' *(ziphirum)* and finally became the Italian *zero.* Zero really meant a positional gap. It did not acquire the indispensable quality of 'infinity' until the rise of perspective and 'vanishing point' in Renaissance painting. The new visual space of Renaissance painting affected number as much as lineal writing had done centuries earlier" (115).

11. The philosopher and mathematician Gottfried Frege links the concept of nothing to the number zero as follows: "Since nothing falls under the concept 'not identical with itself,' I define nought as follows: o is the number which belongs to the concept 'not identical with itself' " (87).

12. The question of whether to restore the gold standard after World War 1 was hotly debated throughout the 1920s in Europe and had wide-reaching consequences for Europe's different economies, as Charles Feinstein, Peter Temin, and Gianni Toniolo point out (45–49). Germany restored the gold standard after the end of the inflation late in 1923.

13. See also in chapter 3 my interpretation of Canetti's novel *Auto-da-fé,* with its protagonist Therese Krumbholz, the "zero-loving" allegorical figure representing the inflation.

14. Those interested in deconstructivist readings will not have missed the many parallels between my discussion and Derrida's assessment of language as an unstable, ultimately self-referential system without any origin. I would like to refer those readers to Brian Rotman's wonderful analysis that accepts the deconstructivist invitation to "treat texts as interpretable results of writing, as if they were circulating money signs, and look at money signs as pieces of writing" (99). My own approach does not build on the theoretical premises of Derridian deconstruction, even though I fully agree that any reading of texts and cultural artifacts has to take into account the open-endedness of texts, their silences, denials, and problematic oppositions.

If we assume that there are parallels between language and money, that money functions to some degree like language, then the painful lessons that the inflation taught people are not that dissimilar from what Derrida tries to teach us about language and writing: that writing is by no means stable, that its value is fluid, that signs refer to other signs and not to any other, anterior object. In that sense, inflation itself acts as a giant deconstructivist force that lays bare all the illusions and volatile assumptions about a monetary system that we silently, be it forced or complacently, make in order to somehow communicate through money.

15. For a more extensive biography see Siegbert Wolf, *Silvio Gesell.*

16. Recently, a small group of contemporary enthusiasts has reprinted Gesell's extensive writings. See Silvio Gesell, *Gesammelte Werke.* For Gesell's place within other theories of moneyless societies see Hugo Godschalk, *Die geldlose Wirtschaft.*

17. The mix of a centrally planned economy with an obsessive demand for "information" for the sake of transparency under the banner of a participatory, "work-based" community in Otto's *Abschaffung des Geldes* invites reflection on certain parallels with the political and cultural realities of the former German Democratic Republic (GDR). As faulty as the economic system of the GDR was, it may have responded to people's emotional longing for control in economic matters that was deeply rooted in the inflation experience. I believe that the East German planned economy with its promise of an "orderly," planned, predictable economic process can in fact be seen as a residual response to the trauma of inflation.

Yet I see also another link that may be less apparent. The anxiety about losing control over economic matters resulted in the urge to centrally record all economic activity and establish a tight economic plan. In the wake of gathering such information, the boundaries between the public and the private would easily get blurred, as we can observe in Otto's case. What we may belittle in Otto's post-inflation, moneyless utopia as quite bizarre became actual, everyday practice in the GDR: the widespread gathering of decidedly personal information by the Staatssicherheit (Stasi). The scope of the Stasi activities was certainly beyond any reasonable grasp. How do we make sense of the fact that the GDR regime employed over a hundred thousand people who created about 6 million personal files over the years? It took about 110 miles of shelves to store these files (Jarausch 173). Can this kind of activity be sufficiently explained by the goal of protecting the state against "subversive elements"? (In that sense, the expansion of the Stasi archives is in itself an inflationary event.)

If we assume that the trauma of the inflation was reenacted in different forms, could we read the activities of the Stasi as such a reaction? In a way, these archives represent the negative form of a currency. McLuhan writes that money is a storehouse of communally achieved work, skill, and experience, and the Stasi files are exactly that—but in a terribly literal sense. Moving beyond the circulating, mediated, and anonymous characteristic of money, the Stasi files negate these qualities of money and yet at the same time comprise a symbolic form of replacement. While money, as I will explain later, is imbedded in a complex network of trust, the Stasi files are a chilling example of a system that knows no trust, that cannot bear anonymity. What continuously circulates in one system, ossifies in the other, is never meant to circulate, and gains its value precisely by noncirculation. In this context, the Stasi archives are an extreme reaction to the trauma-inducing inflationary banknote: the ultimate manifestation of control and power that negates all that is connected with an anonymous money economy. Western states may have been proud of their trading balances, money deposits, and the Bundesbank, but the GDR, whose real currency was not even internationally convertible, had its own treasure, its own dark Nibelungenschatz deep down in the infamous Stasi buildings in Berlin's Normannenstrasse.

18. For a comparison of the Soviet Five-Year Plans and the National Socialist Four-Year Plans see Peter Temin's article "Soviet and Nazi Economic Planning in the 1930's."

19. For an extended discussion of *The Decline of the West* within the context of the Conservative Revolution see Jeffrey Herf, *Reactionary Modernism,*

49–69. An overview of the Conservative Revolution is provided by Stefan Breuer, *Anatomie der Konservativen Revolution*.

20. The trader plays a significant role in other cultural ideologies of the time, most prominently as a figure for establishing differences between British and German cultures in Werner Sombart, *Händler und Helden*.

21. Spengler, *Decline of the West*, 2:5. It should be noted that while Spengler's concept of culture relies heavily on the "race-blood-soil" complex, Spengler did not use these terms as a legitimation of any conceived superiority of a white or even Aryan race (Felken 218).

NOTES TO CHAPTER 5

1. Noel Burch has undertaken an insightful interpretation of the opening scene that stresses the cinematographic innovations of *Dr. Mabuse, the Gambler*. See Burch, "Notes on Fritz Lang's First Mabuse," 4.

2. The notion of "unrestricted narcissism" invites us to interpret the figure of Dr. Mabuse in light of another essay by Freud. The triad of autocratic domination by one extraordinary individual, a form of "hypnosis" or suggestibility, and unconditional obedience by a group of followers is central to Freud's *Group Psychology and the Analysis of the Ego* (1922). Again, the thematic parallels between both texts are remarkable. Both situate an independent and socially autonomous leader figure against a passive mass that expresses both fear of and fascination for this leader. Both are concerned with hypnotic powers in which, according to Freud's theory, the hypnotist steps into the place of the ego: "The ego experiences in a dreamlike way whatever he may request" (114).

Group Psychology and the Analysis of the Ego offers an almost perfect description of Mabuse's character. Freud writes on the figure of the "primal father":

> The members of the group were subject to ties just as we see them today, but the father of the primal horde was free. His intellectual acts were strong and independent even in isolation, and his will needed no reinforcement from others. Consistency leads us to assume that his ego had few libidinal ties; he loved no one else but himself, or other people only in so far as they served his needs. To objects his ego gave away no more than was barely necessary.
>
> He, at the very beginning of the history of mankind, was the "superman" whom Nietzsche only expected from the future. (123)

3. Borrowing from the contemporary discourse of psychology and psychoanalysis, Lang presents all the paraphernalia and rituals that come with hypnosis: the crystal ball; the gaze of the hypnotist; the somnambulistic, dreamlike state of the hypnotized. He shows individuals being transformed into a state of total submission as well as a whole audience succumbing to an exercise in "mass suggestion." Yet in a strictly clinical sense, these "hypnotic" performances have little in common with the practice of actual hypnosis. To be successfully hypnotized, the person has to be cooperative and has to trust the hypnotist. While the audience of Dr. Mabuse, alias Sandor Weltmann, may be readily susceptible to hypnotic experiments, the protagonist usually forces his "hypnotic" powers on his victims against their will, often after lengthy battles of willpower. He "hypnotizes" people who cannot even see him.

4. Ufermann, *Könige der Inflation,* 10. Ufermann's choice to describe inflation as female is hardly arbitrary. It points to an overall tendency to feminize the otherwise abstract dynamics of inflation that I will investigate in chapter 8 of this study.

5. In Oscar Wilde's play *Lady Windermere's Fan,* Cecil Graham asks Lord Darlington, "What is a cynic?" And Darlington answers, "A man who knows the price of everything and the value of nothing."

6. For 1923, see *Archiv für Kriminologie* 79 (1926): 75. For 1924, see *Statistisches Jahrbuch für das Deutsche Reich* (1926): 439. For 1925, see *Statistisches Jahrbuch für das Deutsche Reich* (1927): 491. Quoted in Kreudener, "Entstehung des Inflationstraumas," 272.

7. Paul Lafargue, "Die Ursachen des Gottesglaubens," in *Die neue Zeit* Stuttgart, 1906. Quoted in Benjamin, *Passagenwerk,* in *Gesammelte Schriften,* vol. 5, pt. 1, 621.

8. Benjamin, *Passagenwerk,* in *Gesammelte Schriften,* vol. 5, pt. 1, 617.

NOTES TO CHAPTER 6

1. For detailed information about the relationship between the German coal and steel industry and their personalities see Gerald D. Feldman, *Iron and Steel in the German Inflation,* 3–49.

2. For a stimulating discussion of Jünger's *Der Arbeiter* and the notion of work in our contemporary context see Rainer Hank, *Arbeit—Die Religion des 20. Jahrhunderts,* 87–105.

3. National Socialism vigorously used this phantasm and stressed its underlying anti-Semitic content. In a 1937 speech Reichsarbeitsführer Hierl proclaimed, "Our work camps are fortresses against the Jewish-materialistic concept of work that sees work simply as a money business *[Geldgeschäft]* in which work is a commodity." Quoted in Conze, "Arbeit," 1:214.

4. Erich Reger's documentary novel about the coal and steel industry in the Ruhr region, *Union der festen Hand* (1931), portrays Stinnes in the person of Ottokar Wirtz; and Elisabeth Langgässer's novella *Merkur* narrates the life of an industrialist during the 1920s who also bears strong resemblance to Stinnes. For an overview of literary works that thematize inflation written during the Weimar Republic see Gerald Feldman, "Weimar Writers and the German Inflation," 173–83.

5. See Elke Emrich, "Heinrich Manns Novelle *Kobes,* oder die 'bis ans logische Ende' geführte deutsche Geistesgeschichte," 155–67.

6. H. Mann, *Kobes,* 276. This misogynist scheme also underlies the narrative of Heinrich Mann's first successful novel, *Im Schlaraffenland* (1900).

7. The widespread enthusiasm for Taylorism in Germany in the 1920s has to be seen within the larger context of Fordism and its promise to once and for all overcome the division between work and capital by greatly expanding industrial output. Yet Taylorism, with its minute planning of the worker's every move and task, with its vision of predictability, order, and rhythmic movement, can also be seen as the complete opposite of the inflationary dynamic.

8. By stressing these totalitarian aspects, *Gott Stinnes* could also be read as

an early forerunner of Ernst Jünger's reactionary utopia in *Der Arbeiter,* which I outlined earlier.

9. For an illuminating discussion about the relationship between patriarchy and the exchange value of women, see Luce Irigaray's essay "Women on the Market" in her collection *This Sex Which Is Not One.*

10. See the extensive discussion on gender and inflation in chapter 8.

11. In addition, the flood scenes invite a reading that focuses on the link between male anxiety and the feminized image of masses and floods. Both Klaus Theweleit, in his ground-breaking work *Male Fantasies,* and I have written extensively on this topic.

NOTES TO CHAPTER 7

1. *Disorder and Early Sorrow,* Thomas Mann's first work after finishing *The Magic Mountain,* was written during April 1925, and appeared in *Die Neue Rundschau* in June 1925. For insightful information on the story's context within the works of Thomas Mann, as well as on its reception, see Hans Rudolf Vaget, *Thomas Mann-Kommentar zu sämtlichen Erzählungen,* 210–19.

2. In his 1926 commentary to *Disorder and Early Sorrow* in *Der Bücherwurm,* Thomas Mann defended his realist writing and encouraged his readers to find out for themselves whether his own "untimely theory," "that only the precise and thorough provides real entertainment," still holds true (622).

3. *Disorder and Early Sorrow* obviously contains a strong autobiographical dimension. Four of Mann's six children stood as models for the Cornelius family: Klaus (Bert), Erika (Ingrid), Michael (Beisser), and Elisabeth (Ellie). The figure of the actor Iwan Herzl refers to Klaus and Erika's friend Bert Fischl. Klaus Mann, as Herbert Lehnert and others report, was not flattered by the portrait (256).

Wolfgang Frühwald relates his remarks on the novella to the larger family drama of the Mann family and points out that the harmonious atmosphere in this story stood in stark contrast with the climate of alienation and hidden generational conflicts of the Mann family (56).

4. One has to be careful not to conflate the third-person narrative with the protagonist's view, as Werner Hoffmeister points out (166). In addition, the autobiographical traits of the story have led some scholars to interpret Cornelius as a direct voice of the author. Hoffmeister is right to not only highlight the narrator's ironic and critical comments to the protagonist but also to relate *Disorder and Early Sorrow* to Mann's growing support and commitment to the Weimar Republic.

5. For more information on the so-called Vellon inflation in Spain between 1599 and 1660 see Gaettens, *Geschichte der Inflationen,* 52–73.

6. Mann, *Disorder and Early Sorrow,* 146. Cornelius continues his reflection: "There is something ulterior about it, in the nature of it; that something is hostility, hostility against the history of today, which is still in the making and thus not history at all, in behalf of the genuine history that has already happened— that is to say, death. Yes, passing strange though all this is, yet it is true; true in a sense, that is. His devotion to this priceless little morsel of life and new growth has something to do with death, it clings to death as against life; and that is nei-

ther right nor beautiful—in a sense" (ibid.). This passage, as Herbert Lehnert points out in his interpretation, refers to a philosophical theme that pervades most of Mann's oeuvre: the relationship between love, experience, beauty, and death. Most directly, the passage relates to *The Magic Mountain,* which Mann had just finished (243–45).

7. See especially his essay "Vom Nutzen und Nachteil der Historie für das Leben," in *Unzeitgemässe Betrachtungen II: Vom Nutzen und Nachteil der Historie für das Leben,* 1:243–334.

8. See also Bolkosky, "Thomas Mann's 'Disorder and Early Sorrow,'" 229–30. This interpretation offers some insights, yet lacks any sensibility of Mann's ironic gestures.

9. Scholars such as Konrad Jarausch and Jürgen Kocka problematize the limits of these terminologies. See Jarausch, "Die Not der Geistigen Arbeiter," 281–82; on the notion of *Bildungsbürger* see Kocka and Conze, eds., *Bildungsbürgertum im 19. Jahrhundert,* 1:9–20.

10. Kaes, "Ökonomische Dimension," 309–10. The economic situation during the early 1920s led to a heated debate between authors and publishers. A polemic by Herbert Eulenberg (1876–1949) in *Die Weltbühne* on January 10, 1924, in particular caused a lot of uproar. Eulenberg accused the publishers of having shamelessly exploited the authors during the inflation. Prominent publishers such as Gustav Kiepenheuer, Kurt Wolff, and Victor Goldschmidt rejected these accusations and tried to defend their position. See Schumacher, "Autoren und Verleger in der Inflationszeit," 88–94; and Wittmann, *Geschichte des deutschen Buchhandels,* 315–19.

11. For the most detailed account of how different groups of intellectuals were affected during the inflation see Feldman, *Great Disorder,* 527–55.

12. Among members of the German academia, the *Privatdozenten,* young professors who had not yet been appointed to a regular position and who were teaching more or less part-time, had to endure the harshest economic conditions. Their fate was far removed from Professor Cornelius's situation. Schreiber writes about a survey done among *Privatdozenten* at the University of Göttingen, many of whom reported starvation and chronic diseases among their children due to malnutrition (42).

13. We find the same argument in Simmel's *Philosophy of Money.* Simmel reflects on the deep animosity that most religions harbor against money. He explains this phenomenon by arguing that the power of money as the ultimate means can replace any end and can become a means by itself, thus replacing any transcendental dimension in life (228–38).

For the reversal of "means" and "ends" as a characteristic of prostitution see chapter 8.

14. In my brief introduction of Bourdieu's work, I mostly rely on Randal Johnson's excellent introduction to Bourdieu's *The Field of Cultural Production.*

15. Ibid. Symbolic capital is closely related to cultural capital and refers to the degree "of accumulated prestige, celebrity, consecration or honor and is founded on a dialectic of knowledge *[connaissance]* and recognition *[reconnaissance]*" (7).

16. Even the German court system took for granted that intellectual work was paired with other sources of income from capital or real estate. Schreiber writes,

"Even today the Reichsgericht is of the opinion that intellectual work is primarily not done to earn money [nicht um des Geldverdienens geschieht]" (109).

17. The dichotomy between American "materialism" and the German "pursuit of higher values" is a subtheme that accompanies the discussion about the role of the intellectual. Georg Schreiber in his survey *Die Not der deutschen Wissenschaft und der geistigen Arbeiter,* for example, writes, "The intellectual worker is the administrator and producer of the intellectual capital [geistiges Kapital]. . . . It has always been an advantage of German intellectual work that in contrast to the American and Asian intellectual life it could boast with intellectual billionaires [Milliardäre des Geistes]—even now despite the fact that these billionaires have become economically part of the proletariat" (110).

18. The concept of a *freischwebende Intelligenz,* of intellectuals whose status positions them above particular class interests and who, therefore, can address a social totality and act as mediators between differing social interests, is central to the cultural sociology of Karl Mannheim in his *Ideologie und Utopie* of 1929.

19. See especially Siegfried Kracauer's essay "Kult der Zerstreuung," 311–17.

NOTES TO CHAPTER 8

1. For an insightful analysis of the emergence of a consumer culture see Rosalind Williams's book *Dream Worlds.*

2. The anthology *Women in the Metropolis,* edited by Katharina von Ankum, analyzes many aspects of women's often ambivalent position in this new urban culture.

3. When Freud's psychoanalysis emerged around the turn of the century, it represented in many respects the battleground on which these two visions of modernity met, the one of work and production, the other of desires and consumption. Psychoanalysis provided a range of new heuristic concepts and a vocabulary that linked the internal world of desires and sexuality to social behavior and a modern identity. Equally important, Freud offered scenarios of compromise and proposed strategies of how to counterbalance the forces of desire and repression.

4. There are other examples of such coding throughout this book. Probably most striking is the illustration "Looted Germania" in chapter 3, which I interpret in connection with the topic of shame. It depicts an emaciated woman covering her sex with paper money.

5. It is interesting how the visual representation of the inflation misery differs from the portrayal of the depression in photographs from the early 1930s that were taken in Germany and elsewhere, which usually show lines of unemployed men. I owe this observation to Lisa Schumann.

6. Otto Friedrich's popular historical recollection, *Before the Deluge,* includes an illuminating memory of a middle-class woman that illustrates how the inflation affected women with respect to marriage and class background. The woman recounts:

> There was not a single girl in the entire German middle class who could get *married* without her father paying a dowry. Even the maids—they never spent a penny of their wages. They saved and saved so that they could get married. When the money became

worthless, it destroyed the whole system for getting married, and so it destroyed the whole idea of remaining chaste until marriage.

The rich had never lived up to their own standards, of course, and the poor had different standards anyway, but the middle class, by and large, obeyed the rules. Not every girl was a virgin when she was married, but it was generally accepted that one *should* be. But what happened from the inflation was that the girls learned that virginity didn't matter any more. The women were liberated. (Friedrich 120)

7. Renate Bridenthal and Claudia Coonz report, "In 1925 there were 32,2 million women and 30,2 million men, or 1072 women to 1000 men" (Bridenthal, Grossmann, and Kaplan 45).

8. See here especially Kristine von Soden and Maruta Schmidt, eds., *Neue Frauen.*

9. Frevert, *Women in German History,* 177. Frevert notes the following developments in the structure of the female workforce (334):

	1907 (%)	1925 (%)	1933 (%)
"Assisting Relatives"	35.2	36.0	36.1
Servants and Domestic Staff	16.1	11.4	10.5
Blue-Collar: Trade/Industry	18.3	23.0	22.9
Blue-Collar: Agriculture	14.5	9.2	7.5
White-Collar and Public Official	6.5	12.6	14.8
Self-Employed	9.2	7.7	8.0

10. See Bram Dijkstra's important book *Idols of Perversity.* For a further discussion of male anxieties and modernity, see Klaus Theweleit, *Male Fantasies;* and my own work *Männerbünde und Massen.*

11. See, for example, Thomas Mann, "Erinnerungen aus der deutschen Inflation," 187–88; or Elias Canetti, who in his *Torch in My Ear* evokes a steaming and bubbling witches' cauldron as a description of the cultural atmosphere during the inflation (52).

12. See especially Helmut Brackert, "Unglückliche, was hast du gehofft?" 131–87.

13. Claudia Honegger explores the interplay between social structural changes, the legitimation crisis of the church, and the role of women in the late medieval period in her anthology, *Die Hexen der Neuzeit,* especially 21–151.

14. The medieval myth made its way into canonical literature through the famous *Walpurgisnacht* scene in Goethe's *Faust, Part I.* Mephistopheles leads Faust to a witches' Sabbat on the Brocken (Bocksberg), the highest elevation in the Harz Mountains, where Faust is exposed to a Dionysian scenario. Alan Lareau informed me that during the height of the inflation in 1922, Walther Uering wrote a popular cabaret piece entitled "The Bocksberg Song," equating the turbulent times with the witches' Sabbat on the Bocksberg.

15. Lancre, *Tableau de l'Inconstance,* 119. The French original reads, "Le sabbat est comme une foire de marchands mêlés, furiuex et transportés, qui arrivent de toutes parts. Un rencontre et mélange de cent mille sujets soudains et transitoires, nouveaux à la vérité, mais d'une nouueauté effroyable qui offense l'œil, et soulève le cœur. Parmi ces mêmes sujets, il s'en voit de réel, et d'autres

prestigieux et illusoires: aucuns plaisants (mais fort peu). . . . Les autres dé-
plaisants, pleins de difformités et d'horreur, ne tendant qu'à dissolution, privation, ruine et destruction. Où les personnes s'y abbrutissent et transforment en
bêtes, perdant la parole tant qu'elles sont ainsi" (ibid.).

16. Not surprisingly, in all the material about the inflation I studied, I have
found not a single female profiteer. While there were most certainly a few women
who profited from the inflation, they were neither represented nor mentioned in
contemporary accounts.

17. The older man with one (or more) beautiful young women is a male fantasy that is obviously older than inflation and continues to be in the center of the
imaginary world of *Playboy* and other heterosexual men's magazines.

18. The notion of luxury itself is almost inconceivable without a strongly
gendered context: it is overwhelmingly feminine. This may be a reason why fascist cultural aesthetics, with its obsessive vision of masculinity, has such a non-
relationship to luxury. Is there something like a fascist vision of luxury at all?
The same accounts in part for Stalinist aesthetics.

19. Not surprisingly, Eduard Fuchs in his *Die Frau in der Karikatur* (1928)
talks about a "witches' Sabbat of modern prostitution" that rages through all
classes of German society (422).

20. Among the extensive literature, see, for example, regarding Munich, Sy-
bille Krafft, *Zucht und Unzucht;* regarding Berlin, Hans Ostwald, *Das Berliner
Dirnentum,* or more recently, Reingard Jäkl, *Vergnügungsgewerbe rund um den
Bülowbogen.*

21. See especially Charles Bernheimer, *Figures of Ill Repute,* 8–33.

22. Prostitution remains of central concern for feminist research and has
produced a wide range of academic positions on the subject, as Shannon Bell, in
her book *Reading, Writing, and Rewriting the Prostitute Body,* points out.

For example, Carole Pateman in her *Sexual Contract* critiques liberal social
contract theory and pays special attention to the inequality of the "sexual contract" between the client and the prostitute. Pateman's critique is directed at a
position adopted by some feminists that prostitution is like any other form of
work; in this case the prostitute is selling a sexual service.

On the other hand, this contractual view is vehemently rejected by Catharine
MacKinnon, one of the leading voices in the American antipornography movement. For MacKinnon prostitution is a central metaphor for the fact that "female
sexuality is entirely constructed as an object of male desire." In MacKinnon's
view the prostitute has no agency and therefore no control in her commercial
sexual encounters (Bell 80).

Luce Irigaray, in her essay "Women on the Market," rereads Marx's theory
of commodification and exchange. She constructs three positions for women
within a system of exchange that is controlled by male desire and agency: mother,
virgin, and prostitute: "The mother is pure use value, the virgin pure exchange
value, the prostitute both" (quoted in Bell 90). Irigaray also writes, "In her [the
prostitute's] case, the qualities of woman's body are 'useful.' However, these
qualities have 'value' only because they have been appropriated by a man, and
because they serve as the locus of relations—hidden ones—between men. Prostitution amounts to *usage that is exchanged*" (Irigaray 186).

Finally, Shannon Bell emphasizes a new strain of feminist theory that emerged with postmodernist sensibilities toward marginality and multiplicity as exemplified in the works of Gayle Rubin. Contrary to Catharine MacKinnon's position, the prostitute appears here as a figure with an active voice, as one possible agent within a "pluralist sexual ethics." Bell summarizes: "Rubin writes the prostitute as a sexual minority like the homosexual and prostitution as a dissident sexuality like homosexuality. . . . It is from this constructed position as an outcast group that prostitutes began to construct their own identity" (95).

23. From Marx's "Economic and Philosophical Manuscripts," in *Early Writings,* 156.

24. Walter Benjamin also reflects on the role of money and prostitution. In *Passagenwerk* we find a wonderful quote that relates money not so much to the prostitute but rather to the psychological condition of the client. Benjamin mentions the "dialectical function of money in prostitution that buys desire and at the same time is an expression of shame," and continues: "For sure, the sex of a whore is for sale. But not the shame of her customer. For this quarter of an hour, shame seeks a hiding place and finds a most ingenious one in money itself. . . . The blushing wound on the body of society discharges money and heals. It covers itself with a metallic scab" (614–15).

25. Rita Felski's essay "On Nostalgia: The Prehistoric Woman" in her book *The Gender of Modernity* gives an astute account of Simmel's view of women and modern culture. She detects a "yearning for the feminine as emblematic of a nonalienated, nonfragmented identity" in his work (37). This yearning associates women, on the one hand, both with nostalgia and a position that stands outside modern developments. On the other hand, Simmel views women as a site of resistance, a utopian space. "Homogenous and whole, woman is presented in Simmel's text as serenely free of alienation and contradiction, as the very opposite of a split subject" (48).

For a further discussion of women and femininity within Simmel's sociology see Guy Oakes, "Problem of Women in Simmel's Theory of Culture."

26. See especially my comments on this subject in chapter 7.

27. Hugo Bettauer was well known in Vienna for uncovering several scandals. Being Jewish and advocating sexual liberation made him a target for right-wing extremists. On March 10, 1925, a Nazi sympathizer by the name of Otto Rothstock shot Bettauer point-blank and killed him. See Noveck, "1925: Hugo Bettauer's Assassination," 440–47.

28. In her article on *Joyless Street,* Tracy Myers contextualizes the film within the Austrian postwar society. She quotes a film review contemporary with the film that captures how strongly it resonated with the culture of inflation during the early 1920s. The social-democratic *Vorwärts* described the film as a "a breathtaking portrait of the inflationary period sweeping through Vienna like a devastating torrid wind. We still stand too close to these events, and have experienced them too much in our own bodies, to be able to face them yet with appropriate distance; we are still whipped into fury by the contents of the film, still roused to deep compassion for the countless victims of this pestilence that gnawed at humanity's physical and moral health, still shake our fists at the shameless ex-

ploiters of this crisis and the impudent lechers who everywhere captured their prey" (43–44).

29. Petro, *Joyless Streets*, 201. Petro cites a 1926 report of the German Film Censorship Board that stresses the potential "danger" of female spectator identification as a result of the film's strong melodramatic gesture. The report warns, "The essential content of the film consists of showing how Viennese girls are forced to sell their honor and to earn their bread in brothels as a result of need and the misery of inflation. . . . Through this forced situation, in which the girls are brought without exception into depravity, the impression must emerge that the girl's action is the necessary consequence of misery and need. This must have a demoralizing effect on the female viewer" (213–15).

30. To some degree, Frau Greifer fulfills the cliché of modern-day "witch" in her capacity of organizing regular "orgies" that defy all bourgeois morality.

NOTES TO CHAPTER 9

1. For an overview of the German economy during the mid-1920s see Detlev Peukert, *Weimar Republic*, 118–28; or, within the European context, Charles Feinstein, Peter Temin, and Gianni Toniolo, *European Economy between the Wars*, 54–145.

2. Peukert, *Weimar Republic*, 251–52. There is much debate among economic historians about how much the restrictive fiscal policies of the German government under Chancellor Brüning contributed to the economic disaster of the early 1930s. Germany had abandoned the gold standard in July–August of 1931, yet Brüning insisted on tight monetary policies that contracted the German economy even further. To preserve the value of the mark, he risked steadily rising unemployment that would soon destroy the German democratic system (Feinstein, Temin, and Toniolo 110). I argue that Brüning's counterintuitive deflationary policy of the early 1930s can be sufficiently understood only within the context of the inflation of the early 1920s.

For more information, see also Knut Borchardt, "Das Gewicht der Inflationsangst in den wirtschaftspolitischen Entscheidungsprozessen während der Weltwirtschaftskrise," 233–60.

3. For Gottfried Feder's fascist ideology see his 1933 book *Der deutsche Staat auf nationaler and sozialer Grundlage*.

4. Barkai notes that the Nazis were pragmatic enough never to actually pursue the abolition of interest (24). When the Nazis came to power, Feder's influence on National Socialist economic policy had already declined considerably (26).

5. Reading Carl Schmitt's political philosophy, with its central notions of *Entscheidung* (decision) and the *Ausnahmezustand* (state of emergency), within the context of the inflation could bear interesting results. The heroization of an authoritarian leader who makes a drastic decision and disregards legal limits can easily grow out of the culture of inflation. Dr. Mabuse could be seen as a fictional example.

6. See, for example, Otto Bangert, *Gold oder Blut*.

7. Klemperer gives several examples of the Nazis' use of big numbers. He

notes, "It was astonishing, how shamelessly short-lived the lies behind these numbers were. . . . In September of 1941 the army reported that 200.000 enemy soldiers were encircled in Kiew. A few days later it was reported that 600.000 prisoners were captured in this action—probably all of the civilian population was counted as soldiers" (*LTI* 278).

8. It is interesting to reflect in this context on the verb "decimate," which links the number ten to eradication. According to the *Oxford English Dictionary*, the verb "decimate" meant originally "to select by lot and put to death one in every ten of [a body of soldiers guilty of mutiny or other crime]." Later, this meaning expanded to today's use signifying to kill large numbers.

9. The concept of "repetition compulsion" is central to Freud's theory of trauma that he develops in *Beyond the Pleasure Principle*. A psychoanalytic reading of Canetti's explanation of the Holocaust could certainly be insightful. I am not pursuing such a reading in this epilogue, partly because the complexity and vagueness of Freud's term would require a more extensive discussion than I can give here. In addition, the fact that Elias Canetti wrote *Crowds and Power* specifically to oppose both psychoanalytic theory and Freud would have to be addressed in such a reading.

10. As one example of many anti-Semitic works that link the inflation directly to Jewish financial business, see Alois Dallmayr, *Der große Raubzug*.

11. For insightful discussions of anti-Semitic images and concepts, see, for example, Sander Gilman, *Jew's Body;* and Julius H. Schoeps and Joachim Schlör, eds., *Antisemitismus*.

12. Probably the most moving and precise testimony that documents in minute detail the often minor yet vicious discriminations against Jews, such as the prohibitions against their having pets or visiting libraries, is Victor Klemperer's diary *Ich Will Zeugnis Ablegen bis zum Letzten*.

13. Within the field of German literature, the inflation became the subject of two middle-brow novels that were both written during the 1930s and that gained wide readership throughout Germany's postwar years: Hans Fallada's *Wolf unter Wölfen* (1937) and Erich Maria Remarque's *Der schwarze Obelisk*. Remarque had fled Germany in 1933 and published his novel in exile in 1938. Both novels offer panoramic views of German society during the early 1920s and recount typical situations during the inflation: the social decline and humiliation of the *Bürgertum,* and the actions of clever speculators. Both of them conventional in plot and character development, they reinforced a widely shared collective memory of the inflation and gave their readership a strong sense of experiencing it "just as it happened."

Bibliography

Abelshauser, Werner. "Inflation und Stabilisierung: Zum Problem ihrer makro-ökonomischen Auswirkungen auf die Rekonstruktion der deutschen Wirtschaft nach dem Ersten Weltkrieg." In *Historische Prozesse der deutschen Inflation 1914 bis 1924: Ein Tagungsbericht*, ed. Otto Büsch and Gerald D. Feldman, 161–74. Berlin: Colloqium Verlag, 1978.

————, ed. *Die Weimarer Republik als Wohlfahrtsstaat: Zum Verhältnis von Wirtschafts- und Sozialpolitik in der Industriegesellschaft. Vierteljahresschrift für Sozial- und Wirtschaftsgeschichte.* Beihefte, ed. Werner Conze et al., vol. 81. Stuttgart: Franz Steiner Verlag, 1987.

Abelshauser, Werner, et al., eds. *Deutsche Sozialgeschichte, 1914–1945: Ein historisches Lesebuch.* München: C. H. Beck Verlag, 1986.

Achberger, Friedrich. "Die Inflation und die zeitgenössische Literatur." In *Aufbruch und Untergang: Österreichische Literatur zwischen 1918 und 1938,* ed. Franz Kardnoska, 29–42. Wien: Europaverlag, 1981.

Angell, Norman. *The Story of Money.* New York: Garden City Publishing, 1929.

Ankum, Katharina von, ed. *Women in the Metropolis: Gender and Modernity in Weimar Culture.* Berkeley and Los Angeles: University of California Press, 1997.

Anz, Thomas, and Michael Stark, eds. *Expressionismus: Manifeste und Dokumente zur deutschen Literatur, 1910–1920.* Stuttgart: Metzler Verlag, 1982.

Aristotle. *The Politics.* Ed. Stephen Everson. Cambridge: Cambridge University Press, 1988.

Asendorf, Christoph. *Batteries of Life: On the History of Things and Their Perception in Modernity.* Trans. Don Reneau. Berkeley and Los Angeles: University of California Press, 1993.

Aulhorn, Edith. "Thomas Manns neueste Novelle 'Unordnung und frühes Leid.'" *Zeitschrift für Deutschkunde* 42 (1928): 253–60.

Bajohr, Frank, ed. *Zivilisation und Barbarei: Die widersprüchlichen Potentiale der Moderne.* Hamburg: Christians, 1991.

Balázs, Béla. *Schriften zum Film.* Ed. Helmut H. Diederichs, Wolfgang Gersch, and Magda Nagy. 2 vols. München: Hanser Verlag, 1982.

Balderston, Theo. "Gerald D. Feldman Analyzes the German Inflation." *Central European History* 27, no. 2 (1994): 205–17.

Bangert, Otto. *Gold oder Blut: Wege der Wiedergeburt aus dem Chaos.* München: Verlag Franz Eher Nachfahren, 1930.

Barkai, Avraham. *Nazi Economics: Ideology, Theory, and Policy.* Trans. Ruth Hadass-Vashitz. New Haven: Yale University Press, 1990.

Barnouw, Dagmar. *Weimar Intellectuals and the Threat of Modernity.* Bloomington: Indiana University Press, 1988.

Basler, Otto. "Amerikanismus: Geschichte eines Schlagwortes." *Deutsche Rundschau* 224 (August 1930): 142–46.

Beck, Ulrich. *Die Erfindung des Politischen: Zu einer Theorie reflexiver Modernisierung.* Frankfurt am Main: Suhrkamp Verlag, 1993.

Becker, Gabriele, et al. *Aus der Zeit der Verzweiflung: Zur Genese und Aktualität des Hexenbildes.* Frankfurt: Suhrkamp Verlag, 1977.

Behn, Fritz. "Amerikanismus in Deutschland." *Süddeutsche Monatshefte* 27 (June 1919): 672–74.

Bell, Shannon. *Reading, Writing, and Rewriting the Prostitute Body.* Bloomington: Indiana University Press, 1994.

Benjamin, Walter. *Gesammelte Schriften.* Ed. Rolf Tiedemann and Hermann Schweppenhäuser. Frankfurt am Main: Suhrkamp Verlag, 1991.

———. *One-Way Street and Other Writings.* Trans. Edmund Jephcott. New York: Harcourt, Brace, and Jovanovich, 1978.

———. "The Work of Art in the Age of Mechanical Reproduction." In *Illuminations,* ed. Hannah Arendt, trans. Harry Zohn. New York: Schocken, 1969.

———. "Zentralpark." In *Gesammelte Schriften,* ed. Rolf Tiedemann and Hermann Schweppenhäuser. Vol. 1, pt. 2. Frankfurt am Main: Suhrkamp Verlag, 1991.

Benz, Wolfgang, and Hermann Graml, eds. *Biographisches Lexikon zur Weimarer Republik.* München: C. H. Beck Verlag, 1988.

Berg, Peter. *Deutschland und Amerika, 1918–1929: Über das Amerikabild der zwanziger Jahre.* Lübeck-Hamburg: Matthiesen Verlag, 1963.

Bergmann, Klaus. *Agrarromantik und Großstadtfeindschaft.* Meisenheim am Glan: Hain, 1970.

Berking, Helmuth. *Masse und Geist: Studien zur Soziologie in der Weimarer Republik.* Berlin: Wissenschaftlicher Autoren-Verlag, 1984.

———. *Moderner Antisemitismus in Deutschland.* Frankfurt am Main: Suhrkamp Verlag, 1988.

Berle, Waltraud. *Heinrich Mann und die Weimarer Republik: Zur Entwicklung eines politischen Schriftstellers in Deutschland.* Bonn: Bouvier Verlag, 1983.

Berman, Russell A. *Cultural Studies of Modern Germany: History, Representation, and Nationhood.* Madison: University of Wisconsin Press, 1993.

Bernheimer, Charles. *Figures of Ill Repute: Representing Prostitution in Nineteenth-Century France.* Cambridge: Harvard University Press, 1989.

Bessel, Richard, and E. J. Feuchtwanger, eds. *Social Change and Political Development in Weimar Germany.* London: Croom Helm, 1981.

Bettauer, Hugo. *Die Freudlose Gasse: Ein Wiener Roman aus unseren Tagen.* Vol. 3 of *Gesammelte Werke.* Salzburg: Hannibal Verlag, 1980.

———. *Die Stadt ohne Juden: Ein Roman von Übermorgen.* Vol. 4 of *Gesammelte Werke.* Salzburg: Hannibal Verlag, 1980.

Beutter, Friedrich. *Zur sittlichen Beurteilung von Inflationen: Grundsätze und Massstäbe.* Freiburger Theologische Studien, Vol. 83. Freiburg: Herder Verlag, 1965.

Beyfuss, Edgar, and A. Kossowsky, eds. *Das Kulturfilmbuch.* Berlin: Carl Chryselius'scher Verlag, 1924.

Bialas, Wolfgang, and Georg Iggers, eds. *Intellektuelle in der Weimarer Republik.* Frankfurt am Main: Peter Lang Verlag, 1996.

Biro, Matthew. "Figures of Technology in Weimar Visual Culture." *New German Critique* 62 (1994): 71–110.

Blackbourn, David. "The Mittelstand in German Society and Politics." *Social History* 4 (1977): 409–33.

Blaich, Fritz. *Der Schwarze Freitag: Inflation und Wirtschaftskrise.* München: Deutscher Taschenbuch Verlag, 1985.

Bloch, Ernst. *Erbschaft dieser Zeit.* Frankfurt am Main: Suhrkamp Verlag, 1985.

Boberg, Jochen, et al., eds. *Die Metropole: Industriekultur in Berlin im 20. Jahrhundert.* München: C. H. Beck Verlag, 1986.

Bogdanovich, Peter. *Fritz Lang in America.* New York: Praeger Publishers, 1967.

Bolkosky, Sidney. "Thomas Mann's 'Disorder and Early Sorrow': The Writer as Social Critic." *Contemporary Literature* 22, no. 2 (1981): 218–33.

Bonn, Moritz J. *Geld und Geist: Vom Wesen und Werden der amerikanischen Welt.* Berlin: S. Fischer, 1927.

———. *Das Schicksal des deutschen Kapitalismus: Neue erweiterte Ausgabe.* Berlin: S. Fischer, 1930.

Bookbinder, Paul. *Weimar Germany: The Republic of the Reasonable.* Manchester: Manchester University Press, 1996.

Borchardt, Knut. "Das Gewicht der Inflationsangst in den wirtschaftspolitischen Entscheidungsprozessen während der Weltwirtschaftskrise." In *Die Nachwirkungen der Inflation auf die deutsche Geschichte, 1924–1933,* ed. Gerald Feldman, 233–60. München: Oldenbourg, 1985.

———. *Strukturwirkungen des Inflationsprozesses.* Sonderschrift des IFO-Instituts für Wirtschaftsforschung 38. Berlin: Duncker und Humblot, 1972.

Borneman, Ernest, ed. *Psychoanalyse des Geldes: Eine kritische Untersuchung psychoanalytischer Geldtheorien.* Frankfurt am Main: Suhrkamp Verlag, 1973.

Böß, Gustav. *Die Not in Berlin: Tatsachen und Zahlen.* Berlin: n.p., 1923.

Bourdieu, Pierre. *Distinction: A Social Critique of the Judgement of Taste.* Trans. Richard Nice. Cambridge: Harvard University Press, 1984.

———. *The Field of Cultural Production: Essays on Art and Literature.* Ed. Randal Johnson. Oxford: Polity Press, 1993.

Brackert, Helmut: "'Unglückliche, was hast du gehofft?' Zu den Hexenbüchern des 15. bis 17. Jahrhunderts." In *Aus der Zeit der Verzweiflung: Zur Genese und Aktualität des Hexenbildes,* ed. Gabriele Becker et al., 131–87. Frankfurt: Suhrkamp Verlag, 1977.

Brenner, Ines, and Gisela Morgenthal. "Sinnlicher Widerstand während der Ketzer- und Hexenverfolgungen: Materialien und Interpretationen." In *Aus der Zeit der Verzweiflung: Zur Genese und Aktualität des Hexenbildes,* ed. Gabriele Becker et al., 188–239. Frankfurt: Suhrkamp Verlag, 1977.

Bresciani-Turroni, Costantino. *The Economics of Inflation: A Study of Currency Depreciation in Post-War Germany, 1914–1923.* London: G. Allen and Unwin, 1937.

Breuer, Stefan. *Anatomie der Konservativen Revolution.* Darmstadt: Wissenschaftliche Buchgesellschaft, 1993.

Bridenthal, Renate, Atina Grossmann, and Marion Kaplan, eds. *When Biology Became Destiny: Women in Weimar and Nazi Germany.* New York: Monthly Review Press, 1984.

Brinckmeyer, Hermann. *Hugo Stinnes.* Trans. Alfred B. Kuttner. New York: B. W. Huebsch, 1921.

Brinkmann, Max. *Kleiner Knigge für Schieber.* Berlin: n.p., 1921.

Buchan, James. *Frozen Desire: The Meaning of Money.* New York: Farrar, Straus, Giroux, 1997.

Buck-Morss, Susan. *The Dialectics of Seeing: Walter Benjamin and the Arcades Project.* Cambridge: MIT Press, 1989.

Bullivant, Keith, ed. *Culture and Society in the Weimar Republic.* Manchester: Manchester University Press, 1978.

Bullock, Marcus Paul. *The Violent Eye: Ernst Jünger's Visions and Revisions on the European Right.* Detroit: Wayne State University Press, 1992.

Bunzel, Julius, ed. *Geldentwertung und Stabilisierung in ihren Einflüssen auf die soziale Entwicklung in Österreich.* Schriften des Vereins für Sozialpolitik 169. München: Duncker und Humblot, 1925.

Burch, Noel. "Notes on Fritz Lang's First Mabuse." *Cine-tracts* 4, no. 1 (1981): 1–13.

Burghardt, Anton. *Soziologie des Geldes und der Inflation.* Wien: Hermann Böhlaus Nachfahren, 1977.

Büsch, Otto, and Gerald D. Feldman, eds. *Historische Prozesse der deutschen Inflation 1914 bis 1924: Ein Tagungsbericht.* Berlin: Colloqium Verlag, 1978.

Canetti, Elias. *Auto-da-Fé.* Trans. C. V. Wedgwood. New York: Farrar, Straus, Giroux, 1984.

———. *Crowds and Power.* Trans. Carol Stewart. New York: Farrar, Straus, Giroux, 1984.

———. *Das Gewissen der Worte: Essays.* München: Hanser, 1975.

———. *The Torch in My Ear.* Trans. Joachim Neugroschel. New York: Farrar, Straus, Giroux, 1982.

Caro, Leopold. *Der Wucher.* Leipzig: Duncker und Humblot, 1893.

Caruth, Cathy, ed. *Trauma: Explorations in Memory.* Baltimore: Johns Hopkins University Press, 1995.

Cassirer, Ernst. *Der Mythos des Staates: Philosophische Grundlagen politischen Verhaltens.* 2nd ed. Zürich: Artemis Verlag, 1978.

Charol, Michael. "Intellektuellendämmerung." *Der Kritiker* 2, no. 49–50 (1920): 6–8.

Childers, Thomas. *The Nazi Voter: The Social Foundations of Fascism in Germany.* Chapel Hill: University of North Carolina Press, 1983.

———. "The Social Language of Politics in Germany." *American Historical Review* 95 (1990): 331–58.

Colwell, James. "The American Experience in Berlin during the Weimar Republic." Ph.D. diss., Yale University, 1961.

Conze, Werner. "Arbeit." In *Geschichtliche Grundbegriffe: Historisches Lexikon zur politisch-sozialen Sprache in Deutschland,* ed. Otto Brunner, Werner Conze, and Reinhart Koselleck, 1:154–215. Stuttgart: Klett Verlag, 1972.

Costigliola, Frank. "The 'Americanization' of Europe." In *Consequences of Inflation,* ed. Gerald Feldman et al., 181–209. Berlin: Colloqium Verlag, 1989.

Court, Franklin E. "Deception and the 'Parody of Externals' in Thomas Mann's 'Disorder and Early Sorrow.'" *Studies in Short Fiction* 12 (1975): 186–89.

Craig, Gordon A. *The Germans.* New York: Putnam, 1982.

Czada, Peter. "Ursachen und Folgen der großen Inflation." In *Finanz- und wirtschaftspolitische Fragen der Zwischenkriegszeit,* ed. Harald Winkel, 9–43. Schriften des Vereins für Sozialpolitik 73. Berlin: Duncker und Humblot, 1973.

Dallmayr, Alois. *Der große Raubzug: Darstellung in fünf Heften.* Leipzig: Hammer, 1929.

Derrida, Jacques. *Of Grammatology.* Trans. Gayatri Chakravorty Spivak. Corrected ed. Baltimore: Johns Hopkins University Press, corrected edition, 1998.

Dijkstra, Bram. *Idols of Perversity: Fantasies of Feminine Evil in Fin-de-Siècle Culture.* New York: Oxford University Press, 1986.

Dörmann, Felix. *Jazz.* Wien: Strache, 1925.

Dreßler, Oskar, and Hugo Weinberger. "Die Geschlechtsmoral." In *Geldentwertung und Stabilisierung in ihren Einflüssen auf die soziale Entwicklung in Österreich,* ed. Julius Bunzel, 323–26. Schriften des Vereins für Sozialpolitik 169. München: Duncker und Humblot, 1925.

Eckardt, Wolf von, and Sander L. Gilman. *Bertolt Brecht's Berlin: A Scrapbook of the Twenties.* Garden City: Anchor Press, 1975.

Eggert, Hartmut, Ulrich Profitlich, and Klaus Scherpe, eds. *Geschichte als Literatur: Formen und Grenzen der Repräsentation von Vergangenheit.* Stuttgart: Metzler Verlag, 1990.

Eigler, Friederike. *Das autobiographische Werk von Elias Canetti.* Tübingen: Stauffenburg Verlag, 1988.

Eisner, Lotte. *The Haunted Screen: Expressionism in the German Cinema and the Influence of Max Reinhardt.* Trans. Roger Greaves. Berkeley and Los Angeles: University of California Press, 1973.

Eksteins, Modris. *Rites of Spring: The Great War and the Birth of the Modern Age.* New York: Doubleday, 1990.

Ellis, Howard. *German Monetary Theory, 1905–1933.* Cambridge: Harvard University Press, 1934.

Emrich, Elke. "Heinrich Manns Novelle *Kobes,* oder die 'bis ans logische Ende' geführte deutsche Geistesgeschichte." In *Heinrich Mann: Sein Werk in der Weimarer Republik, Zweites Internationales Symposion Lübeck 1981,* ed. Helmut Koopmann and Peter-Paul Schneider, 155–67. Frankfurt: Klostermann Verlag, 1983.

Epstein, Max. "Spielclubs." *Die Weltbühne: Wochenschrift für Politik, Kunst, Wirtschaft* 15 (1919): 649–54.

Eulenburg, Franz. "Die sozialen Wirkungen der Währungsverhältnisse." *Jahrbücher für Nationalökonomie und Statistik* 67 (November–December 1924): 748–94.

Fallada, Hans. *Wolf unter Wölfen.* Berlin: Rowohlt, 1937.

Feder, Gottfried. *Der deutsche Staat auf nationaler und sozialer Grundlage: Neue Wege in Staat, Finanz, und Wirtschaft.* München: Verlag Franz Eher Nachfahren, 1933.

———. *Das Manifest zur Brechung der Zinsknechtschaft des Geldes.* Diessen: Franz Eher, 1926.

Feinstein, Charles H., Peter Temin, and Gianni Toniolo. *The European Economy between the Wars.* Oxford: Oxford University Press, 1997.

Feldman, Gerald D. *The Great Disorder: Politics, Economics, and Society in the German Inflation, 1914–1924.* New York: Oxford University Press, 1993.

———. *Iron and Steel in the German Inflation, 1916–1923.* Princeton: Princeton University Press, 1977.

———. "The Weimar Republic: A Problem of Modernization." *Archiv für Sozialgeschichte* 26 (1986): 27–48.

———. "Weimar Writers and the German Inflation." In *Fact and Fiction: German History and Literature, 1848–1924,* ed. Gisela Brude-Firnau and Karin J. MacHardy, 173–83. Tübingen: Francke Verlag, 1990.

———, ed. *Die Nachwirkungen der Inflation auf die deutsche Geschichte, 1924–1933.* München: Oldenbourg, 1985.

Feldman, Gerald D., et al., eds. *Die Anpassung an die Inflation.* Veröffentlichungen der Historischen Kommission Berlin, no. 67. Berlin: Walter de Gruyter, 1986.

———. *Consequences of Inflation.* Berlin: Colloqium Verlag, 1989.

———. *Die deutsche Inflation: Eine Zwischenbilanz.* Berlin: Walter de Gruyter, 1982.

Felken, Detlev. *Oswald Spengler: Konservativer Denker zwischen Kaiserreich und Diktatur.* München: C. H. Beck Verlag, 1988.

Felski, Rita. *The Gender of Modernity.* Cambridge: Harvard University Press, 1995.

Ferenczi, Sandor, et al. *Zur Psychonanalyse der Kriegsneurosen.* Leipzig: Wien, 1919.

Fergusson, Adam. *When Money Dies: The Nightmare of the Weimar Collapse.* London: William Kimber, 1975.

Feuchtwanger, Lion. *Erfolg: Drei Jahre Geschichte einer Provinz.* Berlin: Kiepenheuer Verlag, 1930.

Fiske, John. *Understanding Popular Culture.* Boston: Unwin Hyman, 1989.

Flemming, Jens, et al., eds. *Die Republik von Weimar.* 2 vols. Königstein: Athenäum-Verlag, 1979.

Fohrmann, Jürgen, and Harro Müller, eds. *Diskurstheorien und Literaturwissenschaft.* Frankfurt am Main: Suhrkamp Verlag, 1988.

Ford, Henry. *My Life and Work.* New York: Doubleday, 1922.

Francke, Ernst, and Walther Lotz, eds. *Die Geistigen Arbeiter: Zweiter Teil: Journalisten und bildende Künstler.* Schriften des Vereins für Sozialpolitik, vol. 152. München: Duncker und Humblot, 1922.

Frankel, S. Herbert. *Money: Two Philosophies: The Conflict of Trust and Authority.* Oxford: Basil Blackwell, 1977.

Frege Gottfried. *The Foundations of Arithmetic.* Trans. J. L. Austin. Oxford: Blackwell, 1974.

Freimark, Hans. *Die Revolution als psychische Massenerscheinung.* München: n.p., 1920.

Freud, Sigmund. "Mass Psychology and Ego Analysis." In *The Standard Edition of the Complete Psychological Works of Sigmund Freud,* trans. James Strachey. London: Hogarth Press, 1953–1974.

———. *The Standard Edition of the Complete Psychological Works of Sigmund Freud.* Trans. James Strachey. London: Hogarth Press, 1953–1974.

———. *Studienausgabe.* Ed. Alexander Mitscherlich et al. Frankfurt am Main: Fischer, 1975.

———. "The Uncanny." In *On Creativity and the Unconscious: Papers on the Psychology of Art, Literature, Love, Religion,* ed. Benjamin Nelson, 122–61. New York: Harper, 1958.

Frevert, Ute. *Women in German History: From Bourgeois Emancipation to Sexual Liberation.* Trans. Stuart McKinnon-Evans. Oxford: Berg Publishers, 1989.

Friedländer, Saul, ed. *Probing the Limits of Representation: Nazism and the "Final Solution."* Cambridge: Harvard University Press, 1992.

Friedrich, Otto. *Before the Deluge: A Portrait of Berlin in the 1920s.* New York: Harper, 1972.

Frisby, David. *Fragments of Modernity.* Cambridge: MIT Press, 1986.

———. *Georg Simmel.* London: Tavistock Publications, 1984.

Fritzsche, Peter. *Rehearsals for Fascism: Populism and Political Mobilization in Weimar Germany.* New York: Oxford University Press, 1990.

———. "Vagabond in the Fugitive City: Hans Ostwald, Imperial Berlin, and the Grosstadt-Documente." *Journal of Contemporary History* 29 (1994): 385–402.

Fritzsching, L. "Die wirtschaftliche Lage der bildenden Künstler." *Annalen des deutschen Reiches für Gesetzgebung, Verwaltung und Volkswirtschaft (1921/22),* 133–208. München, 1923.

Frühwald, Wolfgang. "Eine Kindheit in München: Die Familie Mann und das Genre der Inflationsliteratur." In *Literaturhistorische Begegnungen: Festschrift zum sechzigsten Geburtstag von Bernhard König,* ed. Andreas Kablitz and Ulrich Schulz-Buschhaus, 43–57. Tübingen: Gunter Narr Verlag, 1993.

Fuchs, Eduard. *Die Frau in der Karikatur.* München: Albert Langen Verlag, 1928. Reprint, Frankfurt: Verlag Neue Kritik, 1973.

Fussell, Paul. *The Great War and Modern Memory.* London: Oxford University Press, 1975.

Gaettens, Richard. *Geschichte der Inflationen: Vom Altertum bis zur Gegenwart.* München: Battenberg, 1982.

Gailus, Manfred. *Pöbelexzesse und Volkstumulte.* Berlin: Europäische Perspektiven, 1984.

Galbraith, John Kenneth. *Money: Whence It Came, Where It Went.* Rev. ed. Boston: Houghton Mifflin, 1995.

Gangl, Manfred, and Gérard Raulet, eds. *Intellektuellendiskurse in der Weimarer Republik: Zur politischen Kultur einer Gemengenlage.* Frankfurt am Main: Campus Verlag, 1994.

Gay, Peter. *Weimar Culture: The Outsider as Insider.* New York: Harper and Row, 1968.

Gerlach, Hildegard, ed. *Hexen, Brocken, Walpurgisnacht.* Sonderausstellung: Faust Museum Knittlingen; Pforzheim: Offizin Rolf Dettling, 1980.

Germanus, Agricola. *Geldwahn und Rettung: Sammlung der in der Zeit vom 7. September bis 31. Januar 1920 erschienen Aufsätze des Germanus Agricola.* Ed. Johannes Dingfelder. München: Verlag "Deutsche Eiche," 1920.

Gesell, Silvio. *Gesammelte Werke.* 18 vols. Lütjenburg: Fachverlag für Sozialökonomie, 1992.

Geyer, Curt. *Die drei Verderber Deutschlands: Ein Beitrag zur Geschichte Deutschlands und der Reparationsfrage von 1920–1924.* Berlin: J. H. W. Dietz Nachfolger, 1924.

Geyer, Martin. *Verkehrte Welt: Revolution, Inflation, und Moderne: München, 1914–1924.* Göttingen: Vandenhoeck und Ruprecht, 1998.

Giese, Fritz. *Girlkultur: Vergleiche zwischen amerikanischem und europäischem Rhythmus und Lebensgefühl.* München: Delphin-Verlag, 1925.

Gilman, Sander L. *Difference and Pathology: Stereotypes of Sexuality, Race, and Madness.* Ithaca: Cornell University Press, 1985.

———. *The Jew's Body.* New York: Routledge, 1991.

Gilman, Sander L., and Jack Zipes, eds. *Yale Companion to Jewish Writing and Thought in German Culture, 1096–1996.* New Haven: Yale University Press, 1997.

Godschalk, Hugo. *Die geldlose Wirtschaft: Vom Tempeltausch bis zum Barter-Club.* Berlin: Basis Verlag, 1986.

Goux, Jean-Joseph. *Symbolic Economies: After Marx and Freud.* Ithaca: Cornell University Press, 1990.

Graf, Oskar Maria. *Gelächter von außen: Aus meinem Leben, 1918–1933.* München: Süddeutscher Verlag, 1980.

———. *Unruhe um einen Friedfertigen.* München: Süddeutscher Verlag, 1975.

Grafe, Frieda, et al. *Fritz Lang.* München: Hanser Verlag, 1987.

Greenberg, Valerie. *Literature and Sensibilities in the Weimar Era: Short Stories in the "Neue Rundschau."* Madrid: J. Porrua Turanzas, 1982.

Grimminger, Rolf, ed. *Hansers Sozialgeschichte der deutschen Literatur vom 16. Jahrhundert bis zur Gegenwart.* 12 vols. München: Hanser Verlag, 1980.

Guttmann, William, and Patricia Meehan. *The Great Inflation: Germany, 1919–1923.* Westmead: Saxon House, 1975.

Guttsman, William L. *Workers' Culture in Weimar Germany: Between Tradition and Commitment.* New York: St. Martin's Press, 1990.

Haber, Franz. *Untersuchungen über Irrtümer moderner Geldverbesserer.* Jena: Verlag von Gustav Fischer, 1926.

Habermas, Jürgen. Foreword to *Philosophische Kultur,* by Georg Simmel. Berlin: Wagenbach Verlag, 1986.

Hake, Sabine. *The Cinema's Third Machine: Writing on Film in Germany, 1907–1933.* Lincoln: Nebraska University Press, 1993.

Halbfell, A. *Staatszerstörung durch Inflation.* Detmold: Verlag der Meyerschen Hofbuchhandlung, 1927.

Halfeld, Adolf. *Amerika und der Amerikanismus.* Jena: Eugen Diederichs Verlag, 1927.

Hall, Robert E., ed. *Inflation: Causes and Effects.* Chicago: University of Chicago Press, 1982.

Hank, Rainer. *Arbeit—Die Religion des 20. Jahrhunderts: Auf dem Weg in die Gesellschaft der Selbstständigen.* Frankfurt: Eichborn Verlag, 1995.

Hansen, Linda. "Middle-Class Consciousness and the German Experience." Ph.D. diss., University of Wisconsin, 1981.

Harbou, Thea von. *Metropolis.* Boston: Gregg Press, 1975.

Harden, Maximilian. *I Meet My Contemporaries.* Trans. William C. Lawton. New York: Henry Holt and Company, 1925.

Haß, Hermann. *Sitte und Kultur im Nachkriegsdeutschland.* Hamburg: Hanseatische Verlags-Anstalt, 1932.

Haß, Ulrike. *Militante Pastorale: Zur Literatur der antimodernen Bewegungen im frühen 20. Jahrhundert.* München: Fink Verlag, 1993.

Hattendorf, Erwin Loewy. *Krieg: Revolution und Unfallneurosen.* Berlin: 1920.

Haupt, Jürgen. "Die Entwertung der Gefühle: Heinrich Manns 'Inflationsnovellen' zur Gesellschaftskrise der zwanziger Jahre." In *Heinrich Mann Jahrbuch,* ed. Helmut Koopmann and Peter-Paul Schneider, no. 6. Lübeck: Amt für Kultur, Hansestadt Lübeck, 1988.

Haxthausen, Charles, and Heidrun Suhr, eds. *Berlin: Culture and Metropolis.* Minneapolis: University of Minnesota Press, 1990.

Heiber, Helmut. *Die Republik von Weimar.* München: Deutscher Taschenbuch Verlag, 1990.

Heller, Heinz B. *Literarische Intelligenz und Film: Zu Veränderungen der ästhetischen Theorie und Praxis unter dem Eindruck des Films 1910–1930 in Deutschland.* Tübingen: Niemeyer Verlag, 1985.

Henning, Friedrich-Wilhelm. *Das Industrialisierte Deutschland 1914 bis 1986.* Paderborn: Schöningh Verlag, 1988.

Hentig, Hans von. *Über den Zusammenhang von kosmischen, biologischen, und sozialen Krisen.* Tübingen: Mohr, 1920.

Hepp, Corona. *Avantgarde, Moderne Kunst, Kulturkritik, und Reformbewegungen nach der Jahrhundertwende.* München: Deutscher Taschenbuch-Verlag, 1987.

Herding, Klaus, and Gunter Otto, eds. *"Nervöse Auffangsorgane des inneren and äußeren Lebens," Karikaturen.* Gießen: Anabas Verlag, 1980.

Herf, Jeffrey. *Reactionary Modernism: Technology, Culture, and Politics in Weimar and the Third Reich.* Cambridge: Cambridge University Press, 1984.

Hermand, Jost, and Frank Trommler. *Die Kultur der Weimarer Republik.* München: Nymphenburger Verlagsanstalt, 1978.

Hermann-Neiße, Max. "Berliner Theaterwirtschaft." *Die neue Schaubühne* 3, no. 4 (1921): 75.

Hirsch, Fred, and John H. Goldthorpe, eds. *The Political Economy of Inflation.* Cambridge: Harvard University Press, 1978.

Hirschfeld, Magnus, and Andreas Gaspar. *Sittengeschichte des Zwanzigsten Jahrhunderts.* Hanau: Schustek Verlag, 1966.

Hitler, Adolf. *Mein Kampf.* München: Verlag Franz Eher Nachfahren, 1933.

Hoffmeister, Werner. "Thomas Manns 'Unordnung und frühes Leid': Neue Gesellschaft, neue Geselligkeit." *Monatshefte* 82, no. 2 (1990): 157–76.

Hohendahl, Peter Uwe. "Nach der Ideologiekritik: Überlegungen zu geschichtlicher Darstellung." In *Geschichte als Literatur: Formen und Grenzen der Repräsentation von Vergangenheit,* ed. Hartmut Eggert, Ulrich Profitlich, and Klaus Scherpe, 77–90. Stuttgart: Metzler Verlag, 1990.

Holtfrerich, Carl-Ludwig. *The German Inflation, 1914–1923: Causes and Effects in International Perspective.* Trans. Theo Balderston. Berlin: Walter de Gruyter, 1986.

Honegger, Claudia, ed. *Die Hexen der Neuzeit: Studien zur Sozialgeschichte eines kulturellen Deutungsmusters.* Frankfurt: Suhrkamp Verlag, 1978.

Horsman, George. *Inflation in the Twentieth Century: Evidence from Europe and North America.* New York: St. Martin's Press, 1988.

Hortleder, Gerd. *Das Gesellschaftsbild des Ingenieurs: Zum politischen Verhalten der technischen Intelligenz in Deutschland.* Frankfurt am Main: Suhrkamp Verlag, 1970.

Hubbard, William. "The New Inflation History." *Journal of Modern History* 62 (1990): 552–69.

Hüppauf, Bernd. "Der Erste Weltkrieg und die Destruktion der Zeit." In *Geschichte als Literatur: Formen und Grenzen der Repräsentation von Vergangenheit,* ed. Hartmut Eggert, Ulrich Profitlich, and Klaus Scherpe, 207–25. Stuttgart: Metzler Verlag, 1990.

———, ed. *War, Violence, and the Modern Condition.* Berlin: Walter de Gruyter, 1997.

Hutter, Michael. "Organism as a Metaphor in German Economic Thought." In *Natural Images in Economic Thought: "Markets Read in Tooth and Claw,"* ed. Philip Mirowski. Cambridge: Cambridge University Press, 1994.

Huyssen, Andreas. *After the Great Divide: Modernism, Mass Culture, Postmodernism.* Bloomington: Indiana University Press, 1986.

Huyssen, Andreas, and David Bathrick, eds. *Modernity and the Text: Revisions of German Modernism.* New York: Columbia University Press, 1989.

Irigaray, Luce. *This Sex Which Is Not One.* Trans. Catherine Porter. Ithaca: Cornell University Press, 1985.

Isherwood, Christopher. *Goodbye to Berlin.* London: Hogarth, 1939.

Jackson, Kevin, ed. *The Oxford Book of Money.* Oxford: Oxford University Press, 1995.

Jacobsen, Wolfgang, Anton Kaes, and Hans Helmut Prinzler, eds. *Geschichte des Deutschen Films.* Stuttgart: Metzler, 1993.

Jacques, Norbert. *Dr. Mabuse, der Spieler*. Berlin: Ullstein, 1920.

———. *Dr. Mabuse: Medium des Bösen*. 3 vols. Hamburg: Rogner und Bernhard, 1994.

———. *Mit Lust gelebt*. Hamburg: Hoffmann und Campe, 1950.

Jäkl, Reingard. *Vergnügungsgewerbe rund um den Bülowbogen: Schöneberg auf dem Weg nach Berlin*. Katalog zur gleichnamigen Ausstellung vom 5.7–16.8. Berlin: n.p., 1987.

Jankovich, Béla von. *Beiträge zur Theorie des Geldes: Auf Grund der Erfahrungen in den Jahren 1914 bis 1925*. Wien: Manzsche Verlags und Universitätsbuchhandlung, 1926.

Jarausch, Konrad H. "Die Not der Geistigen Arbeiter: Akademiker in der Berufskrise, 1918–1933." In *Die Weimarer Republik als Wohlfahrtsstaat: Zum Verhältnis von Wirtschafts- und Sozialpolitik in der Industriegesellschaft*, ed. Werner Abelshauser, 280–99. Vierteljahresschrift für Sozial- und Wirtschaftsgeschichte: Beihefte 81. Stuttgart: Steiner Verlag, 1987.

———. *The Rush to German Unity*. New York: Oxford University Press, 1994.

———. *The Unfree Professions: German Lawyers, Teachers, and Engineers, 1900–1950*. New York: Oxford University Press, 1990.

Jeggle, Utz, et al. *Volkskultur in der Moderne*. Reinbek: Rowohlt, 1986.

Jelavich, Peter. *Berlin Cabaret*. Cambridge: Harvard University Press, 1993.

Jenkins, Stephen, ed. *Fritz Lang: The Image and the Look*. London: British Film Institute, 1981.

Johnson, Randal. "Introduction: Pierre Bourdieu on Art, Literature, and Culture." In *The Field of Cultural Production: Essays on Art and Literature*, by Pierre Bourdieu. Oxford: Polity Press, 1993.

Jünger, Ernst. *Der Arbeiter: Herrschaft und Gestalt*. Stuttgart: Klett-Cotta Verlag, 1982.

Kaempfer, Wolfgang. *Ernst Jünger*. Stuttgart: J. B. Metzler, 1981.

Kaes, Anton. "Cinema and Modernity: On Fritz Lang's 'Metropolis.' " In *High and Low Cultures: German Attempts at Mediation*, ed. Reinhold Grimm and Jost Hermand, 19–35. Madison: University of Wisconsin Press, 1994.

———. "Mass Culture and Modernity: Notes Toward a Social History of Early American and German Cinema." In *America and the Germans*, ed. Frank Trommler and Joseph McVeigh. Philadelphia: University of Pennsylvania Press, 1985.

———. "Die ökonomische Dimension der Literatur: Zum Strukturwandel der Institution Literatur in der Inflationszeit (1918–1923)." In *Consequences of Inflation*, ed. Gerald Feldman et al., 307–29. Berlin: Colloqium Verlag, 1989.

———, ed. *Kino-Debatte: Texte zum Verhältnis von Literatur und Film, 1909–1929*. München: Deutscher Taschenbuch Verlag, 1978.

———. *Weimarer Republik: Manifeste und Dokumente zur deutschen Literatur, 1918–1933*. Stuttgart: J. B. Metzler, 1983.

Kaes, Anton, Martin Jay, and Edward Dimendberg, eds. *The Weimar Republic Sourcebook*. Berkeley and Los Angeles: University of California Press, 1994.

Kaiser, Georg. *Nebeneinander: Volksstück 1923 in fünf Akten*. Potsdam: Kiepenheuer, 1923.

Kampffmeyer, Paul. *Der Fascismus in Deutschland*. Berlin: n.p., 1923.

Kaplan, E. Ann. "Fritz Lang and German Expressionism: A Reading of 'Dr. Mabuse, der Spieler.' " In *Passion and Rebellion: The Expressionist Heritage*, ed. Stephen E. Bronner and Douglas Kellner, 398–408. New York: Universe Books, 1983.

Kästner, Erich. *Fabian: Die Geschichte eines Moralisten.* Stuttgart: Deutsche Verlags-Anstalt, 1989.

Kater, Michael. "The Jazz Experience in Weimar Germany." *German History* 6 (1988): 145–58.

———. *Studentenschaft und Rechtsradikalismus in Deutschland, 1918–1933: Eine sozialgeschichtliche Studie zur Bildungskrise in der Weimarer Republik.* Hamburg: Hoffmann und Campe, 1975.

Kern, Elga. *Wie sie dazu kamen: Lebensfragmente bordellierter Mädchen.* Darmstadt: Luchterhand, 1985.

Kersten, Kurt. "Wirtschaft, Kultur, Intellektuelle." *Die Weltbühne* 19, no. 50 (1923): 583–85.

Keun, Irmgard. *Das kunstseidene Mädchen.* Düsseldorf: Claasen, 1979.

Keynes, John Maynard. *The General Theory of Employment, Interest, and Money.* London: Macmillan, 1936.

———. "Inflation." *Essays in Persuasion.* New York: W. W. Norton, 1963.

———. *A Treatise on Money.* 2 vols. London: Macmillan, 1930.

Kintzelé, Jeff, and Peter Schneider, eds. *Georg Simmels "Philosophie des Geldes."* Frankfurt am Main: Hain, 1993.

Klass, Gert von. *Hugo Stinnes.* Tübingen: Rainer Wunderlich Verlag, 1958.

Klemperer, Victor. *Ich Will Zeugnis Ablegen bis zum Letzten.* Ed. Walter Nowojski. 2 vols. Berlin: Aufbau Verlag, 1995.

———. *LTI: Notizbuch eines Philologen.* Leipzig: Reclam, 1975.

Kocka, Jürgen, and Werner Conze, eds. *Bildungsbürgertum im 19. Jahrhundert.* 4 vols. Stuttgart: Klett-Cotta, 1985.

———. "German History before Hitler: The Debate about the German Sonderweg." *Journal of Contemporary History* 23 (1988): 3–16.

Koktanek, Anton Mirko. *Oswald Spengler in seiner Zeit.* München: C. H. Beck Verlag, 1968.

Kolb, Eberhard. *Die Weimarer Republik.* München: Oldenbourg, 1984.

Kolbe, Jürgen. *Heller Zauber: Thomas Mann in München, 1894–1933.* Berlin: Siedler Verlag, 1987.

Koonz, Claudia. *Mothers in the Fatherland: Women, the Family, and Nazi Politics.* New York: St. Martin's Press, 1987.

Kotze, Hildegard von, and Helmut Krausnick, eds. *"Es spricht der Führer": 7 exemplarische Hitler-Reden.* Gütersloh: Sigbert Mohn Verlag, 1966.

Kracauer, Siegfried. *Die Angestellten: Aus dem neuesten Deutschland.* Frankfurt am Main: Suhrkamp Verlag, 1971.

———. *From Caligari to Hitler: A Psychological History of the German Film.* Princeton: Princeton University Press, 1974.

———. "Kult der Zerstreuung: Über die Berliner Lichtspielhäuser." In *Das Ornament der Masse: Essays,* 311–17. Frankfurt: Suhrkamp Verlag, 1977.

Kraemer, Ernst. *Was ist Technokratie?* Berlin: K. Wolff, 1933.

Krafft, Sybille. *Zucht und Unzucht: Prostitution und Sittenpolizei im München der Jahrhundertwende*. München: Hugendubel Verlag, 1996.

Krannhals, Paul. *Das organische Weltbild: Grundlagen einer neuentstehenden deutschen Kultur*. München: F. Bruckmann, 1936.

Kremeier, Klaus. *Die Ufa-Story: Geschichte eines Filmkonzerns*. München: Carl Hanser Verlag, 1992.

Kroner, Friedrich. "Overwrought Nerves." Trans. Don Reneau. In *The Weimar Republic Sourcebook,* ed. Anton Kaes, Martin Jay, and Edward Dimendberg, 63–64. Berkeley and Los Angeles: University of California Press, 1994.

Kruedener, Jürgen Freiherr von. "Die Entstehung des Inflationstraumas: Zur Sozialpsychologie der deutschen Hyperinflation 1922/23." In *Consequences of Inflation,* ed. Gerald Feldman et al., 213–86. Berlin: Colloqium Verlag, 1989.

Krüger, Dieter. *Nationalökonomen im wilhelminischen Deutschland*. Göttingen: Vandenhoeck und Ruprecht, 1983.

Krüger, Michael. Foreword to *Einladung zur Verwandlung: Essays zu Elias Canettis "Masse und Macht,"* ed. Michael Krüger. München: Hanser Verlag, 1995.

Kunz, Andreas. *Civil Servants and the Politics of Inflation in Germany, 1914–1924*. Berlin: Walter de Gruyter, 1986.

Kupzyk, Erwin. "Postwar Concentration in the German Iron Industry." In *The Weimar Republic Sourcebook,* ed. Anton Kaes, Martin Jay, and Edward Dimendberg, 75–77. Berkeley and Los Angeles: University of California Press, 1994.

Kurucz, Jenö. *Struktur und Funktion der Intelligenz während der Weimarer Republik*. N.p.: Grote'sche Verlagsbuchhandlung, 1967.

Lancre, Pierre de. *Tableau de l'Inconstance des Mauvais Anges et Démons*. Paris: n.p., 1613.

Langgässer, Elisabeth. *Erzählungen*. Hamburg: Claassen, 1964.

Laplanche, Jean, and J. B. Pontalis. *Das Vokabular der Psychoanalyse*. Frankfurt am Main: Suhrkamp Verlag, 1986.

Laqueur, Walter. *Weimar: A Cultural History, 1918–1933*. New York: G. P. Putnam's Sons, 1974.

Lebovics, Herman. *Social Conservatism and the Middle Classes in Germany, 1914–1933*. Princeton: Princeton University Press, 1969.

Lederer, Emil. *Kapitalismus, Klassenstruktur, und Probleme der Demokratie in Deutschland, 1910–1940*. Göttingen: Vandenhoeck und Ruprecht, 1979.

———. *State of the Masses: The Threat of Classless Society*. New York: W. W. Norton, 1940.

Lee, W. R., and Eve Rosenhaft, eds. *The State and Social Change in Germany, 1880–1980*. New York: St. Martin's Press, 1990.

Lehnert, Herbert. "Thomas Manns 'Unordnung und frühes Leid': Entstellte Bürgerwelt und ästhetisches Reservat." *Text und Kontext* 6, no. 1–2 (1978): 239–56.

Lethen, Helmut. "Kracauer's Pendulum: Thoughts on German Cultural History." *New German Critique* 65 (1995): 37–45.

———. *Neue Sachlichkeit, 1924–1932: Studien zur Literatur des "Weissen Sozialismus."* Stuttgart: Metzler, 1970.

———. *Verhaltenslehren der Kälte: Lebensversuche zwischen den Kriegen.* Frankfurt am Main: Suhrkamp Verlag, 1994.

Linse, Ulrich. *Barfüßige Propheten: Erlöser der Zwanziger Jahre.* Berlin: Siedler Verlag, 1983.

———. *Zurück o Mensch zur Mutter Erde.* München: Deutscher Taschenbuch Verlag, 1983.

Lüddeck, Theodor. "Amerikanismus als Schlagwort und Tatsache." *Deutsche Rundschau* 221 (March 1930): 214–21.

Luhmann, Niklas. *Die Wirtschaft der Gesellschaft.* Frankfurt am Main: Suhrkamp Verlag, 1988.

Lyth, Peter J. *Inflation and the Merchant Economy: The Hamburg Mittelstand, 1914–1924.* New York: Berg Publishers, 1990.

Macho, Thomas. "Jäger und Sammler in der Wissenschaft." *Freitag* 6 (August 1993).

Maier, Charles S. *In Search of Stability: Explorations in Historical Political Economy.* Cambridge: Cambridge University Press, 1987.

———. *Recasting Bourgeois Europe: Stabilization in France, Germany, and Italy in the Decade after WW I.* Princeton: Princeton University Press, 1975.

Makropoulos, Michael. "Tendenzen der Zwanziger Jahre." *Deutsche Zeitschrift für Philosophie* 39 (1991): 675–87.

Mann, Heinrich. *Gesammelte Werke in dreizehn Bänden.* Berlin: Aufbau Verlag, 1978.

———. *Kobes: Mit zehn Lithographien von George Grosz.* Berlin: Propyläen Verlag, 1925.

———. "Die Tragödie von 1923." In *Sieben Jahre: Chronik der Gedanken und Vorgänge.* Berlin: Paul Zsolnay Verlag, 1929.

Mann, Klaus. *Der Wendepunkt: Ein Lebensbericht.* Frankfurt am Main: S. Fischer, 1952.

Mann, Thomas. *Disorder and Early Sorrow.* In *Stories of a Lifetime.* vol. 2. London: Secker and Warburg, 1970.

———. "Erinnerungen aus der deutschen Inflation." In *Gesammelte Werke in dreizehn Bänden,* 13:181–90. Frankfurt am Main: Fischer, 1990.

———. *Gesammelte Werke in dreizehn Bänden.* Frankfurt am Main: Fischer, 1990.

———. "Inflation: The Witches Sabbath: Germany 1923." *Encounter* 44, no. 2 (1975): 60–64.

———. "Meine Zeit." In *Gesammelte Werke in dreizehn Bänden,* 8:5–27. Frankfurt am Main: Fischer, 1990.

———. "On Myself." In *Gesammelte Werke in dreizehn Bänden,* 8:51–93. Frankfurt am Main: Fischer, 1990.

Mannheim, Karl. *Ideologie und Utopie.* Bonn: Cohen, 1929.

Marx, Karl. *Capital: A Critique of Political Economy.* Ed. Frederick Engels. Trans. Samuel Moore and Edward Aveling. New York: International Publishers, 1975.

————. *Early Writings.* Trans. T. B. Bottomore. London: C. A. Watts and Company, 1963.

Marx, Karl, and Friedrich Engels. *The Communist Manifesto.* Ed. Paul Beer. New York: Appleton-Century-Crofts, 1955.

Mayer, Dieter. *Linksbürgerliches Denken: Untersuchungen zur Kunsttheorie, Gesellschaftsauffassung, und Kulturpolitik in der Weimarer Republik (1919–1924).* München: W. Fink Verlag, 1981.

Mayer, Theodor Heinrich. *Prokop der Schneider: Roman.* Leipzig: Staackmann, 1922.

Mazlish, Bruce. *The Meaning of Karl Marx.* New York: Oxford University Press, 1984.

McLuhan, Marshall. *Understanding Media: The Extensions of Man.* Cambridge: MIT Press, 1994.

Mehring, Walter. *Der Kaufmann von Berlin: Ein historisches Schauspiel.* Berlin: S. Fischer, 1928.

Mendelssohn Bartholdy, Albrecht. *The War and German Society: The Testament of a Liberal.* Economic and Social History of the World War: German Series, ed. James T. Shotwell. New Haven: Yale University Press, 1937.

Meriodionalis. "Die Not des Geistes." *Die Weltbühne* 19, no. 25 (1923): 709–12.

Miller-Lane, Barbara, and Leila Rupp, eds. *Nazi Ideology before 1933: A Documentation.* Austin: University of Texas Press, 1978.

Modleski, Tania. "Femininity as Mas(s)querade: A Feminist Approach to Mass Culture." In *High Theory/Low Culture: Analysing Popular Television and Film,* ed. Colin MacCabe. Manchester: Manchester University Press, 1986.

Moellendorff, Wichard von. *Konservativer Sozialismus.* Hamburg: Hanseatische Verlagsanstalt, 1932.

Moeller von den Bruck, Arthur. *Das Dritte Reich.* Hamburg: Hanseatische Verlagsanstalt, 1931.

Mommsen, Hans, et al., eds. *Industrielles System und politische Entwicklung in der Weimarer Republik: Verhandlungen des Internationalen Symposiums in Bochum 12.–17. Juni 1973.* Düsseldorf: Droste Verlag, 1974.

Moreck, Curt. *Führer durch das "lasterhafte" Berlin.* Berlin: Divan, 1987.

Morus. "Jahresbilanz." *Die Weltbühne* 18, no. 1 (1922): 20.

Müller, Hans-Harald, and Harro Segeberg, eds. *Ernst Jünger im 20. Jahrhundert.* München: Fink Verlag, 1995.

Muthesius, Volkmar. *Augenzeuge von drei Inflationen: Erinnerungen und Gedanken eines Wirtschaftspublizisten.* Frankfurt am Main: Knapp Verlag, 1973.

Myers, Tracy. "History and Realism: Representations of Women in G. W. Pabst's 'The Joyless Street.'" In *Gender and German Cinema: Feminist Interventions,* ed. Sandra Frieden et al., 2:43–59. 2 vols. Providence: Berg Publishers, 1994.

Naremore, James, and Patrick Brantlinger, eds. *Modernity and Mass Culture.* Bloomington: Indiana University Press, 1991.

Neckarsulmer, Ernst. *Der alte und der Neue Reichtum.* Berlin: F. Fontane Verlag, 1925.

Neckel, Sighard. *Status und Scham: Zur Reproduktion sozialer Ungleichheit.* Frankfurt am Main: Campus Verlag, 1991.

Nelson, Cary, Paula A. Treichler, and Larry Grossberg. Introduction to *Cultural Studies,* ed. Larry Grossberg et al. New York: Routledge, 1992.

Neumann, Robert. *Sintflut: Roman.* Stuttgart: Engelhom, 1929.

Nevin, Thomas. *Ernst Jünger and Germany: Into the Abyss, 1914–1945.* Durham: Duke University Press, 1996.

Niehuss, Merith. "Lebensweise und Familie in der Inflationszeit." In *Die Anpassung an die Inflation,* ed. Gerald D. Feldman et al., 237–77. Berlin: Walter de Gruyter, 1986.

Niemann, Hans-Werner. *Das Bild des industriellen Unternehmers in den deutschen Romanen der Jahre 1890–1945.* Berlin: Colloquium Verlag, 1982.

Niemer, Gotthart. *Das Geld: Ein Beitrag zur Volkskunde.* Breslau: M. and H. Markus, 1930.

Nietzsche, Friedrich. *Unzeitgemässe Betrachtungen II: Vom Nutzen und Nachteil der Historie für das Leben,* 243–334. Vol. 1 of *Sämtliche Werke: Kritische Studienausgabe in 15 Bänden,* ed. Giorgio Colli and Mazzino Montinari. Berlin: Walter de Gruyter, 1988.

Niewyk, Donald L. "The Impact of Inflation and Depression on the German Jew." *Leo Baeck Institute Yearbook* 28 (1983): 19–36.

Nocera, Joseph. *A Piece of the Action: How the Middle Class Joined the Money Class.* New York: Simon and Schuster, 1994.

Notgeld-Poesie: Deutsche Dichtung im Notgeld: Lütckens Illustrierte Geschichte des Notgeldes. Köln, 1921.

Noveck, Beth S. "1925: Hugo Bettauer's Assassination by Otto Rothstock in Vienna Marks the First Political Murder by the Nazis in Austria." In *Yale Companion to Jewish Writing and Thought in German Culture, 1096–1996,* ed. Sander L. Gilman and Jack Zipes, 440–47. New Haven: Yale University Press, 1997.

Oakes, Guy. "The Problem of Women in Simmel's Theory of Culture." In *Georg Simmel: On Women, Sexuality, and Love,* ed. Guy Oakes, 3–62. New Haven: Yale University Press, 1984.

Oelenheinz, Theodor. *Spiegel der deutschen Inflation: Dokumente, Berichte, Urteile.* Leipzig: Verlag Volks-Recht, 1928.

Ortega y Gasset, Jose. *Der Aufstand der Massen.* Trans. Helene Weyl. München: Rowohlt, 1930.

Ortner, Eugen. *Gott Stinnes: Ein Pamphlet gegen den vollkommenen Menschen.* Hannover: P. Steegemann Verlag, 1922.

Ostwald, Hans. *Das Berliner Dirnentum.* 10 vols. Leipzig: Verlag Walther Fiedler, 1905–7.

———. *Das Galante Berlin.* Berlin: H. Klemm, 1928.

———. *Sittengeschichte der Inflation: Ein Kulturdokument aus den Jahren des Marktsturzes.* Berlin: Neufeld und Henius Verlag, 1931.

———, ed. *Kultur- und Sittengeschichte Berlins.* Berlin: H. Klemm, 1924.

Otto, Berthold. *Abschaffung des Geldes: Arbeitswährung, Rechenwirtschaft. Aufgaben und Einrichtungen der volksorganischen Gemeinwirtschaft. Denk-*

schrift an die Denker im deutschen Volk. Berlin: Verlag des Hauslehrers, 1926.

Overesch, Manfred, and Friedrich Wilhelm Saal, eds. *Die Weimarer Republik: Eine Tageschronik der Politik, Wirtschaft, und Kultur*. Augsburg: Weltbild Verlag, 1992.

Pahl, Leslie Ann. *Margins of Modernity: The Citizen and the Criminal in the Weimar Republic*. Ann Arbor: UMI Press, 1993.

Pateman, Carole. *The Sexual Contract*. Stanford: Stanford University Press, 1988.

Petro, Patrice. *Joyless Streets: Women and Melodramatic Representation in Weimar Germany*. Princeton: Princeton University Press, 1990.

————. "Modernity and Mass Culture in Weimar: Contours of a Discourse on Sexuality in Early Theories of Perception and Representation." *New German Critique* 40 (1987): 115–46.

Peukert, Detlev J. K. *The Weimar Republic: The Crisis of Classical Modernity*. Trans. Richard Deveson. London: Penguin Press, 1991.

Pfleiderer, Otto. "Das Prinzip Mark = Mark in der deutschen Inflation 1914 bis 1924." In *Historische Prozesse der Deutschen Inflation 1914 bis 1924: Ein Tagungsbericht*, ed. Otto Büsch and Gerald D. Feldman, 69–82. Berlin: Colloquium Verlag, 1978.

Plessner, Helmuth. *Grenzen der Gemeinschaft: Eine Kritik des sozialen Radikalismus*. Bonn: Bouvier Verlag, 1972.

Pöder, Elfriede. "Spurensicherung: Otto Weininger in der Blendung." In *Elias Canetti: Blendung als Lebensform*, ed. Friedbert Aspetsberger and Gerald Stieg, 57–72. Königstein: Athenäum, 1985.

Poggi, Gianfranco. *Money and the Modern Mind: Georg Simmel's Philosophy of Money*. Berkeley and Los Angeles: University of California Press, 1993.

Pohlmann, Friedrich. *Individualität, Geld, und Rationalität: Georg Simmel zwischen Karl Marx und Max Weber*. Stuttgart: F. Enke Verlag, 1987.

Prümm, Karl. *Die Literatur des soldatischen Nationalismus der zwanziger Jahre, 1918–1933*. Kronberg: n.p., 1974.

Rabinbach, Anson. "The Aesthetics of Production in the Third Reich: Schönheit der Arbeit." *Journal of Contemporary History* 11 (1976): 43–75.

Raphael, Freddy. "Der Wucherer." In *Antisemitismus: Vorurteile und Mythen*, ed. Julius H. Schoeps and Joachim Schlör, 103–17. Frankfurt: Verlag Zweitausendundeins, 1997.

Raphael, Gaston. *Hugo Stinnes: Der Mensch, sein Werk, sein Wirken*. Berlin: Verlag von Reimar Hobbing, 1925.

Rathenau, Walter. *Zur Kritik der Zeit*. Berlin: S. Fischer, 1912.

Reger, Erich. *Union der festen Hand*. Berlin: Rowohlt, 1931.

Reichel, Peter. *Der schöne Schein des Dritten Reiches: Faszination und Gewalt des Faschismus*. München: Hanser Verlag, 1991.

Remarque, Erich Maria. *Der schwarze Obelisk: Geschichte einer verspäteten Jugend*. Köln: Kiepenheuer und Witsch, 1989.

Rentschler, Eric, ed. *The Films of G. W. Pabst: An Extraterritorial Cinema*. New Brunswick: Rutgers University Press, 1990.

————. *The Ministry of Illusion: Nazi Cinema and Its Afterlife.* Cambridge: Harvard University Press, 1996.

Resar, Karl. *Technokratie, Weltwirtschaftskrise, und ihre endgültige Beseitigung.* Wien: C. Barth, 1935.

Reschke, Renate. "'Pöbel-Mischmasch' oder vom notwendigen Niedergang aller Kultur: Friedrich Nietzsches Ansätze zu einer Kulturkritik der Masse." In *Zwischen Angstmetapher und Terminus: Theorien der Massenkultur seit Nietzsche,* ed. Norbert Krenzlin, 14–42. Berlin: Akademie Verlag, 1992.

Richards, Donald Rey. *The German Bestsellers in the Twentieth Century: A Complete Bibliography and Analysis, 1915–1940.* Bern: Herbert Lang, 1968.

Ringer, Fritz K. *The Decline of the German Mandarins: The German Academic Community, 1890–1933.* Cambridge: Harvard University Press, 1969.

————, ed. *The German Inflation of 1923.* New York: Oxford University Press, 1969.

Rittmann, Herbert. *Deutsche Geldgeschichte seit 1914.* München: Klinkhardt und Biermann, 1986.

Rosenberg, Alfred. *Mythos des 20. Jahrhunderts: Eine Wertung der seelisch-geistigen Gestaltenkämpfe unserer Zeit.* München: Hoheneichenverlag, 1937.

Rossbach, J. R. *Die Massenseele.* München: n.p., 1919.

Rosten, Curt. *Das ABC des Nationalsozialismus.* Berlin: Commissionsverlag Schmidt and Company, 1933.

Rotman, Brian. *Signifying Nothing: The Semiotics of Zero.* London: Macmillan Press, 1987.

Sackett, Robert. *Popular Entertainment: Class and Politics, 1900–1923.* Cambridge: Harvard University Press, 1982.

Saenger, Samuel. "Die Not der geistigen Arbeiter." *Neue Rundschau* 34, no. 1 (1923): 276.

Saldern, Adelheid von, and Sid Auffarth, eds. *Wochenend und schöner Schein: Freizeit und modernes Leben in den Zwanziger Jahren.* Berlin: Elefanten Press, 1991.

Sargent, Thomas J. *Rational Expectations and Inflation.* New York: Harper Collins, 1986.

Sauer, Wolfgang. "Weimar Culture: Experiments in Modernism." *Social Research* 30 (1972): 254–84.

Schacht, Hjalmar. *Die Magie des Geldes.* Düsseldorf: Econ, 1966.

Schäfer, Hans-Dietrich. *Das gespaltene Bewußtsein.* München: Hanser Verlag, 1981.

Scherpe, Klaus, ed. *Die Unwirklichkeit der Städte: Großstadtdarstellungen zwischen Moderne und Postmoderne.* Reinbek: Rowohlt, 1988.

Schickele, Rene. *Die neuen Kerle: Komödie in drei Aufzügen.* Basel: Mohrstadt, 1924.

Schlachter, Gail, ed. *The Weimar Republic: A Historical Bibliography.* Santa Barbara: ABC-Clio Information Services, 1984.

Schlegel, Friedrich. *Philosophical Fragments.* Trans. Peter Firchow. Minneapolis: University of Minnesota Press, 1991.

Schlüter, Hans. "Das Jahr 1923." *Neue Rundschau* (1931): 524–44.

Schmitt, Carl. *Die geistesgeschichtliche Lage des heutigen Parlamentarismus.* Berlin: Duncker und Humblot, 1926.

Schmuckler, Nathan, and Edward Marcus, eds. *Inflation through the Ages: Economic, Social, Psychological, and Historical Aspects.* New York: Brooklyn College Press, 1983.

Schneider, Michael. "Deutsche Geschichte in Krieg und Währungskrise." *Archiv für Sozialgeschichte* 26 (1986): 301–19.

Schoeps, Hans Joachim. *Zeitgeist der Weimarer Republik.* Stuttgart: E. Klett, 1968.

Schoeps, Julius H., and Joachim Schlör, eds. *Antisemitismus: Vorurteile und Mythen.* Frankfurt: Verlag Zweitausendundeins, 1997.

Scholdt, Günter, ed. *Dr. Mabuse: Roman—Film—Dokumente.* St. Ingbert: W. J Röhrig Verlag, 1987.

Schönemann, Heide. *Katalog zur Ausstellung: Fritz Lang. Filmbilder. Vorbilder.* Berlin: Verlag Edition Hentrich, 1992.

Schrader, Bärbel, and Jürgen Schebera. *The "Golden" Twenties: Art and Literature in the Weimar Republic.* New Haven: Yale University Press, 1988.

Schreiber, Georg. *Die Not der deutschen Wissenschaft und der geistigen Arbeiter: Geschehnisse und Gedanken zur Kulturpolitik des Deutschen Reiches.* Leipzig: Quelle und Meyer, 1923.

Schriften des Vereins für Sozialpolitik. Die Zukunft der Sozialpolitik: Die Not der Geistigen Arbeiter: Jubiläumstagung des Vereins für Sozialpolitik in Eisenach 1922. Vol. 163. München: Duncker und Humblot, 1923.

Schultze, Ernst. *Not und Verschwendung: Untersuchungen über das deutsche Wirtschaftsschicksal.* Leipzig: F. A. Brockhaus, 1923.

Schumacher, Martin. "Autoren und Verleger in der Inflationszeit." *Vierteljahresschrift für Sozial- und Wirtschaftsgeschichte* 58 (1971): 88–94.

Schumpeter, Joseph A. *Das Wesen des Geldes.* Göttingen: Vandenhoeck und Ruprecht, 1970.

Schütz, Erhard. *Romane der Weimarer Republik.* München: Fink Verlag, 1986.

Schwilk, Heimo, ed. *Ernst Jünger: Leben und Werk in Bildern und Texten.* Stuttgart: Klett-Cotta, 1988.

Segeberg, Harro, ed. *Vom Wert der Arbeit: Zur literarischen Konstitution des Wertkomplexes "Arbeit" in der deutschen Literatur (1770–1930).* Tübingen: Niemeyer, 1991.

Shell, Marc. *The Economy of Literature.* Baltimore: Johns Hopkins University Press, 1978.

Simmel, Georg. "The Metropolis and Mental Life." In *Classic Essays on the Culture of Cities,* ed. Richard Sennett, 47–60. Englewood Cliffs: Prentice, 1969.

———. "Money in Modern Culture." Trans. Mark Ritter and Sam Whimster. *Theory, Culture, and Society* 8 (1991): 17–31.

———. *On Women, Sexuality, and Love.* Trans. Guy Oakes. New Haven: Yale University Press, 1984.

———. *Philosophie des Geldes.* Ed. David Frisby and Klaus Christian Köhnke. *Gesamtausgabe.* vol. 6. Frankfurt am Main: Suhrkamp Verlag, 1991.

———. *The Philosophy of Money*. Trans. Tom Bottomore and David Frisby. 2nd ed. London: Routledge, 1990.

———. *Schriften zur Philosophie und Soziologie der Geschlechter*. Ed. Heinz-Jürgen Dahme and Klaus Christian Köhnke. Frankfurt am Main: Suhrkamp Verlag, 1985.

———. *Zur Psychologie der Scham: Schriften zur Soziologie*. Ed. Heinz-Jürgen Dahme and Otthein Rammstedt. Frankfurt am Main: Suhrkamp Verlag, 1983.

Simplicissimus: Eine satirische Zeitschrift München, 1896–1944. Exhibition Catalogue. Haus der Kunst München, 19 November 1977 to 15 January 1978. München: Haus der Kunst, 1978.

Sinzheimer, Ludwig, ed. *Die Geistigen Arbeiter: Erster Teil: Freies Schriftstellertum und Literaturverlag*. Schriften des Vereins für Sozialpolitik, vol. 152. München: Duncker und Humblot, 1922.

Sloterdijk, Peter. *Critique of Cynical Reason*. Trans. Michael Eldred. Minneapolis: University of Minnesota Press, 1987.

Soden, Kristine von, and Maruta Schmidt, eds. *Neue Frauen: Die Zwanziger Jahre*. Berlin: Elefanten Press, 1988.

Sombart, Werner. *Der Bourgeois: Zur Geistesgeschichte des modernen Wirtschaftsmenschen*. München: Duncker und Humblot, 1913.

———. *Händler und Helden: Patriotische Besinnungen*. München: Duncker und Humblot, 1915.

———. *Die Juden und das Wirtschaftsleben*. München: Duncker und Humblot, 1918.

———. *Liebe, Luxus, und Kapitalismus: Über die Entstehung der modernen Welt aus dem Geist der Verschwendung*. Berlin: Klaus Wagenbach Verlag, 1983.

Southern, David B. "The Impact of the Inflation: Inflation, the Courts, and Revaluation." In *Social Change and Political Development in Weimar Germany*, ed. Richard Bessel and E. J. Feuchtwanger. London: Croom Helm, 1981.

Spengler, Oswald. *The Decline of the West*. Trans. Charles F. Atkinson. 2 vols. New York: Alfred Knopf, 1950.

———. *Neubau des deutschen Reiches*. München: Beck Verlag, 1924.

———. *Preußentum und Sozialismus*. München: Beck Verlag, 1921.

Sprenger, Bernd. *Das Geld der Deutschen: Geldgeschichte Deutschlands von den Anfängen bis zur Gegenwart*. Paderborn: Schöningh Verlag, 1991.

Stark, Michael, ed. *Deutsche Intellektuelle, 1910–1933: Aufrufe, Pamphlete, Betrachtungen*. Heidelberg: Verlag Lambert Schneider, 1984.

Stieg, Gerald. "Elias Canetti als Zeitzeuge." In *Experte der Macht: Elias Canetti*, ed. Kurt Bartsch and Gerhard Melzer, 28–37. Graz: Droschl, 1985.

Sturm, Georges. "Mabuse, ein Bild der Zeit—Ein Spiel mit dem Bild." In *Dr. Mabuse: Medium des Bösen*, ed. Michael Farin and Günter Scholdt, 3:336–59. Frankfurt: Rogner und Bernhard bei Zweitausendeins, 1994.

Stürmer, Michael, ed. *Die Weimarer Republik: Belagerte Civitas*. Königstein: Verlagsgruppe Athenäum, Hain, Scriptor, Hanstein, 1980.

Tatar, Maria. *Lustmord: Sexual Murder in Weimar Germany*. Princeton: Princeton University Press, 1995.

Temin, Peter. "Soviet and Nazi Economic Planning in the 1930's." *Economic History Review* 44, no. 4 (1991): 573–93.

Theweleit, Klaus. *Male Fantasies*. Trans. Stephen Conway. 2 vols. Minneapolis: University of Minnesota Press, 1987.

Thurow, Lester C. *The Future of Capitalism: How Today's Economic Forces Shape Tomorrow's World*. New York: William Morrow and Company, 1996.

Tischer, Gerhard. *Wirtschaft ohne Zins und Steuern*. Halle: n.p., 1932.

Toller, Ernst. *Hoppla, wir leben*. Potsdam: G. Kiepenheuer, 1927.

Tormin, Walter. *Die Weimarer Republik*. Hannover: Fackelträger Verlag, 1977.

Trevithick, James Anthony. *Inflation: A Guide to the Crisis in Economics*. Harmondsworth: Penguin, 1980.

Trommler Frank. "Arbeitsnation statt Kulturnation? Ein vernachlässigter Faktor deutscher Identität." In *Kontroversen, Alte und Neue: Akten des VII. Internationalen Germanisten Kongresses Göttingen 1985*, ed. Albrecht Schöne, 9:220–29. Tübingen: Niemeyer, 1986.

———. "Inflation, Expressionismus, und die Krise der literarischen Intelligenz." In *Consequences of Inflation*, ed. Gerald Feldman et al., 287–305. Berlin: Colloqium Verlag, 1989.

Ufermann, Paul. *Könige der Inflation*. Berlin: Verlag für Sozialwissenschaft, 1924.

Ungern-Sternberg, Roderich von. *Geldwertschwund und sozialer Friede*. Frankenstein in Schlesien: E. Philipp, 1926.

Vaget, Hans Rudolf. *Thomas Mann-Kommentar zu sämtlichen Erzählungen*. München: Winkler Verlag, 1984.

Veeser, Harold, ed. *The New Historicism*. New York: Routledge, 1989.

Vietta, Silvio. *Die literarische Moderne*. Stuttgart: Metzler Verlag, 1992.

Vogt-Praclik, Kornelia. *Bestseller in der Weimarer Republik, 1925–1930: Eine Untersuchung*. Herzberg: Verlag Traugott Bautz, 1987.

Waechter, Norbert. *Im geldlosen Staate*. Graz: n.p., 1926.

Webb, Steven B. *Hyperinflation and Stabilization in Weimar Germany*. New York: Oxford University Press, 1989.

Weber, Alfred. *Die Not der geistigen Arbeiter*. München: Duncker und Humblot, 1923.

Weil, Marianne, ed. *Wehrwolf und Biene Maja: Der deutsche Bücherschrank zwischen den Kriegen*. Berlin: Ästhetik und Kommunikation, 1986.

Weininger, Otto. *Geschlecht und Charakter: Eine prinzipielle Untersuchung*. Wien: Wilhelm Braumüller Verlag, 1904.

Welskop-Deffaa, Eva Maria. "Die 'Inflationsnovelle' aus dem 'Triptychon des Teufels': Ein wirtschaftsgeschichtlicher Essay zur Nachwirkung der Inflation im Frühwerk Elisabeth Langgässers." In *Consequences of Inflation*, ed. Gerald Feldman et al., 307–30. Berlin: Colloqium Verlag, 1989.

Wertheimer, Paul. *Menschen von heute: Schauspiel in drei Akten*. Wien: Rikola, 1923.

White, Hayden. "The Question of Narrative in Contemporary Historical Theory." *History and Theory* 23 (1984): 1–33.

Widdig, Bernd. *Männerbünde und Massen: Zur Krise männlicher Identität in der Literatur der Moderne*. Opladen: Westdeutscher Verlag, 1992.

Wilkinson, James. "A Choice of Fictions: Historians, Memory, and Evidence." *PMLA* 111 (1996): 80–92.

Willett, John. *Expressionism.* London: Weidenfeld and Nicolson, 1970.

———. *The New Sobriety, 1917–1933: Art and Politics in the Weimar Period.* London: Thames and Hudson, 1982.

———. *The Weimar Years: A Culture Cut Short.* London: Thames and Hudson, 1984.

Williams, Rosalind. *Dream Worlds: Mass Consumption in Late Nineteenth-Century France.* Berkeley and Los Angeles: University of California Press, 1982.

Wittmann, Reinhard. *Geschichte des deutschen Buchhandels: Ein Überblick.* München: Beck Verlag, 1991.

Wolf, Siegbert. *Silvio Gesell: Eine Einführung in Leben und Werk eines bedeutenden Sozialreformers.* Münden: Fachverlag für Sozialökonomie, 1983.

Wolff, Rudolf, ed. *Heinrich Mann: Das essayistische Werk.* Bonn: Bouvier Verlag, 1986.

Wulf, Peter. *Hugo Stinnes: Wirtschaft und Politik, 1918–1924.* Stuttgart: Klett-Cotta, 1979.

Zacharias, Gerhard. *Der Dunkle Gott: Die Überwindung der Spaltung von Gut und Böse. Satanskult und Schwarze Messe.* 3rd ed. Wiesbaden: Limes Verlag, 1982.

Zammito, John Henry. "Art and Action in the Metropolis: The Berlin Avant-Garde, 1900–1930." Ph.D. diss., University of California, 1978.

Zelizer, Viviana A. *The Social Meaning of Money.* New York: Basic Books, 1994.

Zweig, Arnold. *Novellen.* Berlin: Aufbau Verlag, 1961.

Zweig, Stefan. "Die unsichtbare Sammlung: Eine Episode aus der deutschen Inflation." In *Insel-Almanach auf das Jahr 1927.* Leipzig: Insel, 1927.

———. *The World of Yesterday: An Autobiography.* London: Cassell, 1987.

Index

Text:	10 on 13 Sabon
Display:	Sabon
Composition:	G & S Typesetters, Inc.
Printing and binding:	Thomson Shore